Troubleshooting Your PC

FOR

DUMMIES®

2ND EDITION

by Dan Gookin

WILEY

Wiley Publishing, Inc.

Troubleshooting Your PC For Dummies®, 2nd Edition

Published by
Wiley Publishing, Inc.
111 River Street
Hoboken, NJ 07030-5774

WILEY

About the Author

Dan Gookin has been writing about technology for 20 years. He has contributed articles to numerous high-tech magazines and written more than 90 books about personal computing technology, many of them accurate.

He combines his love of writing with his interest in technology to create books that are informative and entertaining, but not boring. Having sold more than 14 million titles translated into more than 30 languages, Dan can attest that his method of crafting computer tomes does seem to work.

Perhaps Dan's most famous title is the original *DOS For Dummies,* published in 1991. It became the world's fastest-selling computer book, at one time moving more copies per week than the *New York Times* number-one best seller (although, because it's a reference book, it could not be listed on the *NYT* best seller list). That book spawned the entire line of *For Dummies* books, which remains a publishing phenomenon to this day.

Dan's most recent titles include *PCs For Dummies,* 9th Edition; *C All-in-One Desk Reference For Dummies; Dan Gookin's Naked Windows XP; Buying a Computer For Dummies,* 2005 Edition; and *Dan Gookin's Naked Office.* He also publishes a free weekly computer newsletter, "Weekly Wambooli Salad," full of tips, how-tos, and computer news. He also maintains the vast and helpful Web page www.wambooli.com.

Dan holds a degree in communications and visual arts from the University of California, San Diego. He lives in the Pacific Northwest, where he enjoys spending time with his four boys in the gentle woods of Idaho.

Publisher's Acknowledgments

We're proud of this book; please send us your comments through our online registration form located at www.dummies.com/register/.

Some of the people who helped bring this book to market include the following:

Acquisitions, Editorial, and Media Development

Project Editor: Rebecca Whitney

Acquisitions Editor: Gregory Croy

Technical Editor: Lee M. Musick

Editorial Manager: Carol Sheehan

Media Development Supervisor: Richard Graves

Editorial Assistant: Amanda Foxworth

Cartoons: Rich Tennant (www.the5thwave.com)

Production

Project Coordinator: Emily Wichlinski

Layout and Graphics: Carl Byers, Andrea Dahl, Lauren Goddard, Denny Hager, Stephanie D. Jumper, Barry Offringa, Heather Ryan

Proofreaders: TECHBOOKS Production Services, Leann Harney, Joe Niesen, Dwight Ramsey, Charles Spencer

Indexer: TECHBOOKS Production Services

Publishing and Editorial for Technology Dummies

    Richard Swadley, Vice President and Executive Group Publisher

    Andy Cummings, Vice President and Publisher

  Mary Bednarek, Executive Acquisitions Director

    Mary C. Corder, Editorial Director

Publishing for Consumer Dummies

    Diane Graves Steele, Vice President and Publisher

    Joyce Pepple, Acquisitions Director

Composition Services

    Gerry Fahey, Vice President of Production Services

    Debbie Stailey, Director of Composition Services

Contents at a Glance

Table of Contents

Introduction

· ·

*W*ow! This book made it to the second edition. Who'd have thunk that there was that much PC trouble out there?

Ah. The innocent. The naïve. The newbies. . . .

For the uninitiated, I have news for you: Trouble lurks around your computer like teenagers at the mall. That's why you need this book! It uncovers the secrets and the power lurking beneath the goofy-colored Windows shell. Trouble will run scared and naked as you merely show this book's cover to your computer monitor. No more waiting on hold to get the answers! No more reinstalling Windows! The truth, well, it's in here!

Computers aren't supposed to die or crash or hang or bomb or toss a hissy fit for no apparent reason. But, as any computer owner knows, computers often don't do what they're told. In *it-was-working-yesterday* syndrome, for some reason your computer decides that today is a different day and so it will act up. And in the *who-owns-the-problem?* issue, you have to decide whether the printer isn't working because of the printer itself or because of Windows or because of the application that's trying to print. I won't even bore you with random Internet-disconnect problems, dead mice, monitors thrust into stupid mode, and a myriad of other problems — because these and other issues are all adequately covered, cured, and remedied throughout this handy little book.

Oh! And that *Dummies* thing? Face it: Anyone who uses a computer feels intimidated enough. It's not that you're a dummy, but dealing with these plastic and silicon monsters certainly makes anyone *feel* like a dummy. Relax! It's the *For Dummies* approach that lets you recognize that it's *you* who is in charge of your PC's destiny. You can tame the beast! This book shows you how.

About This Book

This is a problem-solving book. After all, if *every* problem mentioned in this book were to land on a computer at one time, even I would toss the thing out the window and take up yodeling or log rolling instead. The idea here is simple: You have a problem, and you look up the solution.

You can use the index to discover where solutions to specific problems lie, or you can just browse through Part II, which covers many solutions based on the particular piece of the PC that's being troubled. Each section within a chapter mentions the problem and covers potential solutions. Sample sections include

- In the presence of unwelcome silence
- Fixing missing Hibernation mode
- The whatever-submenu on the Start menu is missing!
- The mouse is getting s-l-o-w
- Things to check when the printer isn't printing
- Where did the download go?
- Why doesn't it shut down?
- "Windows doesn't remember my password!"

And many, many more. You don't have to learn anything. You don't have to complete worksheets or take quizzes. Just find your problem, look up the answer, and follow a few quick and easily explained steps, and you're back on your way with a working computer in no time.

How This Book Works

This book explains how to do things in a step-by-step manner. Occasionally, solutions have a large number of steps, or sometimes you have only one or two things to do, but, fortunately, it's all numbered and explained in a cheerful and entertaining manner.

Whenever you're told to type something, that something appears in **special** type. For example:

1. Type **WINVER** in the box.

This instruction tells you to type the text **WINVER** into the box. The next step may be to click the OK button with the mouse or press the Enter key. But all you need to worry about for this step is to type **WINVER**.

The steps tell you exactly which button to click or which gizmo to tickle with the mouse:

2. Click the OK button.

Sometimes, these steps are shortened:

3. Click OK.

This line still means "Click the OK button with the mouse."

Keyboard shortcuts or key-combination commands are given like this:

Press the Alt+F keys on the keyboard.

This line means to press and hold the Alt key on your keyboard and then tap the F key. Release the Alt key. It works the same way as pressing Shift+F to type a capital letter *F*, but the Alt key is used rather than Shift.

Likewise, you may use the Ctrl key in combination with other keyboard characters.

The key between the Ctrl and Alt keys in the lower-left corner of your keyboard is the Windows key, which is abbreviated as "Win" throughout this book. So, whenever you see

Win+F

it means to press and hold the Win key and then tap the F key.

Choosing items from the menu works like this:

Choose Edit⇨Paste.

This line means to use the mouse to click the Edit menu and then click again to choose the Paste item from that menu. (You can also use the keyboard to work the menus, in which case you press the Alt key and then the underlined letter of the menu or command to choose that command.)

What You're Not to Read

I just can't help being technical at times. So, when I break into a high-tech song, I let you know. Reading that material may increase your knowledge for playing computer trivia, but, otherwise, such asides and tidbits are written because — after 20 years of writing computer books — *I just can't help myself!*

The trivia and asides are always marked as optional reading. Don't bother trying to figure out what's important and what's just the author babbling.

Foolish Assumptions

I must assume a few things about you, O dear, gentle reader: You use a computer. Specifically, you use a computer (or PC) that runs the Windows operating system, Windows XP Edition, either the Home or Professional version. This book mentions the SP2 update where appropriate.

This book assumes that you're using Windows XP in the graphical XP mode. That is, not the Windows Classic or NT mode. The difference is in the way you log in to Windows as well as the Start button's menu display.

The name of the menu on which your programs are located is called the All Programs menu in this book. In some versions of Windows XP, this menu appears as Programs only.

In this book, I assume that you view the Control Panel in Classic mode. To switch to Classic mode, look on the left side of the Control Panel window, in the Control Panel task pane area. Choose the link labeled Switch to Classic View to see things as this book describes them.

This book doesn't cover previous versions of Windows. For information on Windows 98 and Windows Me, try to find this book's first edition.

How This Book Is Organized

This book contains four major parts to whet your troubleshooting appetite. Each part contains chapters that help further explain the part subject. Then, each chapter is divided into individual sections that address specific issues. Everything is cross-referenced. You don't have to read the entire book, from front to back. You may start reading anywhere and receive the full enjoyment that you would if you were to start on the first page or wherever the binding falls open when you try to lay this book on its back.

Part 1: What the @#$%&*!?

The chapters in this part of the book serve as a handy introduction to the entire notion of troubleshooting your PC. I give you some explanations, some quick things to try, plus helpful tips and advice on where to go when you can't find the answers.

Part II: Troubleshooting Minor Irks and Quirks

The chapters in this part make up the book's core. Each chapter covers a specific aspect of the computer, either some piece of hardware or something you do, such as use the Internet. Each chapter contains general troubleshooting information and some specific (and common) questions and answers along with their possible solutions.

Part III: Preventive Maintenance

Nothing beats being prepared. The chapters in this part tell you how to best prepare for the potential of PC peril and how to optimize your system, and you get some general good advice on what to do "just in case."

Part IV: The Part of Tens

The traditional *For Dummies* Part of Tens contains several chapters with some good advice, all bundled into neat lists of ten.

Icons Used in This Book

This icon flags something I would consider a tip (though just about all the information in this book falls into the Tip category).

This icon serves as a special reminder to do something or to remember something.

This icon serves as a special reminder not to do something or to definitely not forget something.

This infamous icon alerts you to the presence of highly technical stuff discussed in the text nearby. It's optional reading only!

Where to Go from Here

Read on! If you don't know where to start, start at Chapter 1, which is why I made that text Chapter 1 and not Chapter 4.

The first part of the book serves as a basic orientation, and Chapter 2 is an excellent introduction to some immediate troubleshooting fixes you can try. Otherwise, look up the problem and find the solution. It's in here somewhere.

As an author, I agree to support my books. If you have any questions about this book or need something explained further, you can e-mail me at dgookin@wambooli.com. That's my real e-mail address, and I do respond to every e-mail sent to me. I cannot, however, troubleshoot your computer for you! That's what this book is for! But I can help answer questions about the book or just say "Hello, thank you for writing," if that's all you want.

I also offer a free weekly newsletter, which you can subscribe to. The newsletter offers updates, news, Q&A, how-tos, opinions, and lots of supplemental information to this and all my books. It costs nothing, and it contains no ads or junk. Check it out, at

www.wambooli.com/newsletter/weekly/

Enjoy the book!

Part I
What the
@#$%&*!?

In this part . . .

There is a lightbulb in Livermore, California — the Centennial Light. The lightbulb has been burning for more than 100 years. Solid. Steady. Fivescore years of luminosity. Amazing. (You can visit the lightbulb at www.centennialbulb.org.)

The Centennial lightbulb is an exception. Lightbulbs are not expected to illuminate for more than a given amount of time, often less than a year. If you've ever bought a light-bulb, you know and accept this fact. You don't operate under the assumption that just because some bulb in Livermore has glowed happily for more than a century, you will see the same performance from the lightbulbs you buy at Home Depot. That would be ridiculous. Even so, most people expect their computers to behave flaw-lessly from the moment they come out of the box to some mythical PC death date several years hence.

The ugly truth: There is no such thing as, nor will there ever be, any computer that runs flawlessly for any length of time. No, only the Centennial Light owns the market on electronic longevity. Computers? They crash. That's reality. The chapters in this part of the book show you how to deal with it.

Chapter 1

It's Not Your Fault! Well, It Might Be Your Fault (How to Tell Whether It's Your Fault)

• •

In This Chapter

▶ Discovering whether it's your fault

▶ Investigating what causes PC problems

▶ Emotionally dealing with a crash

• •

During my 20-odd years of helping folks use their computers, I have noticed one unfortunate and common belief:

> *People tend to blame themselves for just about anything that goes wrong inside a PC.*

This is not always true, of course. Computers crash for a number of reasons, and most of the time it's really not your fault. Yet, when the computer sometimes does something strange or unexpected, even I catch myself saying "What did I do now?"

Alas, the sad truth is that with a computer, you should expect the unexpected. So, before you plan on doing any troubleshooting, please set the proper frame of mind. Rather than immediately jump to the what-have-I-done? conclusion, practice saying the following mantra:

Oh, my. The computer is behaving in a random and unexpected manner. I suppose that I shall have to look into this to see what can be done to remedy the situation.

TECHNICAL STUFF

Computer foul-up terms not worth memorizing

Glitch: Whenever the computer does something strange or unexpected or behaves in a manner inconsistent with normal operation, that's a *glitch.* Glitches happen to everyone. Often, you fail to notice a glitch unless it does something that directly affects what you're doing. For example, you don't notice a sound glitch until you try to make your computer squawk. The sound may have not been working for weeks, but you notice it missing only when you otherwise would expect it. Such is the agony of the glitch.

Bug: A *bug* is an error in a computer program. Despite the efforts of the best programmers, most computer software is riddled with bugs. Bugs are what cause computer glitches. Bad bugs can cause a computer to *hang* or *crash.* Note that most of the worst bugs happen when you mix two programs together and they interact in some new and unexpected way. The term comes from the early days of computing, when a real bug (a moth) got stuck in the circuitry.

Hang: A totally unresponsive computer is said to be *hung,* or *hanged.* You could also use the term *frozen,* though *hang* is the accepted term used by computer nerds for generations.

Crash: *Crash* is another term for a dead computer — specifically, what happens to a hard drive when it ceases operation. A crash is typically more sensational than a hang. Remember that a *hang* is a freeze. A crash is typically accompanied by spectacular warning messages or weird behavior (and may indicate more than just a dying hard drive). In fact, a crashed computer may still be teasingly functional. Only the foolhardy continue to use a crashed computer.

There. It's totally neutral, merely an observation coupled with a determination on your behalf to fix things. With that proper attitude set, you're ready to begin your troubleshooting odyssey.

Computers shouldn't crash, of course. They're not designed to. Really! But they do, for two reasons, neither of which is really your responsibility:

- ✔ The software has bugs in it.
- ✔ There is an utter lack of cooperation.

Why It's Not Your Fault

It can be argued (and it is, by software and hardware developers) that *using* software is your fault. Yes, you can stumble across a bug. Zip-flash! The program crashes, and your data is gone, and you attempt seppuku with a letter opener. Stuff happens. Is it really your fault? No. You were the trigger, but the fault isn't your own. Put that letter opener away!

Why do computers have bugs?

In the real world, bugs — or, more accurately, *insects* — are a necessary part of the ecosystem. In a computer system, bugs are evil and entirely unnecessary. Yet they exist.

A *bug* is an error in a computer program. It's an accident, caused by an oversight on the part of the programmer, sloppy programming, or a lack of anticipation. For example, a programmer may not anticipate that a user may have a last name that's more than 25 characters long and that when you type that 26th character, the program waltzes off into La-La Land. Or, the programmer may type variable_AM1 when he really meant to type variable_AM2 or something similar.

No programmer creates bugs on purpose. In fact, most programming involves *removing* bugs as opposed to writing new code. So, a programmer types a set of instructions, runs them, fixes them, runs them, fixes them, and back and forth until all the bugs are (hopefully) worked out. Programmers even invite others *(beta testers)* to check their programs for bugs. After all, the programmers can't possibly figure out every possible way their software will be used. The object is to make the final product as bugfree as possible.

When you discover a bug, which is the case with most PC trouble, you should report it to the software developers. They're the ones — not you — responsible for fixing the bug!

In addition to bugs is the lack-of-cooperation issue. Software and hardware vendors can check their products in only certain PC configurations. Chances are — given the tremendous number of people who own computers and all the software and hardware combinations you can have — that somehow you will stumble across that one particular blend that wreaks havoc in the computer. Is that your fault? Technically, no, because the manufacturer should build reliable stuff.

So there you have it. The computer is a device that's not designed to crash, but through the odd chance of a software bug or some weird software-hardware mixture, it does crash, and crash often. Yes, I would quite agree that the reason it happens is *not* your fault.

How It Possibly Could Be Your Fault

You're not off the hook!

Rarely in my travels have I found someone who has somehow influenced the computer to go wacky. In fact, only a few things have been known to be directly related to human problems. These causes are covered in this section.

You did something new to the computer

Computers are very conservative; they don't like change. The most stable computer I have in my office has only Microsoft Word installed on it. Nothing else is used on that computer — not the Internet, no games, no nothing! The computer still crashes, but not as often as other systems in my office.

The key to having a more stable computer is *not* to install new software or hardware. Unfortunately, this advice is nearly impossible to follow. It's not that the mere act of installing something new causes the computer to crash. No, it's just that installing something new introduces another combination into the system — a new potion into the elixir, so to speak — and an incompatibility or conflict may come from that. It's what I call the it-was-working-yesterday syndrome.

For example, one of my readers writes in and says, "The sound is gone from my computer! I had sound yesterday, but today it's all gone!" The first thing I ask is whether the person installed any new hardware or software. The answer is generally "Yes," and that's what prompted the problem.

Sometimes, you can forget that you have installed new stuff, which makes the problem seem random. After all, the computer is acting goofy, and it's easy to overlook that you downloaded some corny animation from the Internet yesterday. Yet that one change was enough to alter the system.

- ✔ Yes, if you had one computer for every program, you would probably live a relatively crashfree high-tech existence. But I don't recommend spending your money that way.

- ✔ Try to keep track of the times that you add, update, or change the hardware and software in your computer system.

- ✔ If possible, do research to determine the new stuff's compatibility with your existing computer system. Do that *before* you install. The manufacturer's or developer's Web page lists known technical issues.

- ✔ These types of new hardware and software installations are why utilities such as System Restore are so popular. For more information, see the section in Chapter 4 about using System Restore.

You were bad and deleted files you shouldn't have deleted

Delete only those files you created yourself. It's when people go on file-hunting expeditions that they can get into trouble. In fact, deleting a swath of files is typically the *only* reason I recommend reinstalling Windows. After all, if you

TIP

Creating a system log file

One way I keep track of my computer's foibles is to create a *system log file.* That's nothing fancy, just a plain text file in which I jot down any changes, updates, modifications, or other non-productive things I do on the computer.

The log file is created by right-clicking the mouse on the desktop. From the pop-up menu, choose New⇨Text Document. The New Text Document icon appears; immediately rename it by typing **Log File.txt** or something equally descriptive. Then, keep that icon parked on your desktop for quick and easy access.

When you change something on your computer, add an entry to the file: Double-click to open the

Log File icon. At the end of the file, add your text. For example:

```
March 10 -- Updated printer
     driver software
```
or
```
March 11 -- Downloaded screen
     saver
```

That way, you can review the changes you have made to your computer and correlate them to any new bugs the system may have. You may be amazed at the "coincidences" between your log file and any problems with the computer.

---

surgically remove a great portion of your operating system, reinstalling is the only way to get it back. (For all other problems, you generally have a solution *other than* reinstalling Windows.)

Here is what's okay to delete:

- ✔ Files (icons) in the My Documents folder
- ✔ Files in any folders in the My Documents folder
- ✔ Any folders created in the My Documents folder or its subfolders
- ✔ Zip files you have downloaded and installed

That's it!

Never, ever, delete any other files anywhere else on your computer. I know that you may want to! The urge may be irresistible! You may go on a "cleaning" binge and yearn to mow down files like some crazed gardener with a high-speed weed whacker. Don't!

- ✔ Oh, and you can delete any shortcut icons you may find. Deleting a shortcut icon doesn't delete the original file.
- ✔ You can delete any icon on the desktop. Most are shortcuts anyway.
- ✔ You can also delete items from the Start menu, though I recommend against it.

✔ Zip files are also known as *compressed folders* in Windows.

✔ Most programs you download come in zip file archives. After you extract the files, you can delete the zip file archive.

✔ I create a special folder, called Downloads, in the My Documents folder. (I suppose that I should call it My Downloads, just to fit in with everything else.) That's where I store all my downloaded files, zip files, and e-mail attachments. It's also a great folder to clean out to free up some space on the hard drive.

✔ No, I don't ever recommend reinstalling Windows. See Chapter 20 for the reasons.

Other ways to remove files you didn't create yourself

The main complaint I get with my "Delete only those files you created yourself" maxim is that people find on the computer other files that they're just itching to delete themselves. These files include

✔ Internet cookies

✔ Temporary files (especially temporary Internet files)

✔ Wallpapers and extra media files

✔ Programs that are unwanted or no longer used

✔ Pieces of Windows they want to get rid of

✔ Stuff I can't think of right now

Avoid the temptation to manually delete these files! It gets you into trouble!

"But, Dan!" you whine, "a friend said that it's okay to manually delete my Internet cookies!"

Well . . . there are proper ways to delete the cookies, rid yourself of temporary files, clean and scour unwanted programs, and remove things you don't need. Use those proper ways! Do not attempt to manually delete things yourself. You will get into trouble if you do.

✔ See Chapter 18 for information on dealing with cookies.

✔ Also see Chapter 23 for information on properly removing unwanted files from your computer.

✔ It's not your fault that the computer crashes — especially if you follow my advice in this section!

TIP

Things to say when the computer crashes

Frack! Wonderful, forceful, yet completely G-rated term. Sounds like you-know-what, but utterly non-offensive. Has that quasi-German feel to it.

Oh, come on. . . . As though the computer could hear you, but at least shifts the blame from yourself to the device. (My personal variation is "Come on, you pig!" for when the computer is behaving stubbornly slow.)

What the —? A natural and common response to an unexpected situation. Can be followed by "Frack" or a frack-like equivalent.

Please! Please! Please! Pleading with the computer is very emotional, but it really doesn't help. Most users typically follow the pleading with "Oh, you sorry son-of-a-[female dog]."

You stupid @#$%&!? piece of @#$%!! Very definitely getting it out of your system, this satisfying phrase just feels good to say. Note how blame is placed entirely on the computer. That's keeping the proper perspective.

How old is your PC?

The older your computer is, the more likely it is to crash. I have no idea why. Systems that run stable for years may suddenly experience a growing number of glitches. It happens so often that I refer to it as "tired RAM." And, alas, no electronic equivalent of Geritol is available for your PC's tired RAM.

When your PC gets old, you have to prepare for inevitable quirkiness from it. You can try replacing the parts piece by piece, but eventually you wind up spending more on parts than you would for an entirely new system. No matter how much you love your computer, when it comes time for it to go, let it go.

- ✔ The average computer lasts between four and six years.

- ✔ If you're in business, plan on replacing your PCs every four years. The boost in productivity from the new models alone is worth the expense.

- ✔ For the home, keep your PC as long as you can. If it still works, great! Even if you do buy a new system, you can still use the old system for the kids to do homework or play games.

- ✔ I have a "bone yard" full of old computer pieces and parts. It's not all junk either; recently, I used parts from several old computers to create a file server for my network.

- ✔ The main problem with older computers: parts! I have an older PC that can only "see" 8GB of hard drive storage, yet the smallest hard drive I can find for sale is 20GB. Oops.

- ✔ The first things to fail on any old PC are the things that move the most, such as any disk drive, the mouse, or the keyboard.

- ✔ A failing hard drive is typically the sign of a PC entering its twilight years. You will notice that the disk drive takes longer to access files and that Check Disk (or similar disk utilities) begin to report more disk errors and bad sectors. See Part III for information on what to do next.

- ✔ Mice can fail long before the rest of the computer. This problem may not be a portent of the PC's ultimate demise; see Chapter 13 for more mouse information.

- ✔ When your PC does die, bid it adieu. Salvage what you can; no point in tossing out the monitor, mouse, keyboard, modem, or other "pieces parts" that could work on another computer. Properly dispose of the rest of the computer according to the PC disposal laws of your locality.

What You Can Do about It

Whether it's your fault or not, it's your job to do something about a computer glitch. This book is your best tool for helping you find a solution, so the next step is to continue reading.

Before you do, be aware that you go through certain emotional phases as you experience and deal with your computer's often irrational behavior. I have categorized them in chronological order:

- ✔ **Guilt:** Despite my insistence, just about everyone feels guilty when the computer fouls up. "Is it my fault?" "What did I do?" Even after years of troubleshooting other people's computers, I still blame myself. It must be a human gene or some instinct we have — probably proof that mankind was created by robots from another planet eons ago.

- ✔ **Anger:** Yeah, hit the monitor! Get it out of your system. "Stupid PC! Stupid PC! Why do you *always* crash when I'm doing something important! Arghghgh!" Yes, you have a right to expect obedience from your personal electronics. Too bad the drones in the manufacturer's Human Usability Labs don't express their anger so readily.

- ✔ **Fear or depression:** "This dumb thing will never work." Wrong! This book helps you eliminate your fear and get over the depression phase.

- ✔ **Acceptance:** Hey, it's a computer. It crashes. It could be your fault, but chances are that it's something else. You must deal with the problem. Be stronger and wiser than the computer.

✔ **Confidence:** "I have *Troubleshooting Your PC For Dummies!* I can solve any problem!" This book lists many solutions to many common glitches, but also helps you to troubleshoot just about any problem. And I have rarely met a PC problem that cannot be solved, some simply by restarting your computer.

✔ **Success:** Your computer is back to normal, and everything is right with the universe. World peace is just around the corner! It's raining money! And bluebirds will help you get dressed in the morning. Let's all sing.

Chapter 2

Stuff to Try First

I have yet to meet a computer problem that doesn't present me with a bouquet of panic as I open the door. That's fine. Get over it. Then, rather than dwell on the whos, whys, or hows of the problem, try a few of the quick-and-dirty techniques presented in this chapter to see whether you can remedy the situation. Then, get on with your work!

Some Quick Keyboard Things You Can Do

The keyboard is the computer's ears. After you have tried shouting at the thing, do some typing instead. The computer most definitely "hears" that. Well, unless the keyboard is dead. But there are ways around that as well!

Test the keyboard

To see whether the keyboard is responding, press the Caps Lock key. If the keyboard is alive and well, the Caps Lock light blinks on and off as you tap the Caps Lock key. That shows you that the keyboard is alive and paying attention.

Figure 2-1 illustrates where you find the Caps Lock key and Caps Lock light on most computer keyboards. (Some may be exceptions.)

Caps Lock light

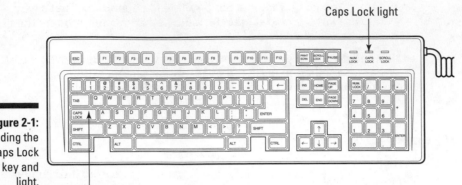

Figure 2-1: Finding the Caps Lock key and light.

Caps Lock key

✔ If the keyboard is dead, use the mouse to restart the computer, a subject covered later in this chapter. Restarting the computer awakens most snoozing keyboards.

✔ Alas, in some cases the keyboard can be alive, yet the computer is ignoring what it's saying. I have seen this situation more often with USB keyboards than with the keyboards that plug directly into a keyboard port on the PC. In these cases, the Caps Lock light does indeed blink on and off, but the computer is still deader than a doornail. Time to restart the computer.

✔ More keyboard troubleshooting information is offered in Chapter 13.

Use Ctrl+Z for immediate file relief

If you ever botch a file operation — moving, deleting, copying, renaming — *immediately* press the Undo key combination, Ctrl+Z. That undoes just about any file operation you can imagine.

✔ You must be prompt with the Ctrl+Z key press. The Undo command undoes only the most recent file operation. If you delete a file and then rename a file, the Undo command undoes only the renaming. You have to find another solution for any earlier problems that need fixing.

✔ Most people forget that editing items and submenus on the Start menu is really a *file* operation. When you screw up something on the Start menu, such as dragging an icon off the Start menu and onto the desktop, pressing Ctrl+Z fixes it right away. Remember that!

✔ Whoops! You cannot undo a Shift+Delete file operation. That's why Windows warns you that deleting a file in that manner renders the file permanently deleted.

✔ If Ctrl+Z, or the Undo command, doesn't work, give up. It means that either it's too late to undo the operation or the operation wasn't undoable in the first place. You have to try something else.

Escape! Escape!

The Esc key on your keyboard is called Escape for a reason: It often gets you out of tight situations! Most scary things that happen on a PC can instantly be canceled or backed away from by pressing the handy Esc key.

Using the keyboard in Windows when the mouse doesn't work

Windows needs a mouse, so if you can't get your mouse to work, you need to rely on the keyboard to finish up whatever tasks you can and then restart the computer. Here are some handy key combinations you can use in place of some mouse techniques:

Ctrl+S: Saves a document to disk. Always save! If you can't work the commands in the Save As dialog box, just save the file wherever you can; you can move it to a better location the next time you start Windows or recover the mouse.

Esc: Cancels a dialog box; closes some windows.

Enter: Does the same thing as pressing the OK, or "default," button in a dialog box.

Tab: Moves between various gizmos in a dialog box. Try using the arrow keys or spacebar to activate the gizmos.

Alt+F4: Closes a window.

Win (the Windows key): Can be used to pop up the Start menu. You can then use the arrow keys and Enter to select items from the menu.

Ctrl+Esc: Pops up the Start menu when you have an older computer keyboard without a Windows key.

You can use other keys all throughout Windows to do just about anything the mouse can do, but that's missing the point here: When something is amiss, you should try to save your stuff and then restart Windows. Don't use a dead mouse as an excuse to show off your keyboard skills.

See the section nearby on restarting Windows when the mouse doesn't work. That typically fixes most mouse problems.

The Drastic Measure of Restarting Windows (Yet It Works)

Drastic is perhaps too severe a word. To me, it conjures up images of amputation or — worse — having to drink a barium shake. Ick. Yet, for some cosmic reason, the "drastic" step of restarting Windows tends to work out many of the more frustrating and seemingly devious computer foibles.

✔ *Restart* is the term used by Microsoft. Old-timers may use the term *reset* or even *reboot* to describe the same thing.

✔ Real old-timers may even call it a *warm boot*. Boots were popular with early computer users, though many of them chose to wear sandals.

Restarting Windows

Believe it or not, a simple restart of Windows can fix most problems: mouse, keyboard, modem, network, or graphics. Try it! If it doesn't work, you can move on to other solutions offered later in this book.

To restart Windows, follow these steps:

1. **Click the Start button.**

2. **Choose Turn Off Computer.**

   The Turn Off Computer dialog box appears, shown in Figure 2-2.

Figure 2-2: Various options for quitting Windows.

3. **Choose Restart.**

After successfully completing these steps, Windows shuts everything down and immediately restarts. Hopefully, that clears up whatever dilemma existed.

Maybe you want to wait for that download

If you're connected to the Internet and downloading a program, you may want to wait a bit before restarting Windows. Even if the keyboard is dead and the mouse doesn't work, sit back and watch the download. If the data is still moving, you're okay. Wait for the download to complete. Then, after the information is fully received (or sent), you can attempt to restart Windows.

The reason this strategy works is that Windows can do several things at once. Although the

mouse or keyboard may be dead, and other programs are running amok, the Internet connection may not be affected. Information may still fly in or out despite other parts of the computer playing possum. If you're lucky, you may get that file downloaded and not have to start over.

To determine whether the download is working, keep an eye on the progress meter. If it's moving, the data is flying. Good. Otherwise, if the meter is still for a few minutes, go ahead and restart Windows.

- ✔ If you have any unsaved documents open, you're asked to save them before Windows restarts.

- ✔ Be sure to remember to remove any floppy disk from Drive A; otherwise, your computer may restart from that disk.

- ✔ Some CD discs can be used to start the computer as well. If your PC is configured to allow a CD to start the computer, you should remove that CD from the drive.

- ✔ Refer to Chapter 8 for more solutions to startup problems.

- ✔ Close any command-prompt (DOS) windows before you restart. Any command-prompt programs that are still running halt the shutdown process in its tracks. You must properly quit the command-prompt program and then try to restart Windows.

- ✔ If you're connected to the Internet, the act of restarting Windows disconnects you. That means if you're doing anything on the Internet, such as downloading a file, the task is interrupted and you have to start over when the computer comes back on.

- ✔ You must restart Windows! Don't just log off. You must choose the restart option as described in this section.

- ✔ Sometimes, you may even have to turn the computer off to fix the problem. See the later section "Restarting when everything is dead."

Restarting Windows when the mouse is dead but the keyboard is alive

If the mouse pointer is stuck to the screen like some dead bug on a car's windshield, you have to rely on the keyboard to restart Windows. This task isn't as hard as it seems (and I suppose I'm saying that because of my years of experience in doing this):

1. **Press the Win key to pop up the Start menu.**

   If your keyboard lacks a Win key, press the Ctrl+Esc key combination.

2. **Press U to choose the Shutdown command.**

3. **Use the arrow keys to highlight and select the Restart option.**

4. **Press the Enter key.**

If you're prompted to save any documents, do so. Don't fret if you can't work the Save As dialog box; just save the document to disk and worry about relocating the file after the computer starts (and the mouse is, hopefully, back in action).

- ✔ You can also use the steps in this section when the mouse is behaving in a stubborn or slow manner.

- ✔ If you have a USB mouse (one that connects to the PC by using a USB port rather than the mouse port), the problem may be with another USB device misbehaving. Consider disconnecting the USB scanner, disk drive, or other USB device to see whether that action remedies the stuck or sluggish mouse.

- ✔ You can use the computer's hard drive light as a way to read its pulse. When the hard drive light is flashing, the computer is still alive and working. If the light is dead, or if the light pulses regularly over a *long* period, the computer most likely is locked up.

- ✔ Be patient! The computer may be unbearably slow. Even so, as long as you're getting a response, it's better to shut down properly than to just unplug the sucker.

Restarting when everything is dead

Ah! Life at the end of Dismal Street. The keyboard is clacking, but the computer is slacking. You could roll the mouse to the North Pole and back, but the mouse pointer on the screen is oblivious. Time to be severely drastic:

1. **Press the computer's power button to turn it off.**

   If briefly pressing the power button doesn't work, press and hold it for several seconds. On some computers, this press-and-hold action turns off the power.

   Yes, if things appear hopeless, just unplug the PC. Or — better still — flip the switch on the surge protector (or power strip or UPS).

2. **After the computer is off, wait a few seconds.**

   Honestly, I don't know why you wait, but you should. One tech guy told me that you wait to ensure that the hard drives properly "spin down," which is analogous to my washing machine, where I definitely don't want to stick my hand in there until the thing has done its spin-down.

   Another techy type told me that you have to wait for the RAM to drain. I don't recall whether he was intoxicated, but it sounds good to me.

   Finally, I think that the wait period prevents some people from doing a quick on-off double flip of the power switch, which has the potential of damaging some of the computer's components. No, it's just best to wait a spell before turning the thing on again.

3. **Turn the computer back on.**

   Punch the button on the computer or turn the power strip or UPS back on. If you do the latter, you may still have to thump the computer's power button to wake it up.

Hopefully, the restart resurrects your keyboard or mouse and gets you back on your way. If not, you can try ever more things, as covered in this book.

- ✔ Older PCs had big red switches or on-off rocker buttons that really, really, did turn off the power. Amazing.

- ✔ Some older PCs even had reset buttons, which you could use rather than power switches to wake up dead or even catatonic PCs. I miss reset buttons.

- ✔ Yes, I know: Some computer cases still have reset buttons on them. But the buttons don't seem to work like they did in the old days. Alas.

What to do about "restart guilt"

Many people feel this pang of guilt when they're forced to restart their computer — even when they have no other course of action. I call it *restart guilt*. It most likely occurs because older versions of Windows came back to life with an ominous message:

```
Windows was not shutdown properly.
```

Oh, no! Which computer gods have ye offended? Peril! Doom!

What kind of idiot would just turn off a computer?

Obviously, if the computer is dead, the mouse is dead, and the keyboard is dead, if all hope is lost and that Costco-size jug of gin is looking good, what else can you do? You have to just turn off the computer. You're no idiot to act that way. No, all the warnings and the reason for calling the drastic step of turning off a computer "improper" have their roots in the old days of DOS.

It was common years ago for people to use the reset button to quit a DOS program. Because DOS could run only one program at a time, pressing the reset button or Ctrl+Alt+Delete was often the fastest way to start another program. So, when some DOS user was done with

WordPerfect, for example, he would whack the reset button (or rapidly flip the power switch off and on), DOS would restart, and he would be off to run another program. This was bad.

It was bad because when programs are not allowed to properly shut down, file fragments and lost clusters begin to litter the hard drive. One such system I serviced had 20 percent of the hard drive's space wasted with lost clusters. So common was this practice that the warning message was added to Windows to ensure that people wouldn't get lazy again and just turn off their computers, rather than properly shut them down. And, it has worked — almost too well.

Happily for everyone, the folks at Microsoft recognized restart guilt and removed the "Windows was not shutdown properly" message from the most recent versions of Windows. Even so, the computer recognizes that it was improperly shut down and performs a quick check of the system to ensure that everything is okay. (Specifically, the Check Disk program is run to ensure that there was no file or disk damage.)

Don't feel guilty about this! If you're forced to unplug the computer to get its attention, so be it. I'm sure that computer scientists in the 1950s eventually had to resort to unplugging their mammoth systems to wrest control when something went haywire. You're no different. (Well, you may not be wearing a white lab coat while you compute.)

- The Check Disk program (or utility) scans the computer's hard disks for errors, missing files, corrupted data, and other annoying things. In the case of shutting down a computer improperly, Check Disk locates the lost file clusters that inevitably appear during an improper shutdown. The lost file clusters are deleted, which is the best course of action to take.

- Also see Chapter 22 for soothing words of advice when you just can't get the computer to quit all by itself.

- If the computer starts in Safe mode, you may have a hardware glitch or some other anomaly that needs fixing. Flip on over to Chapter 24 for more information.

- No, it's not required or necessary to restart in Safe mode after any crash or system reset.

Chapter 3

Telling a Hardware Problem from a Software Problem

*1*t happens countless times a day, every day of the week: You phone technical support for your printer. After wading through the bog of voice-mail menus, you finally get to a tech person who says "Oh, that's a Windows problem." So you phone Microsoft and someone there says "You really need to call your computer dealer because you didn't buy Windows directly from us." And then you phone your dealer, who says "That's a printer problem." And so it goes.

The reason for the tech-support confusion (which may or may not be genuine) is that no one quite knows whether you have a hardware or software problem. If it's a hardware problem, the printer (or hardware) manufacturer can help you. If it's a software problem, the software developer should help you. When you're troubleshooting things yourself, knowing the hardware-software difference can save you oodles of time in tracking down the solution to the problem. This chapter shows you how.

Whose Problem Is It?

Step 1 in any troubleshooting investigation should be eliminating the possibility that you have a hardware problem. After all, if the device is working properly, you can fairly assume that it's the software controlling the device that's fouling things up.

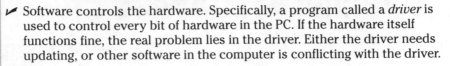

- *Hardware* is anything physical in your computer. If you can touch it, it's hardware.

- Even the disk drives are hardware. The programs *(software)* are encoded on the disks, but that doesn't transform the disks into software.

- Software controls the hardware. Specifically, a program called a *driver* is used to control every bit of hardware in the PC. If the hardware itself functions fine, the real problem lies in the driver. Either the driver needs updating, or other software in the computer is conflicting with the driver.

- Drivers are also known as *device drivers.*

Is it a hardware problem?

Specific examples of hardware and software problems (plus their solutions!) are located throughout Part II of this book. Generally speaking, however, hardware problems crop up suddenly and are not random.

For example, when the printer breaks, it stops working. That's a hardware problem. But, if you cannot print when you use Outlook Express though you can print in every other program, that's a software problem. The printer is being affected by one particular program, Outlook Express. Otherwise, the hardware apparently works just fine.

If the computer shuts itself off half an hour after you start using it — no matter which programs you run — that's a hardware problem. It isn't random. It's generally one half-hour, and it's most likely caused by something getting too hot inside the case — again, hardware.

If the tray on the CD-ROM drive no longer slides open — yup: hardware.

The Enter key doesn't work. Hardware.

Only when the problem seems more random or unpredictable is the software to blame, though that's not a hard-and-fast rule (which is one reason that troubleshooting is so tough).

How hardware fails

Hardware can fail electronically or physically. Both ways are fairly easy to spot.

Electronic failure of hardware usually happens within one month of purchase. If the electronics don't work, were cheap, or were improperly assembled or installed, or the hardware is just bad, it fails right away. That's good because the warranty on just about any computer covers such failures, and whatever goes kaput is replaced free of charge.

The physical failure of hardware happens only when the hardware moves. Fortunately, a PC has few moving parts on it: the disk drives and keyboard.

When a disk drive stops spinning, it's dead! It needs replacement. Fortunately, the disk drive usually has a period of intermittent errors, stops and starts, and hits and misses before this happens, which gives you plenty of warning.

Removable disk drives may have problems with their doors or eject mechanisms, which are obvious to spot.

Finally, the keyboard can fail. Cheap ones can go quickly, usually all at once. The better-made keyboards may lose a key here and there, but they can be fixed. Well, better than fixing, any keyboard can be replaced, and it's inexpensive to do so.

- ✔ A cheap keyboard is one that utterly lacks a "clack" or "click" when you type; the keys feel mushy. That's because the keyboard is most likely a touch-membrane model with spring-activated keys. If the membrane, which is like a flimsy rubber sheet, breaks, the keyboard is finished.

- ✔ Nearly all hardware is replaceable, which is often cheaper than fixing things. For example, a CD-ROM drive can be fixed, but often it's just cheaper to get a newer, better CD-ROM drive as a replacement.

- ✔ Avoid repair outfits that attempt to fix electronic components. Yes, even electronic components (the motherboard, plug-in cards, and so on) can easily and cheaply be replaced if they're damaged. I speak from experience here: I paid a guy close to $1,000 to solder new chips to an old laser printer's motherboard. The cost of a new laser printer at the time? $1,200 — an expensive lesson.

Is it a software problem?

Of the two types of problems, hardware and software, software is more common because it's the software that does everything in a computer.

Alas, software trouble is more devious than hardware trouble. Consider that most software has unknown bugs in it and no software developer fully tests programs in all possible configurations. Tracking the problem can be *tough*.

The good news is that software problems can be predictable. If you find that choosing some option in a program causes the computer to lock up — and it behaves that way time and time again — it's a software bug. If the mouse stops working in only one program, it's a software problem.

The insidious thing, of course, is that it may not be that particular program causing the problem. For example, Internet Explorer may lock up tight whenever you visit a certain Web page, but it may be a Web plug-in that's causing the thing to crash — very nasty, but at least you have properly identified the problem as software and not as hardware.

Some good questions to ask yourself

To help determine whether you have a software problem or a hardware problem, consider asking yourself some basic questions:

✔ Have you installed any new hardware recently?

✔ Have you installed any new software recently?

Remember that computers don't like change. Change introduces new elements into the mix. Sometimes, something works without a hitch. But, if you have a busy computer — one with lots of software installed and many peripherals — adding something new may be that final pebble in the gears that grinds your PC to a halt.

✔ Adding something new introduces the it-was-working-yesterday syndrome.

✔ The reason for the popularity of such utilities as System Restore in Windows XP and Norton GoBack is that they effectively uninstall new hardware and software and restore your computer to the state it was in when it last worked best.

✔ See Chapter 4 for more information on using the System Restore utility.

✔ Remember that adding new hardware also adds new software. Most hardware requires *device drivers* in order to work. This explains why it's tough sometimes to determine whether it's the hardware that doesn't work or whether it's just the software not cooperating.

Another unfortunate software problem: Viruses

A sad fact of computing is that some software programs are specifically designed to do nasty things to your computer. Called *viruses* or *worms,* they can arrive piggyback on a simple e-mail message and open like a mushroom cloud, to distribute havoc and chaos everywhere in your computer system.

The best way to fight viruses is with antivirus software. Windows isn't supplied with any antivirus software, so you have to pick up a third-party product. I recommend Norton AntiVirus because it's simple to use and easy to install. It's available at most software stores or over the Internet.

See Chapter 24 for more information on fighting viruses as well as other nasty Internet problems.

Hardware Things to Check When You Smell Trouble

The first things to check when you suspect hardware trouble are the connections, cables, and whatnot that link all the various pieces and parts of your PC:

✔ Is everything properly plugged in and receiving power? (Are the power strip on-off switches in the On position, for example?)

✔ Are cables snuggly plugged into their sockets?

✔ Are cables snuggly plugged into the *proper* sockets? (The mouse and keyboard ports look identical on every PC, but *there is a difference!*)

✔ Are *both ends* of the cable connected?

I could relate a story from my old computer consulting days: Once upon a time, I made $60 in two minutes by plugging a modem's phone cord into a phone jack in the wall. The business wasn't happy paying my fee, but the people there learned an expensive lesson.

Listen!

Is the computer making noise? All computers have internal fans designed to regulate the temperature inside the box. If the fan goes, the computer gets too hot and fails.

Do you hear the fan? Poke your head around the back to see whether the fan is spinning, just to be sure. If not, you have hardware trouble.

✔ Not all PCs have a fan. The Apple iMac computers come without a fan. I know that some older microcomputers and laptops come without internal fans. I suppose that a PC here or there could be without a fan, so if you know of one, please don't write in to tell me that I'm wrong.

✔ Some PCs can get hot even with the fan spinning. For such systems, you can get fan "upgrades" by adding a second fan to the PC's case.

✔ Laptops have internal fans, but they still run notoriously hot. To help keep your laptop cool, consider an external cooling pad. The pad contains several fans, and you set your laptop atop the thing. The result is a cooler-running and much happier laptop.

✔ Sometimes, the fan is integrated into the power supply. In that case, you need to buy a new power supply to replace the fan.

Figure 3-1:
Don't try this
at home.

✔ If you have to wait for the power supply to arrive in the mail, but still need to use the computer, you can operate it without the case's lid, as shown in Figure 3-1. See how I have used a little fan to help keep the PC's innards cool? I don't recommend this solution for the long term.

Touch!

Is the computer hot? Electronics do get hot, but they're designed to dissipate the heat. Heat is a Bad Thing for electronics. It causes errors. In fact, your computer manual probably has a "recommended operating temperature" guide somewhere — maybe even on the console's back panel.

✔ If the computer is hot, turn it off. Get it fixed.

✔ Also check a peripheral's power brick to see whether it gets too hot. Power bricks (more properly, *transformers*) do get warm, but should never be hot. If they're hot, they're broken and need to be replaced.

✔ Heat also refers to the room temperature. Generally speaking, the hotter the room, the more likely the computer is to malfunction. If it's hotter than 80 degrees where your computer sits, turn the thing off.

Check the monitor

To do a quick check of the monitor, first ensure that it's properly connected and turned on: A monitor plugs into both a power source and the computer. A CRT, or "glass," monitor plugs directly into a socket. LCD monitors typically plug into a power brick (transformer) and then into the wall socket.

The monitor may look dead, but the brightness may just be turned down all the way. Fiddle with the knobs to try to get a reaction.

Modern monitors are quite smart. If yours doesn't receive a signal from the computer, it displays a message telling you so. It says "No input" or "No signal" or something cryptic and obtuse, but conveys the general meaning of "I'm not connected to anything sending me a signal."

Some monitors have more than one input. My Mitsubishi monitor has an A-B switch for viewing output from more than one source. Some high-end monitors have both VGA and BNC connectors for the signal, plus corresponding buttons on the panel to choose either one.

- ✔ It's quite common for the power light on a monitor to turn green when the monitor is up and running. When the monitor isn't receiving a signal, the light turns yellow or flashes.

- ✔ The light also turns yellow when the computer is in Sleep, Stand By, or Hibernate mode.

  Speaking of which, tap the Ctrl or Enter key on the keyboard to see whether the computer is just sleeping and has shut down the monitor.

- ✔ On some computers, you have to punch the Power/Sleep button to wake it up.

- ✔ If you still have your hearing, most CRT (glass) monitors make a high-pitched whistle, to indicate that they're on. The top of the CRT monitor is also warm to the touch.

Other hardware tricks to try

This book is full of hardware tricks and tests you can use to determine whether your problem is hardware or software. See the proper chapter in Part II for more information on specific pieces of hardware.

Using Software to Check for Hardware Problems

Don't you hate it when you install some game or new piece of software in the computer and you invariably get this question: "Which type of graphics system does this computer have?" I feel like shouting at the program, "Hey! You're *in there!* Why don't you just look around and find out!?"

It's quite possible to use software to test the computer's hardware. Smart software knows where to poke around and what kind of responses are expected. If something is amiss, software can generally report it. After all, why not make the computer do the work. Isn't that what it's for?

The Device Manager

Windows comes with a handy tool called the *Device Manager,* which you can use to detect any hardware errors that are bugging Windows. You see, despite its lousy reputation, Windows is quite tolerant of sloppy hardware. Many claim that it's a fault of Windows — and it may be, but that's not my point: Checking with the Device Manager generally confirms that you have a hardware problem.

To display the Device Manager's window, heed these steps:

1. **Open the Control Panel.**

   You may find a link to the Control Panel from the Start button's menu.

2. **Open the System Properties icon.**

3. **Click the Hardware tab.**

4. **Click the Device Manager button.**

The Device Manager is shown in Figure 3-2.

In Figure 3-2, you see the telltale sign that something is wrong with the computer: The display adapter (graphics card) in this computer isn't working properly. The circle (which is yellow) flags any misbehaving hardware right there in the Device Manager window. Further examination shows that the display adapter needs a new driver.

So, is it a hardware or software problem? Officially, it's software because the Device Manager recommends getting a new driver. It seems like a hardware problem because the hardware isn't being recognized, so the device is being ignored by Windows. But it's really a software issue.

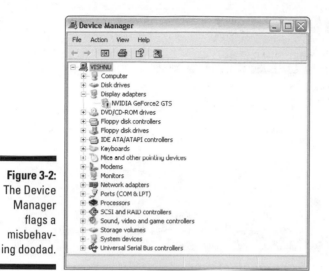

Figure 3-2:
The Device
Manager
flags a
misbehav-
ing doodad.

✔ See Chapter 24 for more information on how to use the Device Manager.

✔ You can find information on how to reinstall a device driver (software) in the various chapters of Part II that deal with specific devices (video and sound, for example).

Diagnostic tools

In addition to the Device Manager (see the preceding section), you can use software diagnostic tools to determine the status of just about any hardware component in your system. So, when you suspect trouble, you can run the diagnostic program to determine whether your hardware is operating properly.

Because these tools are a hardware thing, they generally come with the hardware itself and are not a part of Windows. To find the tools, look for the bonus disks that came with your computer when it was new. Otherwise, you can find the disks with the hardware device inside the box it came in.

For example, my network card's diagnostic program came on the floppy disk that accompanied the network card. Figure 3-3 shows the Diagnostic tool in use. Certain video cards also come with diagnostic and troubleshooting tools. You must look for them!

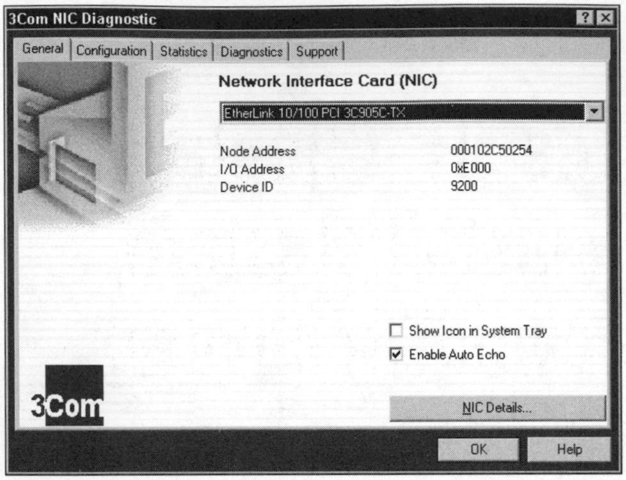

3Com NIC Diagnostic

General | Configuration | Statistics | Diagnostics | Support

Network Interface Card (NIC)

EtherLink 10/100 PCI 3C905C-TX

Node Address	000102C50254
I/O Address	0xE000
Device ID	9200

☐ Show Icon in System Tray
☑ Enable Auto Echo

3Com

NIC Details...

OK   Help

Figure 3-3:
A network
card
diagnostic
tool.

The PC itself may have a diagnostic tool in its *Setup* program, the program
that's run when the computer first starts. A message appears, such as "Press
the <F2> key to enter Setup." (The key to press could be any key. Commonly,
the Delete key or F1 is also used.) Inside the Setup program, you may find a
diagnostic tool you can use to test all the PC's components.

✔ One thing you cannot test for in most PCs is the RAM. Programs must
run in RAM, so a diagnostic program that tests RAM is a questionable
thing in the first place. How can the program test memory if the program
must reside in memory to begin with?

✔ Computers with failing RAM are generally a total mess anyway. It's best
to have your dealer or the manufacturer test your PC's RAM; it has the
proper equipment to give your computer's memory a good once-over.

✔ Diagnostic programs were all the rage in the early 1990s — not that
anyone needed them suddenly; it was just one of those computer crazes.
(And, it's probably why the TV show *Star Trek: The Next Generation* used
the word *diagnostic* more than any other computer term of the day.)

✔ You can get two types of diagnostic programs. One is only a report
program. It simply reports what hardware resources you have in your
computer. The program doesn't test anything. The other type of diagnostic program tests your hardware and reports the results.

✔ It's funny how the word *diagnostic* tends to lose its meaning the more
you say it.

Chapter 4

The "R" Chapter (Reinstall, Restore, Recycle, Recovery)

*T*his chapter is brought to you by the letter *R*. Many happy words begin with *R,* like *recovery.* And *rescue.* Good words like *repair* and *restore.* How about *refund, rejoice,* and *recreation? Really!*

I don't know why most of the handy tools and helpful troubleshooting tricks are associated with R words. In fact, it didn't dawn on me until I finished writing this chapter. (Its original title was "Escape from Doom and Peril with These Fine Utilities," which is a good title, but not as catchy.) After writing about Restore, Reinstall, Recycle, and Recover, I just couldn't help myself.

Enough recess! Remember your resolve! Read on!

Restoring from the Recycle Bin

To ease the panic that sets in when you can't find a file, you need to do two things: First, use the Find or Search command to try to locate the file (this topic is covered in Chapter 9); second, check the Recycle Bin to see whether the file was accidentally deleted:

1. Open the Recycle Bin icon on the desktop.

2. Choose View⇨Details.

These steps display the Recycle Bin window, similar to what's shown in Figure 4-1. Information about the deleted files appears in four columns: name, location, date, and size. Those labels help you quickly locate files you have deleted, as covered in this section.

✔ The Search command in Windows, the one you would normally use to locate lost files, doesn't look in the Recycle Bin. Keep that in mind!

✔ To recover a deleted file, click it and choose File⇨Restore from the menu.

✔ To recover more than one file, press the Ctrl key and hold it down as you click the files you want to restore.

✔ You must restore a file to its original location, the folder from which it was deleted. If you need to move the file to a better location, do so *after* restoring it. (Make a note of the location to where the file is restored.)

✔ You cannot restore files that were deleted using the Shift+Delete keystroke. Those files cannot be recovered by using any of the tools in Windows. (Various third-party tools, such as Norton Utilities, may be able to recover these files.)

✔ Rubbish is yet another R word, underused by Americans but right at home in the commonwealth.

Figure 4-1: Setting up the Recycle Bin for file recovery.		

Recycle Bin

File Edit View Favorites Tools Help

Back · · Search Folders

Address Recycle Bin Go

Recycle Bin Tasks
- Empty the Recycle Bin
- Restore all items

Other Places
- Desktop
- My Documents
- My Computer
- My Network Places

Details
Recycle Bin
System Folder

Name	Original Location	Date Deleted ▼	Size
sample.zip	C:\Documents ...	4/4/2002 12:42 AM	74 KB
samp80.jpg	C:\Documents ...	3/24/2002 3:28 PM	38 KB
samp80.jpg	C:\Documents ...	3/24/2002 3:28 PM	38 KB
lost45.jpg	C:\Documents ...	3/24/2002 2:11 PM	32 KB
lost02.jpg	C:\Documents ...	3/24/2002 2:11 PM	30 KB
02_071.jpg	C:\Documents ...	3/21/2002 9:02 PM	10 KB
M0405.bmp	C:\Documents ...	3/17/2002 4:57 PM	1 KB
F2108n.bmp	C:\Documents ...	3/17/2002 4:57 PM	803 KB
F1605.bmp	C:\Documents ...	3/17/2002 4:57 PM	1,299 KB
F1103n.bmp	C:\Documents ...	3/17/2002 4:57 PM	1,407 KB
S2801.bmp	C:\Documents ...	3/4/2002 2:06 PM	412 KB
M2808.bmp	C:\Documents ...	3/4/2002 2:06 PM	2 KB
M2807.bmp	C:\Documents ...	3/4/2002 2:06 PM	7 KB
M2806.bmp	C:\Documents ...	3/4/2002 2:06 PM	11 KB
M2805.bmp	C:\Documents ...	3/4/2002 2:06 PM	11 KB
M2804.bmp	C:\Documents ...	3/4/2002 2:06 PM	13 KB
M2803.bmp	C:\Documents ...	3/4/2002 2:06 PM	11 KB
M2802.bmp	C:\Documents ...	3/4/2002 2:06 PM	12 KB
M2801.bmp	C:\Documents ...	3/4/2002 2:06 PM	13 KB
F2807.bmp	C:\Documents ...	3/4/2002 2:06 PM	669 KB
F2806.bmp	C:\Documents ...	3/4/2002 2:06 PM	539 KB
F2805.bmp	C:\Documents ...	3/4/2002 2:06 PM	846 KB
F2804.bmp	C:\Documents ...	3/4/2002 2:06 PM	539 KB
F2803.bmp	C:\Documents ...	3/4/2002 2:06 PM	564 KB

Showing more columns in the Recycle Bin

For some reason, I don't feel that pretty icons show me enough information when it comes to the serious issue of restoring a file. That's one reason I prefer Details view for the Recycle Bin (refer to Figure 4-1). If you want even more information displayed about the dormant files, you will be pleased to know that the number of columns displayed, and therefore the information about each file, is adjustable.

To see more columns in the Recycle Bin window, such as the Type column, choose

View➪Choose Details from the menu. In the Choose Details dialog box, put a check mark next to the columns you want to view in the Recycle Bin window. You can scroll through the list to see the variety of information that's available. (Obviously, checking every item would make the window quite wide.)

Click OK to when you're done with your selections.

Restoring a file you deleted recently

To find a file that you suspect was just deleted, click the Date Deleted heading in the Recycle Bin window (refer to Figure 4-1). When the triangle next to Date Deleted points *down*, the most recently deleted files appear at the *top* of the list: Scroll to the top of the list and pluck out the files you want recovered.

Restoring a deleted file when you know its name

To locate a file by name, click the Name heading in the Recycle Bin window. That sorts the files alphabetically by name, either from A to Z or from Z to A, depending on how many times you click the Name heading.

To quickly scroll to a given filename, type its first letter on the keyboard. To find all files beginning with N, for example, press the N key.

Restoring a deleted file when you know which application created it (by file type)

Searching for files by type allows you to locate a file when you don't know its name but you do remember which program created it. To do so, click the Type heading in the Recycle Bin window to sort the files by their file type (or by which program created them).

Using System Restore

The System Restore utility in Windows is an excellent way to recover from just about any mishap, but specifically it works best for those it-was-working-yesterday situations. With System Restore, you can turn back the clock on your entire computer system — yes, back to the good old days when things were working normally.

Knowing when to set restore points

The System Restore utility lets you take your computer back in time only by setting various *restore points*. Windows sets them automatically as you use your computer. More importantly, you should set them yourself *before* you make any extensive changes to the system.

For example, set a restore point before you add or upgrade any hardware or software. Set a restore point before you mess with any Windows settings — graphics, sounds, or wallpaper. Set one before you modify your Internet or network settings or when editing the Start menu, rearranging files, uninstalling programs — before doing just about anything other than getting your work done, set a restore point. You will thank yourself later.

Setting a restore point

Never rely on Windows to automatically set a restore point for you. To do the job manually, heed these steps:

1. **Start System Restore.**

   From the Start menu, choose Programs➪Accessories➪System Tools➪System Restore.

   If System Restore doesn't start up, it's either disabled or you have another problem with your computer. See Chapter 21 for information on troubleshooting System Restore.

   The System Restore display is rather dry and dull, so I'm not putting an illustration of it in here. Yet.

2. **Choose the option labeled Create a Restore Point.**

3. **Click the Next button.**

4. **Enter a restore point description.**

   The restore point description appears when you later use System Restore. Therefore, it helps to be descriptive here.

Good restore point descriptions are "Installing new Zip drive," "Changing resolution for new monitor," "System acting funny," and anything that may remind you in the future of what the problem could be.

Bad restore point descriptions are "Installing" and "Stuff" and "Chad is singing again, and if I pretend I'm busy doing something on the computer, perhaps he will go away."

5. **Click the Create button.**

   The new restore point is created, and the current day, date, and time appear on the screen. Nifty.

6. **Click the Close button.**

   You're done. System Restore closes its window and sneaks off.

Now you can proceed to mess with your system or add a new gizmo or application. Those are the times when the system may not behave as you have expected. Not to worry! You have the safety net of a recent restore point, which you can bring the system back to if things don't work as expected.

- ✔ Don't neglect using the restore point description! It's valuable information that may come in handy later if something goofs up.

- ✔ Windows attempts to create automatic restore points as long as you leave the system on for a length of time. I leave my computers on 24 hours a day, so I notice restore points created just about every day, typically around midnight.

- ✔ Windows may not, however, create restore points if System Restore is disabled or has been disabled by a computer virus. See Chapter 21 for information on what to do in that case.

Restoring the system

When things don't go as planned or your PC suffers from it-was-working-yesterday syndrome, you can attempt a system restore. (My first advice is to restart Windows, which is covered in Chapter 2, and then do a System Restore.)

Follow these steps to restore your system:

1. **Close any open windows or programs, to safely save any unsaved information.**

   Restoring the system restarts the computer, so it's best to close and save now before you begin the restore process. See Chapter 21 for a nifty tip on shutting down programs.

2. **Start System Restore.**

   From the Start menu, choose Programs➪Accessories➪System Tools➪ System Restore.

   If there is a problem or System Restore doesn't start, see Chapter 21 for help.

3. **Choose the option labeled Restore My Computer to an Earlier Time.**

4. **Click the Next button.**

5. **Pick the date you want to take the computer back to.**

   If you have set a specific restore point, choose the date where you set that restore point.

   If more than one restore point is set on a date, as shown in Figure 4-2, choose it from the list.

   Sometimes, System Restore may fail if you choose a restore point too far in the past. In that case, consider selecting more recent restore points and working your way back to restore the system to an earlier date.

6. **Click the Next button.**

   Read the scary warning. The bottom line is that the System Restore process is fully reversible, so if System Restore makes things worse, you can undo its changes.

7. **Click the Next button.**

   Windows restores, restarts, and. . . .

   Hopefully, things wind up just fine, and the kinks are worked out of the system. After the system restarts, a screen eventually appears and tells you "Restoration Complete," with a summary of what happened.

8. **Click the OK button.**

I have suggested this operation to many of my readers with computer problems, and most of the time it meets with tremendous success. If not, further troubleshooting is needed. In fact, if System Restore doesn't fix the problem, it's most likely a hardware problem that needs further attention (replacement, for example).

Undoing a System Restore

If the System Restore operation fails to address the issue or you just would rather have not performed the operation in the first place, you can undo the changes: Start System Restore and on the first screen select the option Undo My Last Restoration. Click the Next button and continue through the steps to undo whatever it was that System Restore had done.

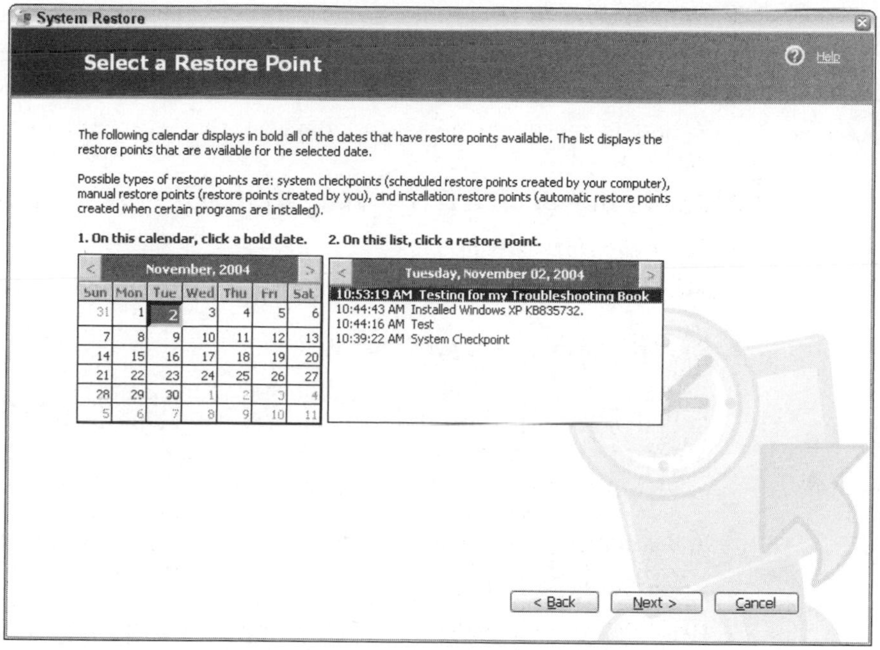

System Restore

Select a Restore Point　　　　　　　　　　　　　　　　　　　(?) Help

The following calendar displays in bold all of the dates that have restore points available. The list displays the restore points that are available for the selected date.

Possible types of restore points are: system checkpoints (scheduled restore points created by your computer), manual restore points (restore points created by you), and installation restore points (automatic restore points created when certain programs are installed).

1. On this calendar, click a bold date.　　　2. On this list, click a restore point.

<	November, 2004					>
Sun	Mon	Tue	Wed	Thu	Fri	Sat
31	1	2	3	4	5	6
7	8	9	10	11	12	13
14	15	16	17	18	19	20
21	22	23	24	25	26	27
28	29	30	1	2	3	4
5	6	7	8	9	10	11

<	Tuesday, November 02, 2004	>
10:53:19 AM Testing for my Troubleshooting Book		
10:44:43 AM Installed Windows XP KB835732.		
10:44:16 AM Test		
10:39:22 AM System Checkpoint		

< Back　　　Next >　　　Cancel

Figure 4-2:
Choose the
restore
point here.

Restoring Files from a Backup

Backing up a hard drive used to be a required (though bothersome) necessity for anyone using a computer. In the early days, hard drives were not only expensive, but they were also often unreliable. Backing up your data ensured that a safety copy existed.

Backup is more of a lost art now. I bemoan this topic even more in Chapter 25. See that chapter if you want to hear my caterwauling about why people don't back up.

Of course, if you do back up, you have the benefit of owning that second, safety copy of your stuff. It means that you can *restore* files or even your entire system from the backup copy.

Information in this section describes how to restore files from a backup. This information is based on the Windows backup program, though it's loosely similar to all backup programs.

✔ Backing up is the process of creating a duplicate of the information on your computer's hard drive. The backup itself is the copy. See Chapter 25 for more detailed information.

➤ Tools such as System Restore would be completely unnecessary now if more people made backups of their hard drives.

➤ For the restore operation to work, you must have a recent backup handy.

Restoring a single file, folder, or folders

If you can't find a particular file or have lost it or permanently deleted it, you can always recover it from a recent backup. Follow these (general) steps:

1. **Start the Backup program.**

   To start Backup in Windows, click the Start button and choose Programs➪ Accessories➪System Tools➪Backup. If you're using another backup program, start it in whatever manner necessary.

2. **Enter Restore mode.**

   In Backup, you first must click the Next button in the Backup or Restore Wizard. Then, on the next screen, you choose the item labeled Restore Files and Settings. Click the Next button to continue.

   In other backup programs, you may have to click the Restore tab or switch to whichever part of the program deals with restoring files from the backup archive. In some cases, you may even need to start a separate Restore program, run separately from the main backup program.

3. **Select the backup media or location.**

   Backing up can be done to a second hard drive, flash media drive, a disk drive on the network, Zip disk, CD-R or CD-RW disc, or any type of removable disk. This step involves not only inserting that media into the drive (or device) but also telling the backup program where to look for it.

   For Windows Backup, a list of recent backups is displayed in the What to Restore window.

4. **Choose the backup set.**

   Often, multiple backups are stored on a single disk. This step involves choosing the most recent backup from which you will restore files.

   In Figure 4-3, the Windows Backup program shows the most recent backup sets. The last one is chosen from the list.

5. **Browse to find the files or folders you want to restore.**

   An optional step in some backup programs is to pick and choose which files you want to restore. For example, you may have deleted only one file, in which case you need to restore only one file. The restore operation should let you choose which specific files you can restore.

   In cases of dire disaster, all files are restored.

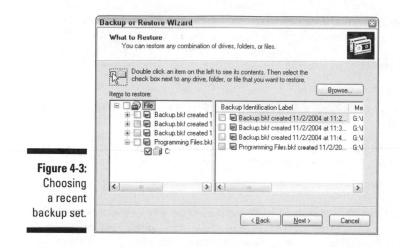

Figure 4-3:
Choosing
a recent
backup set.

In Figure 4-4, you see how the Backup program in Windows is manipulated to select only one file for restoring: Folders are shown in the left window, files on the right. Files or folders to be restored have a check mark by them. In Figure 4-4, only the file named CLEAR.C is selected for restoring.

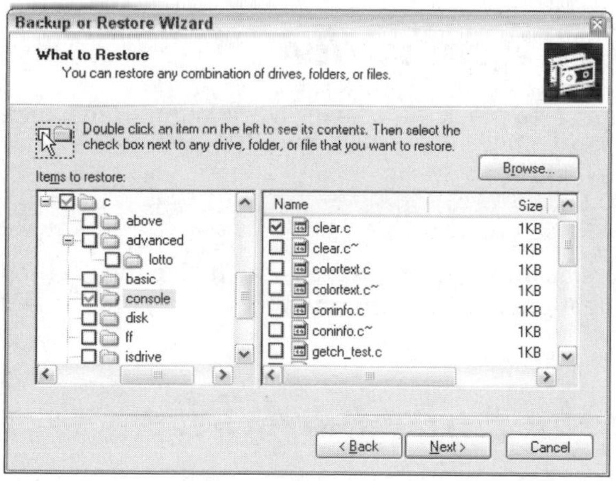

Figure 4-4:
Plucking out
a single file
to restore.

6. Review the summary.

As the Backup program prepares to read the backup media and restore the file, there are still a few options you may consider. One is whether to restore the backup files to their original locations. Doing so overwrites any files of the same name already at those locations, so you must be careful.

In Windows Backup, if you elect to restore files to a new location, click the Advanced button in the Backup or Restore Wizard. By doing so, you're pelted with an array of options for restoring the file. Otherwise the file is restored in the manner described in the wizard's window.

7. **Complete the operation.**

   Perform whatever deed necessary to make the restore take place: Click the Start or Go or Restore button.

   If the files are stored across several disks, you're asked to replace disks as the restore operation continues.

   And you're done.

I would say that of all the utilities I have ever used on any computer, the restore half of Backup is the most satisfying. It's not enough knowing that you have the backup copy. It's a great feeling when you actually get to restore a file and recover something that you thought was lost forever.

Be careful about overwriting existing files when you restore a folder! Make sure that you *really* want to restore the entire folder and all its contents before you choose a Replace All option. (You cannot recover any file that has been overwritten.)

Restoring an application

Alas, it's fairly difficult to pluck out a single application from a backup disk set. Applications in Windows don't really install themselves in a specific place. Therefore, trying to locate all the bits and pieces of a program that may be scattered all over a hard drive is a questionable operation.

Rather than restore an application, just reinstall it. See the section "Reinstalling applications," later in this chapter.

Restoring the entire hard drive

When disaster strikes, you can use your backup disks to restore your entire hard drive — for example, if your computer is infected with one of those nasty, nonremovable viruses. Or, suppose that your 12-year-old "computer genius" cousin decides to "optimize" your Windows folder. It's those severe times that call for a full hard drive restore operation.

Restoring a full hard drive involves these steps:

1. Create special boot disks to reinstall the operating system, or disks you can use to run the backup program and restore files.

2. Reformat the hard drive (often included with Step 1).

3. Boot with the special boot disks to restore files from the backup to the hard drive. Or, reinstall the operating system and then the backup program to restore the hard drive.

4. Restore from any partial or incremental backups since the last full hard drive backup.

Those steps are not only scary, they're also time-consuming! That is why I don't recommend such an operation for silly things. Unfortunately, most of the tech-support people working today recommend the reformat-restore operation like it's routine. It's not.

✔ Most backup programs come with a special boot disk, or they let you create your own disk, so that you can start the computer, run the program, and restore files when the hard drive may be utterly corrupted.

✔ Windows Backup program doesn't need a special restore disk. Just reinstall Windows onto the new hard drive and then use the Backup program to restore the backup files from your backup disks.

✔ Most PCs now come with a boot image, or Restore, CD, which you can boot on the computer to reinstall the system the way it appeared when you first bought the computer. Just stick the CD into the drive and restart the computer. If you're presented with the option to start from the CD, do so. That restores the entire system. After that point, you can reinstall your backup program and then restore the rest of your computer system from the backup disks.

✔ If your computer didn't come with restore disks, contact the manufacturer to find out what to do in the event of total disk disaster.

Reinstalling Stuff

Sometimes, the solution to a problem is as easy as reinstalling software. You just find the original copy or distribution disks or CDs, pop 'em in the computer, and reinstall. Problem fixed (most of the time).

✔ A special instance where reinstalling isn't what I recommend is for your computer's operating system, Windows. Too often, "reinstalling Windows" is presented as a solution by lazy tech-support people — especially when a better, less-time consuming, and less-destructive option is available. (Reinstalling Windows is one of my pet peeves, which I bemoan throughout this book.)

✔ Another thing to reinstall is a *device driver*. That's the software used by Windows to control a piece of hardware. Because reinstalling a device driver is specific to the hardware you're troubleshooting, that information is located elsewhere in this book. Use the index to locate the hardware for which you need a new device driver.

Reinstalling applications

Consider reinstalling an application for any of the following reasons:

✔ The application is behaving in a manner inconsistent with the way it once behaved.

✔ All the files "owned" by that application are now owned by something else, something you don't want them to be owned by.

✔ Files belonging to the application were deleted so that the application no longer runs or displays error messages as it starts.

✔ The application was accidentally uninstalled.

✔ The application was infected with a virus.

✔ The application develops a longing to tour the world's beaches and find "the perfect wave."

There may be more reasons as well. In my experience, I have had to reinstall only two programs. One was a graphics program that apparently didn't like another graphics program I later installed. Reinstalling the first program fixed the incompatibilities. The second instance was an older program that no longer worked, but somehow reinstalling it fixed things up nicely.

To reinstall your application, simply insert the Install or Setup disk in the proper drive. Go ahead and install the program over itself; you rarely need to remove or uninstall the original from the hard drive. (Only if the Setup program tells you that the original needs to be removed do you need to do so.)

✔ Generally speaking, consider visiting the Web page for the application's developer. Check for a FAQ list or any tech support you can find online that maybe has a specific solution to your problem.

✔ The support Web page for all Microsoft products is http://support.microsoft.com.

Bringing back bits of Windows

For problems involving Windows applets (Calculator, Paint, and FreeCell, for example), the solution is often to uninstall and then reinstall the program. This isn't as common as it once was, but it often clears up small, annoying problems that may happen with those common Windows programs.

The first step to reinstall a Windows applet is to uninstall it. Follow these steps:

1. **Open the Control Panel's Add/Remove Programs icon.**

   An Add/Remove Programs dialog box appears.

   In the Windows XP category view, click the Add or Remove Programs link to open the Add/Remove Programs dialog box.

2. **Click the Add/Remove Windows Components button on the left side of the window.**

   Please wait. The Windows Components Wizard appears.

3. **Choose the main category from the scrolling list.**

   You find most applets in the Accessories and Utilities category.

4. **Click the Details button.**

   This step displays whatever group of programs is held inside a category. The Accessories and Utilities category contains both the Accessories and Games categories. (It's funny that no Utility category is in there.)

5. **When you finally get down to the bottom level, locate on the list the program you want to uninstall.**

6. **Remove the check mark by that program, as shown in Figure 4-5.**

   This step selects the program for removal.

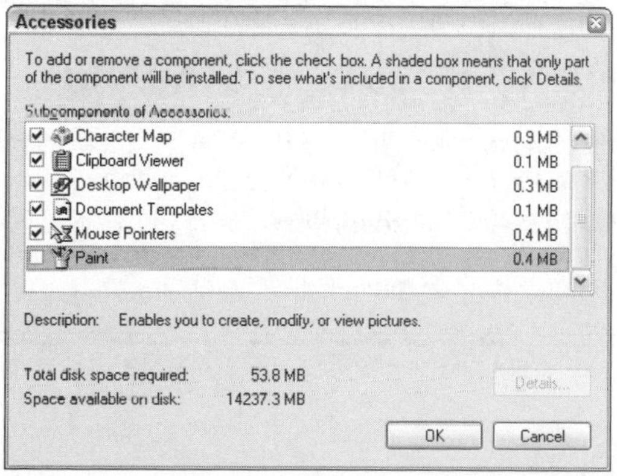

Figure 4-5:
Uninstalling
a Windows
applet.

7. **Click OK to close the various dialog boxes until you return to the main Add/Remove Programs dialog box. Then click OK to close it.**

8. **Restart Windows.**

   This step is optional, though it does officially remove the previously installed files. If you don't restart Windows, they may still be on the hard drive. Better not chance it: Restart Windows (refer to Chapter 2 for details).

   After restarting your computer, you reinstall the program, to give Windows a fresh — and, hopefully, better-running — copy. Now, you need to reinstall the program you just removed. Continue.

9. **Repeat Steps 1 and 2.**

   You want to be in the Windows Components Wizard.

10. **Repeat the steps you just took to remove the applet (Steps 3 through 6), and this time add the applet back in (reinstall).**

11. **Click OK to close the various sub-dialog boxes.**

12. **Click OK to close the Add/Remove Programs Properties dialog box.**

   Windows may ask for the CD-ROM to be inserted so that it can reinstall the programs. If your computer came with Windows preinstalled, the files are found on the hard drive.

After reinstalling, the program should work just fine. At least, that has been my experience.

  ✔ If Windows is unable to locate the files, try looking for them in the Windows\Options\CABS folder on Drive C.

  ✔ Uninstalling unused programs is another way to conserve hard drive space. This topic is covered in Chapter 23.

The Windows XP Recovery Console

The final R for this chapter stands for Recovery; specifically, a tool called the Windows Recovery Console. Sadly, the Recovery Console isn't for everyone. It's a command-line utility, ugly like the days of DOS. In fact, you may never use it; instead, it might be your guru or a tech-support person who wrestles with the thing. For this reason, I have hidden information about the Recover Console near this book's rump, in Chapter 24. Read there if you dare.

Chapter 5

Your Last Resort: Tech Support

*W*hen you buy a computer, purchase software, or sign some type of agreement for a service (such as the Internet), you should get some form of support. I recommend service and support over brand names and discounts any day of the week. Support is there to help you if things don't work as expected and to fix things when stuff invariably breaks. It's a good thing; worth the extra expense.

Alas, the quality of technical support has dwindled over the past several years. It has grown expensive and often intolerant, especially of the needs of beginners. Although you find good support departments here and there, technical support for consumer computers is rapidly getting a reputation as bad as the computer manuals of days gone by.

This chapter shows you the ups and downs of technical support and why you should use it only as a last resort.

✔ In the computer biz, there's a difference between technical support and customer service. *Customer service* deals with sales, sale support, product questions before purchase, and product return. *Technical support* is where you go when you have questions or problems with a product. Know the difference before you make the call!

✔ Looking for proper service and support is the fourth of five steps to take when you're buying a computer. See my book *Buying a Computer For Dummies* (Wiley Publishing, Inc.) for more information.

When to Use Tech Support

This advice is simple: Use tech support as a last resort, if at all.

✔ Most problems are easily "fixable" without having to call support.

✔ Use this book to help you troubleshoot many of the common computer foibles that everyone experiences.

✔ Technical support is also available for any peripheral or add-on hardware you may buy. In that case, call the manufacturer, as listed in your manual or on your invoice.

✔ Above all, you *paid* for support when you bought the product. They owe it to you. If you can fix it yourself, great. But don't feel guilty about calling support when you need it.

Boring tech-support history that you don't have to read

In the old days, technical support was purely technical. By that, I mean that the only people who would call tech support were technicians themselves, the office computer guru, a programmer, or a hacker. They knew computers. And, the folks giving the technical support were typically the software programmers or product engineers themselves. They knew the answers, and, more importantly, the people calling knew the right questions to ask. The system worked rather well.

As computers became more of a consumer commodity, tech support changed to accommodate more beginners. In fact, the folks at the old DOS WordPerfect toll-free tech-support line told me that the most common phone call they received was by someone who hadn't yet taken the product out of the box. Sure, those people needed help, and in those days the WordPerfect folks were willing to help them. (Sadly, the bean counters eventually took over, and WordPerfect had to cut back on its technical support.)

Computer companies now have to justify having technical support. The toll-free numbers are almost gone. Free support has dried up except for the first 90 days. After that, you have to pay a flat-rate toll, a per-call fee, or a per-minute fee. Even then, paying the fee doesn't guarantee that your problem gets solved or even that you don't have to wait on hold.

Yes, there's a time limit

Technical support is often "farmed out" to businesses other than the original manufacturer or developer. So, although you may think that you're calling the software developer, hardware manufacturer, or online service, you really end up being connected to some other company, one that specializes in handling technical support.

For the most part, the people answering the tech-support phones are knowledgeable about the product and capable of solving the problems. Unfortunately, because they base their business on the number of calls answered per hour (or per shift), their financial goal is beating the clock, as opposed to really solving your problem.

The average amount of time a typical tech-support person has to deal with your problem is 12 minutes, more or less. After that, he's under tremendous pressure to "dump" you. I have experienced this situation too often myself. And, my readers have related to me the disappointing results of being dumped: After 12 minutes, the person simply says "Reinstall Windows" or "Reformat the hard drive" and then hangs up. Most definitely, that is *not* the solution to your problem. It's the solution to *his* problem, which is to get rid of you before the 12 minutes are up.

When you phone tech support, keep an eye on the clock. If you have spent more than 12 minutes and no solution is working or the tech-support person suggests reinstalling Windows or reformatting the hard drive, you should protest. Ask to speak to a supervisor. Often, the supervisors aren't under the same time limitations as the grunts who have to answer the phones. That should lead to an answer.

Before you call tech support

Using a computer is a tough thing. These beasts are not simple. Anything can and does go wrong. The tech-support people know this, and they brace themselves for anything. They have to! Callers range from the timid beginner who still has the computer in the box to the hacker whose computer has been utterly disassembled and desoldered. You can make the tech-support person's job easier by doing a little research before you call. Follow my suggestions:

Find out who owns the problem. Narrow things down. Is it hardware or software? That way, you can call the proper place. Refer to Chapter 3 for more on making this determination.

Try as many solutions yourself as possible. Use this book to help you troubleshoot as much as possible. Tech-support people are blown away if you have already looked in the Device Manager or worked in the System Configuration Utility. They may have you look there again — if so, be patient. (They're typically following a script and must check things off before taking you to the next level.)

Determine whether the problem is repeatable. Be prepared to demonstrate to tech support that the bug isn't random and can be reproduced. I did this once, and the tech-support guy was amazed when the same foul-up happened on his computer.

Be prepared to give information, and lots of it. Do your homework before you call. This book tells you many places to look for solving problems. Go through those steps and gather as much information as possible. You don't have to spill it all at once to the tech-support person, but have it ready for when you're asked.

Finally, it pays to know which number to call. This is something I find frustrating: The tech-support number is typically hidden somewhere in the manual. Sometimes, it's right up front or in a tech-support index. But most often it's in a not-so-obvious place.

- ✔ When you find the tech-support phone number, flag it! Highlight it. Better still, write it in the front of the manual. Add it to your Address Book. You can even spray-paint it on the wall.

- ✔ See Chapter 24 for more information on the Device Manager and the System Configuration Utility (MSCONFIG).

Finding your version of Windows

One important thing to relate to tech support is which version of Windows you have. It also helps to know the version of any application or utility that you figure is causing the problem.

To find out the Windows version, follow these steps:

1. **Right-click the My Computer icon on the desktop.**

2. **Choose Properties from the pop-up menu.**

   The General tab in the System Properties dialog box lists all the information about Windows that you need to know, as shown in Figure 5-1. Beneath the System heading are listed the Windows version (or release) and then, below that, the edition and then the specific version.

   In Figure 5-1, the computer is running Windows XP, Professional Edition, Version 2002, Service Pack 2.

3. **Close the System Properties dialog box.**

You don't have to cough up *all* the information displayed on the General tab in the System Properties dialog box. Offer only what they ask for. For example, don't spew off the serial number unless they request it.

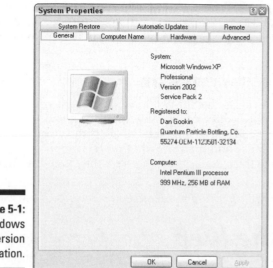

Figure 5-1:
Windows
version
information.

Finding the version number in an application program

Windows may not be the problem. It may be some other program you run. In that case, you may need to tell the tech-support person which version of that program you're running. This information is *not* the same thing as the version number for Windows; each piece of software has its own version number.

To find out the version of any specific application, choose the Help➪About command. (The About command is usually followed by the program's name.) That command displays a dialog box with the program's full name, release, and version information — and maybe even a quick button to click for connecting to tech support.

Making the call

Phone them up. Wait on hold. Listen to the silly music.

Be prepared to talk to a screener before you get true tech support. Sometimes, an initial person breaks in and gets your name, phone number, customer ID, and serial or registration number, and a description of the problem before you speak with a live tech.

Do some doodling in the Paint program while you wait.

When the techie answers, calmly and politely explain the problem. Then, follow the instructions as best you can. Don't bother saying "But I already tried this." Just follow along and, hopefully, your problem will be solved.

✔ For some reason, when you opt to pay for tech support, it happens sooner and faster than when it's "free" support.

✔ Keep an eye on the clock. Do this for two reasons. First, if you're paying for the call, you probably want to check the time you spend waiting on hold. Second, after the call starts, you need to keep an eye out for the 12-minute period to elapse and then see whether tech support is giving you the brush-off. (See the sidebar "Yes, there's a time limit," earlier in this chapter.)

Tech Support on the Web (Better than You Think)

As long as your problem isn't with the Internet in the first place, you can find some excellent tech support freely available on the Web. Most software developers and hardware manufacturers have support areas on their Web sites. There, you can review common questions and answers, troubleshoot products, e-mail questions, or download new software solutions. In fact, it's only after checking the Web that I bother calling tech support by phone.

Finding the manufacturer's Web site

After discovering whether the problem is hardware or software, your next step is to find a Web site to seek out technical support. Sometimes, this part is easy: Choose Help⇨About or Help⇨Support from the menu, and often the developer's Web page is listed right there. Neat-o.

For hardware manufacturers, the problem is a bit rougher. First, if the hardware came with your computer, contact the computer manufacturer (the computer manufacturer commonly lists contact information in the System Properties dialog box):

1. **Right-click the My Computer icon.**

2. **Choose Properties from the pop-up menu.**

   The System Properties dialog box dangles open.

3. **If necessary, click the General tab.**

4. **Click the Support button.**

   A dialog box is displayed that lists tech-support and contact information.

If this trick doesn't work, you have to hunt down the hardware manufacturer by using a search engine, like Google:

```
http://www.google.com/
```

Just type the manufacturer's name into the text box and click the Search button on the Google main page. Somewhere within the results is the page you're looking for.

When you get to the manufacturer's page, look for a technical-support link. Then, you can begin the process of searching for the information you need.

✔ You should also use these steps for finding support information for any extra hardware you buy for your computer. If the tech-support Web page isn't listed in the manual, use the Internet to search for the Web page.

✔ Be sure to use as few words as possible when you search for information on the Internet. Be direct: "S3 graphics driver upgrade" or "missing icon," for example.

✔ Another tip: If you search broadly at first, check to see whether any options can refine your search or "search within results." For example, if the search results on the tech-support Web page yield 400 answers, consider searching through those answers for something more specific to your situation.

✔ If you bought your computer locally, just phone the dealer for support. This is one case where it's easier to call and bug them than to use a Web page. But, for manufacturers, going to the Web page is easier by far.

✔ Also check on the manufacturer's Web page for an FAQ — Frequently Asked Questions — list.

Using the Microsoft Knowledge Base

Microsoft has perhaps the most extensive and exhaustive troubleshooting database on the Internet. They call it the Microsoft Knowledge Base, and it's similar to information the Microsoft tech-support people use when you phone them (and pay) for an answer.

Visit the Knowledge Base by typing this address:

```
http://support.microsoft.com/
```

Type a brief, punchy question or problem description; for example, "Windows shutdown" or "Missing toolbar." Click the button, and soon a list of potential solutions appears, perhaps one of which will save your butt.

✔ Definitely, definitely, most definitely use the Microsoft Knowledge Base *first,* before phoning up Microsoft.

✔ Much of the information in the Knowledge Base is a rehash from what you find in the Windows help system. To use the help system in Windows, choose Help and Support from the Start button's menu.

✔ Note that some problems have multiple solutions. Each one is for a different system configuration, so try to match your computer's configuration to the best possible solution.

✔ It helps to know Microsoft-ese when you're typing questions for the Knowledge Base. For example, you may use the word *hang,* but the Knowledge Base uses the word *freeze.* Be sure to try another, similar word if your initial search yields no results.

Downloading a new driver

Occasionally, your Internet search ends with the task of installing new software to make things work right. For example, to fix that CD-ROM glitch, you may need new software — a *driver.* To get rid of a printer problem or to make your printer happy with other software, you may need a new printer driver. Whatever the reason, your task is to download and install new software. Here's my advice for getting that done:

✔ Bookmark the Web page! Press the Ctrl+D key combination to add the Web page to your Favorites list. You do this just in case things go wrong and you need to return.

✔ Print any instructions for installing the new software. In Internet Explorer, choose File⇨Print to print the current Web page.

✔ When you have found the software you need, you click a link so that the software can be sent to you online *(downloaded).* A Save As dialog box appears. In that dialog box, choose a memorable location for the file. I use a folder named Downloads, which is created in the main My Documents folder.

✔ If the download fails or Windows tells you that it's "corrupted," you have to try again. If the file is still corrupted after the second download, contact the developer and tell someone there that something is wrong with the file.

✔ Drivers control hardware, so, to learn more about installing specific drivers, see the index in this book for the hardware in question. Instructions for installing or updating drivers are included throughout this book.

✔ Drivers should be free. I have found only one Web site where they wanted to charge me for a new driver — and for hardware I already owned. I immediately tossed out the hardware and bought something else. I wrote a letter to the hardware manufacturer's president — not that it did any good. Don't be suckered into paying for a driver or software upgrade.

Windows XP and Remote Assistance

I have answered technical and troubleshooting questions from my readers for more than a dozen years now. The biggest hurdle in trying to help someone is not being able to see what that person sees on the screen.

For example, someone may write, "The buttons are wrong; they're all over the screen." After two or three exchanges of e-mail, I discovered that the reader's taskbar was on the top edge of the screen, not on the bottom. Now, had I been standing right there looking at the screen, it would have been a click and a swipe of the mouse to fix things. But, via e-mail, it took four or five messages to get things right.

Being there is a big part of getting proper tech support. To help out, Windows XP has a feature named Remote Assistance. By using Remote Assistance, you can allow anyone on the Internet who also has Windows XP to take control of your computer and see what you see on the screen. That makes it a heck of a lot easier to fix things, as this section demonstrates.

 ✔ I recommend using this feature only if you really, really trust the person who's looking at your computer. If so, you may find a ready solution for some of your PC's problems.

 ✔ Remote assistance isn't worth diddly squat if your computer cannot connect to the Internet.

 ✔ Speaking of the Internet, the faster the connection, the more effective remote assistance is. I have done it with 56K modems at about 49 Kbps true speed, and it was tolerable, but not ideal.

 ✔ Sadly, the Remote Assistance feature isn't available on Windows 98 or Windows Me.

Setting up your system for remote assistance

Before asking for remote assistance, ensure that this option is turned on. After all, you can't let anyone else in when your computer lacks a door for someone to walk through. Follow these steps to ensure that Remote Assistance is activated:

1. **Open the Control Panel.**

   You can get to this window from the Start button's menu, or from any Windows Explorer or folder window's Address bar drop-down list.

2. **Double-click to open the System icon.**

3. **Click the Remote tab in the System Properties dialog box.**

4. **Click to put a check mark by the item labeled Allow Remote Assistance Invitations to Be Sent from This Computer.**

5. **Click the OK button.**

   The System Properties dialog box bows out.

Your PC is now set up for remote assistance.

You can also disable the Remote Assistance feature by repeating these steps and removing the check mark. I recommend doing this after you get remote help, to keep your computer secure.

Getting someone to help you

Obviously, you don't want just anyone barging into your PC to give you "assistance." The person must be properly invited. Follow these general steps:

1. **Get on the Internet.**

   You gotta be on the Internet for this to work; connect to the Internet as you normally do.

2. **Find someone to help you!**

   Ideally, the person must be another Windows XP user signed up for the Windows Messenger program. That way, the operation works smoothly on both ends (and that's the only configuration I have tested).

   Phone that person up and tell her to get online and to connect to the Windows Messenger program. Then, she needs to wait while you set things up on your end.

3. **Summon the Help and Support Center.**

   You can choose Help and Support from the Start menu or press the Win+F1 key combination.

   On the right side of the Help and Support Center window, you see the heading Ask for Assistance.

4. **Click the link to invite or ask a friend for help (the exact text may vary).**

   A special, Remote Assistance screen opens.

   If you're warned that your computer isn't set up for remote assistance, refer to the preceding section for information on setting things up.

5. **Pick your pal out of the Windows Messenger list.**

   The person should appear on the list, per your instructions from Step 1. This is the easiest way to get help from someone. You can try sending him an e-mail message, but things just work better when both of you are online and connected with Windows Messenger.

6. **Invite the person to help.**

   A message is sent to your pal, who is fortunately already connected, per Step 1. The pal has to accept the invitation, in which case you see a Waiting for a Connection dialog box.

   Eventually, you're asked whether you want the person to view your screen and chat with you. Click the Yes button, or take whatever step necessary to invite that person to help.

   The Remote Assistance dialog box appears, as shown in Figure 5-2. This is your control panel for granting the person access to your computer. It's also where you can chat while you're connected.

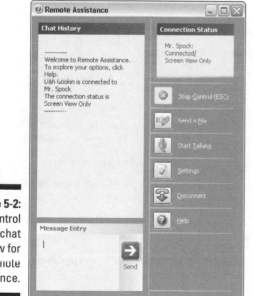

Figure 5-2:
Your control panel/chat window for remote assistance.

On the other system, the person is receiving a snapshot of what your screen looks like.

The person may chat with you via the chat window and have you do things, which she can see on her computer. Or, she may opt to control your computer for herself, in which case she can move your mouse and type things. If so, you see the dialog box shown in Figure 5-3.

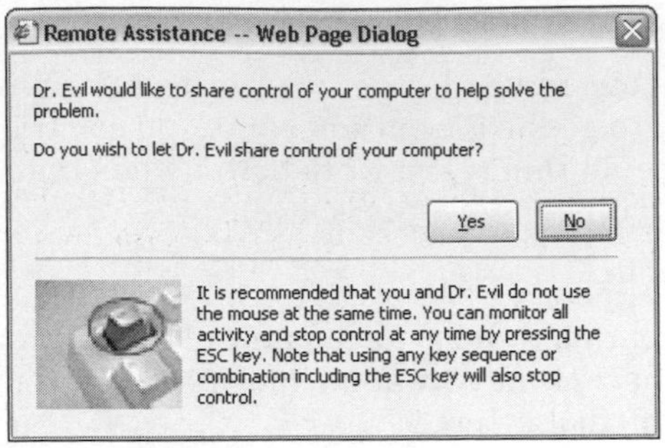

Figure 5-3:
Allowing
the other
person to
control your
computer.

> Remote Assistance -- Web Page Dialog
>
> Dr. Evil would like to share control of your computer to help solve the problem.
>
> Do you wish to let Dr. Evil share control of your computer?
>
> [Yes]   [No]
>
> It is recommended that you and Dr. Evil do not use the mouse at the same time. You can monitor all activity and stop control at any time by pressing the ESC key. Note that using any key sequence or combination including the ESC key will also stop control.

7. **Click the Yes button to allow the other person to control your computer.**

   You can cancel what the other person is doing at any time by pressing the Esc button on your keyboard.

   Hopefully, everything goes well and she fixes your problem without discovering where you hide the filthy pictures on your computer.

8. **When you're done, click the Disconnect button in the Remote Assistance dialog box.**

9. **Close any windows you may have opened.**

Hopefully, whatever problems you have had were solved by the nice Remote Assistance person.

- ✔ If you have Windows XP, you probably have already signed up for your .NET ("dot-net"), Passport, and Windows Messenger accounts.

- ✔ No one can get into your computer unless you invite him.

- ✔ You can cancel the connection at any time by clicking the Disconnect button or pressing the Esc key.

- ✔ If you don't want the person to meddle with certain areas of your hard drive, such as your personal finance folder, let him know ahead of time.

- ✔ Yes! It's *slow* over plain modems! It's very slow, but workable.

Performing remote assistance on another system

To help out another Windows user, start by arranging the Remote Assistance session. The person should let you know when you need to be online and ready to help. Follow these steps:

1. **Connect to the Internet.**

2. **Start up the Windows Messenger.**

   The person contacts you via the Windows Messenger program. You have other ways to contact people, such as by sending them e-mail and so forth, but it's much easier if you're already in Windows Messenger.

3. **Wait for the invite to appear on the screen.**

   It appears like any other pop-up message in Windows Messenger.

4. **When the invitation appears, click it.**

   A Conversation (chat) window appears, similar to the one shown in Figure 5-4. But, unlike in a normal chat window, you find an invitation to help the other person via remote assistance.

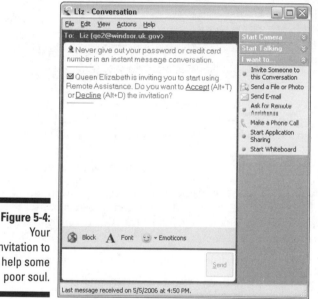

Figure 5-4:
Your invitation to help some poor soul.

5. **Click Accept.**

   The connection is made to the other computer, and the Remote Assistance window appears, which details what the other person sees on his screen, as shown in Figure 5-5.

   At this point, you can type in the Chat History window (on the left side of the window in Figure 5-5) and tell the other person to do things. What he sees on his screen shows up in the window so that you can see what's going on.

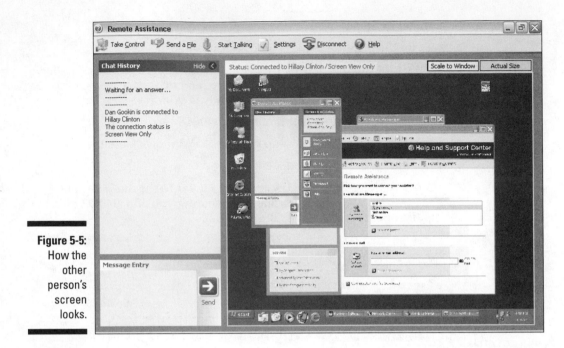

Figure 5-5:
How the
other
person's
screen
looks.

Click the Actual Size button to see the image clearly; otherwise, the Scale to Window option squishes everything to fit in the Remote Assistance window.

6. **To take over the other computer, click the Take Control button.**

   This step allows you to use your mouse and keyboard to manipulate the other computer. The results are displayed in the Remote Assistance window. Note that the person has to say Yes to the Take Control question before you can take over.

7. **Press the Esc key when you're done controlling the computer.**

8. **Click the Disconnect button to break the connection when you're done troubleshooting.**

   Be sure to close any other windows that may be left open.

Again, the idea here isn't to mess with the computer, but rather to *see* what he sees. In fact, it's often better to tell the person what to do and then watch the results than try to work a mouse over a slow modem connection.

Part II
Troubleshooting Minor Irks and Quirks

The 5th Wave   By Rich Tennant

Maintenance is chagrined to find out the squeak in Clark's disk drive is really a whistle in Clark's nose.

In this part . . .

Face it: Even at times of brutal desperation, human beings are essentially lazy. It's nothing to feel guilty about, and nothing worth "getting over." It's just one of those random and ugly facts about people. For example, only in the movies does the good guy go back and rescue his stumbling girlfriend when the monster is chasing them. In real life, the guy runs to the shelter and bends over all red-faced, panting and wheezing. Then, only after someone hands him a cold beer does he wonder, "Hey! Where's Linda?"

Why experience the solution when you can just look it up instead? It's human nature to prefer the ready-made solution. After all, so many computer problems are common or similar enough that someone somewhere must have had the same thing happen to them. Then, all you need to do is look up that answer and get on with your life. That's the function of the chapters in this part of the book. They're organized into problem areas, scenarios, or specific hardware or software. Look up a common question. Get an answer. Get on with your life.

Chapter 6

"This Just Bugs Me!"

- -

- -

*I*t's difficult to find any computer glitch that doesn't fall under the category of This Just Bugs Me. Even so, I tried to compile a short list of my top few favorite annoying PC or Windows problems plus their solutions. Obviously, I couldn't list *everything* that bugs you with your computer; there aren't enough trees in the world to produce the paper needed to print *that* particular book.

> ✔ Yes, even though a particular problem may be on your personal This Just Bugs Me list, it may not be in this chapter.
>
> ✔ See the index or use the table of contents to discover in which chapter the problem and solution lie.

Funny Startup Noises

Oh, those startup noises just make me laugh!

Well, no, not really. I suppose that I should say *peculiar* or *unexpected* noises as opposed to funny noises. No, if the computer made funny noises, the troubleshooting process would be far more entertaining.

Officially, the computer makes only the following noises when it starts (I leave it up to you to determine whether you think they're funny):

✔ The fan inside the computer case whirs to life and makes a soft, warbling drone. The fan (and sometimes you have more than one) is responsible for keeping the console's components cool.

✔ The hard drive spins up to speed, which makes a high-pitched humming sound that few people over 40 can hear.

✔ The computer beeps once as it comes to life. The single beep means that everything is okay. It's like the computer gets all excited and — golly, gee! — if this were an MGM musical from the 1940s, the computer would burst into song and have a big dance number with all the other office equipment. But, no: It's just a beep. That's the best Mr. PC can do.

The computer could make additional noises, funny or no:

✔ The monitor may honk when it comes to life. Especially for larger CTR (glass, not LCD) monitors, you may hear a loud honking noise. Actually, it's more of an "UNK" noise than a car horn tootling. This is normal.

✔ CRT monitors generally make a high-pitched whistling sound. Again, if you're over 40, there's no point in trying to hear it.

✔ The printer may hum a few bars of "Oink-grunt-oink" as it comes to life.

✔ Zip drives, as well as other external disk drives, honk and whir when they're first initialized.

✔ The scanner may also power up and play "Clink, grindily grind."

That's pretty much it for the early-morning computer cacophony. You're most likely familiar with all these noises and note that something's wrong when a noise goes missing or a new noise gets introduced.

✔ No, sadly, wearing earplugs merely masks the symptoms. It doesn't solve any noise-related problems.

✔ See Chapter 10 for information on troubleshooting sound problems other than startup sounds.

In the presence of unwanted noises

Noise problems are invariably hardware related, especially at startup. New noises generally indicate a problem with whichever device seems to be making the noise. Alas, these problems must be fixed by your dealer or the computer manufacturer. Especially if the computer is still under warranty, avoid a homebrew solution.

✔ If the computer beeps more than once, the beeps indicate a problem with the computer's startup electronics. This problem must be fixed by your dealer or the manufacturer. Tell them what the beep pattern was: several short beeps or long-short beeps, for example.

✔ Beeps may also sound off after you upgrade some hardware. That's simply the computer's acknowledgement that its basic configuration has changed. The extra beeps are typically accompanied by a text message on the screen explaining that new hardware has been found (or something like that).

✔ Hard drives can get louder over time. That means that their bearings are giving out. Of course, the real question is *when* will they give out. A hard drive in one of my systems was loud for an hour after I turned the computer on, but then it got quiet. So the problem could be intermittent. See Part III of this book for more disk drive information.

✔ Spinning parts in the computer can be affected by the weather. If it's an especially cold morning and the furnace hasn't quite heated up your office, the hard drives may peal an especially annoying squeak on startup. This squeak should go away when things heat up.

✔ A squealing monitor needs to be fixed by a professional. Or replaced. Or told that squealing doesn't work and that it has to find another, more polite way to ask for assistance.

✔ You can replace a pinging fan yourself, if you're good with electronics. In some cases, however, replacing the fan involves replacing the entire power supply, which can be done by anyone handy with a screwdriver or who has ever set up a backyard barbecue. Even so, if the system is still under warranty, have the dealer or manufacturer fix it.

✔ Here's another good way to repair a noisy fan: Clean it! Unplug your computer and open its case. Then, take a vacuum and suck out all the dirt, hair, and byte-bunnies that accumulate in all PCs. Ensure that you also clean the vents that the fan blows air through.

✔ Never open or try to repair a PC's power supply or the monitor. Despite whatever noises they make, these items cannot be fixed by mere mortals.

In the presence of unwelcome silence

Whether the computer makes too much noise or no noise at all, it's still a hardware problem, one most effectively repaired by your computer dealer or manufacturer. Worse, a missing sound typically means a dead something-or-other inside your computer. Pee-yew! So, the unwelcome silence is followed by more error messages and trouble. Take the thing in and get it fixed.

- ✔ Some computers don't beep when they first start up. Other computers may beep only if they're connected to speakers.

- ✔ One day, the sound stopped entirely in my old IBM PC. I heard no beep at startup and no music when I played my favorite game. The next time I opened the case, I discovered the problem. I was living in a rather decrepit apartment in El Cajon, California, and a mouse family (the rodent type) had moved into my computer and built a cozy nest atop the warm hard drive. The speaker apparently bothered them, so they *ate* the speaker's cardboard cone. I solved the problem by replacing the speaker and then moving to another apartment complex.

The Display Is Stuck in "Dumb" Mode

I believe dumb mode to be the lowest possible resolution on a modern computer monitor: 640 by 480 pixels. This mode renders everything on the display *very large,* and it doesn't give you much screen real estate to get any work done. Obviously, it's a problem that needs fixing.

- ✔ Dumb mode may also be caused by your computer entering Safe mode when it starts up. Not only does Windows alert you when Safe mode first starts, but you also see the words *Safe Mode* appear in the four corners of the screen.

- ✔ See Chapter 24 for more information on Safe mode.

- ✔ Yes, I am aware that even lower graphic resolutions are available (320 by 160, for example). The 640-by-480 resolution is the lowest mode supported by Windows. So there.

Checking the screen resolution

Before jumping to any conclusions, see whether you can fix the resolution the way the manual says to (if there were a manual):

1. **Right-click the desktop.**

2. **Choose Properties from the pop-up menu.**

   This step summons the Display Properties dialog box, which you can also get to via the Control Panel.

3. **Click the Settings tab.**

   In the bottom of the dialog box, you find a slider gizmo, used to change the resolution from Less to More. Figure 6-1 gives you an idea of what's where.

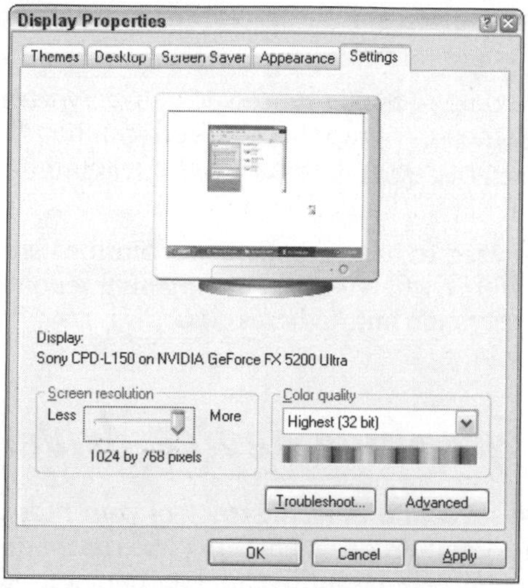

Figure 6-1:
Setting the
proper
screen
resolution.

4. **Adjust the resolution higher.**

   Grab the slider gizmo and try moving it to the right. The resolution displayed below the gizmo tells you the potential screen resolution. The preview window gives you an idea of how the new setting affects the display.

   If nothing works, you need a new display driver. See the next section.

5. **Click the Apply button to test the new setting.**

   Unlike the OK button, the Apply button lets you preview your changes without closing the Display Properties dialog box.

   If you don't like the new settings or they don't seem to work, return the resolution to its old setting.

6. **Click the OK button.**

   This step locks in the new resolution and banishes the Display Properties dialog box.

In the long list of who-does-what in Windows, *you* are the one in charge of screen resolution. You can pick and choose whichever resolutions the Display Properties dialog box lets you. No program, not even Windows itself, can change that resolution to something else. After you have made a setting, it sticks that way.

The only time the resolution changes is if a problem occurs with the display driver or, occasionally, if some games change the resolution and then don't change it back after you close them. (That's becoming less of a problem, however.)

- ✔ More is not always better. If you set the resolution too high, you may lose the number of colors available.

- ✔ Higher resolutions also tend to flicker more and cause eyestrain. Only the highest-speed, high-memory graphics adapters can handle the higher resolutions. If you're in doubt, don't set the resolution to higher than 1024-by-768.

- ✔ LCD monitors are optimized to handle specific resolutions, such as 800-by-600 or 1024-by-768 or whatever else the manual recommends. Trying other resolutions yields butt-ugly results.

Updating your graphics device driver

Dumb mode is often caused by Windows losing track of your PC's graphics device driver. How can the computer lose something like that? I don't know. But I do know that human beings are far more capable than computers and they often lose important things like eyeglasses or car keys. Anyway.

Without a specific driver, Windows uses what's known as the *standard VGA* driver, which gives you only 640-by-480 boring and dumb pixels to play with — not enough.

Fortunately, although Windows has lost track of the video driver, the driver most likely still exists on your computer. The solution is to go to your graphics adapter's Properties dialog box and reinstall the existing driver software. You can do that in two ways.

First, you can do a System Restore to reinstall the video driver: Go back in time to when you remember the display working properly. It could be yesterday or last Friday or whenever you last used your computer. Refer to the Chapter 4 discussion on using System Restore.

Second, and whenever System Restore doesn't work, you can follow these steps to manually replace the computer's graphics device driver:

1. **Right-click the desktop.**

2. **Choose Properties from the pop-up menu.**

   This step displays the Display Properties dialog box. You can also see this dialog box by opening the Display icon in the Control Panel. (Right-clicking the desktop is quicker.)

3. **Click the Settings tab.**

   This is gloriously illustrated in Figure 6-1. Gaze upon its beauty.

4. **Click the Advanced button.**

   A rather technical-looking dialog box appears, which is to be expected because the button was (after all) labeled Advanced.

5. **Click the Adapter tab.**

   The true power behind your computer's graphics is the graphics adapter hardware, not the monitor. The Adapter tab lists information about the graphics hardware installed inside your computer.

6. **Click the Properties button.**

   Deeper and deeper down the rabbit hole. . . .

7. **Click the Driver tab inside your graphics adapter's Properties dialog box.**

   Though each graphics adapter's Properties dialog box is different, each one has a Driver tab, similar to what you see in Figure 6-2.

Figure 6-2:
Install or update the video driver here.

8. **Click the Update Driver button.**

   This step starts a wizard, which looks for a better driver than the silly one you're using now.

9. **Obey the wizard!**

   Follow each step the wizard offers, by clicking the Next button after each step.

   The wizard may ask to search the Windows Update service. If so, ensure that your computer is on the Internet or ready to be connected. Note that this step isn't necessary if you're merely reinstalling the graphics driver already on your computer.

The wizard attempts to locate a better driver for your graphics adapter. Chances are, for this particular problem, that Windows will find the driver already on your computer. If so, use that driver, and everything will be fine.

10. **Take whatever steps are necessary to finish installing the driver.**

    This step may include finding the original Windows CDs or the CDs that came with your computer or graphics adapter that contain drivers. It may also involve restarting your computer.

In some cases, Windows may not be able to find a better driver. If so, consider visiting the Web page for the graphics adapter or the computer manufacturer to see whether you can find and download a newer or better device driver.

 ✔ If your computer has two display adapters, it's a guessing game to determine which one is the one that requires a new driver. My advice: Update them both.

 ✔ If the display is still in dumb mode after you restart Windows, visit the Display Properties dialog box to see whether you can then change the resolution to something higher (refer to the preceding section).

Annoying Programs in the System Tray/ Notification Area

One of the most vexing issues that vexes even the most vexless PC user seems to be those ugly little booger icons in the *system tray,* or what Windows XP calls the *system notification area,* shown in Figure 6-3. Whatever. It's littered with teensy icons collecting like dust bunnies under the sofa.

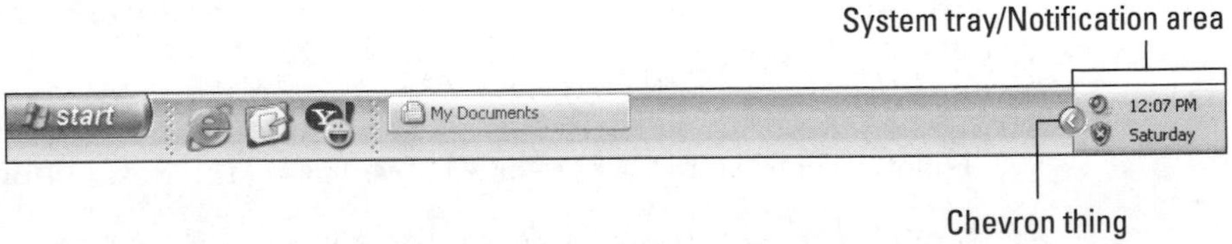

Figure 6-3: Finding the system tray/ notification area.

Although many people seem to tolerate the miscellaneous miscreants, a few downright can't stand the boogers and want to stomp them out of existence. If that's you, heed the advice given in this section.

✔ The system tray/notification area is on the far right end of the taskbar, and the taskbar sits on the bottom of the screen.

✔ In Windows XP, the icons in the system tray/notification area are hidden if they're not used. The chevron-thing button (refer to Figure 6-3) can be clicked to show all the icons.

✔ The term *notification area* is new with Windows XP. Before that, the area was referred to as the *system tray.* I use both terms.

"So what the heck are those icons, anyway?"

Each icon appearing in the system tray or notification area represents some program running in Windows — usually, a utility or some other "background" operation or *process.* The icon offers you a way to check that program's progress or to get quick access to its settings or more information. And that sounds really nice.

In real life, however, the system tray/notification area has become an electronic hippie commune for any old random icon that wanders by. After seeing about ten or so icons there, I begin to think "What the heck is this?" It's from that thought that the urge to purge grows into an obsession.

Required icons for the system tray/ notification area

What do you need to have in the system tray/notification area? Nothing. There's no requirement, and if you're crafty enough, you can eliminate *all* icons from that area. (A blank box remains, but that's it.)

Killing off teensy icons in the system tray/notification area

Apparently, word got to Microsoft that the system tray was bugging people, so Windows XP contains a handy, built-in trick for manually hiding all the icons and system tray/notification area detritus. Here's what to do:

1. **Right-click the mouse in the notification area.**

   Don't click an icon in the notification area — click in the notification area proper. If this step confuses you, just click the time shown in the notification area.

Beware of utilities to help you manage system tray icons

When I present the answers to system tray/notification area icon problems in my free weekly newsletter, a few people respond that tools are available to help manage the icons. Beware of these tools! I have tried a couple, and I was not happy with the results.

One such utility interfered with the way some of my programs operated, which forced me to

delete the utility in order to restore my sanity. Another program merely hid the system tray, which wasn't a good solution.

My advice: Try my techniques described in this chapter before you resort to some other solution.

2. **Choose Properties from the pop-up menu.**

   If you don't see the Properties command, you have clicked an icon and not in the notification area proper.

   If you're successful, you see the Taskbar and Start Menu Properties dialog box, as shown in Figure 6-4.

3. **Ensure that the Taskbar tab is up front in the Taskbar and Start Menu Properties dialog box.**

   Refer to Figure 6-4. The bottom part of the dialog box deals with the notification area.

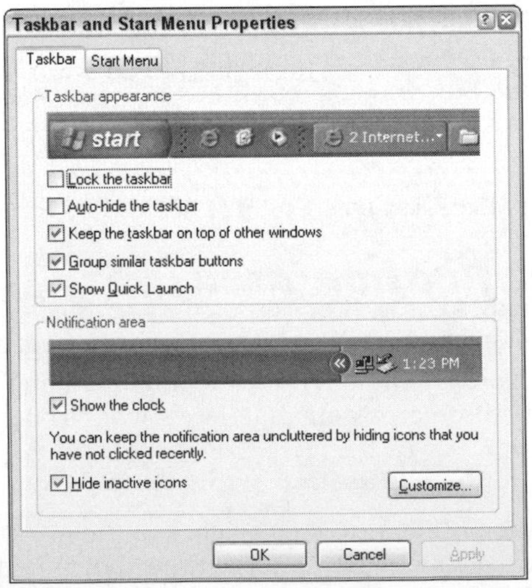

Figure 6-4:
The Taskbar and Start Menu Properties dialog box.

4. **If you don't want the clock to be displayed, uncheck the box by the option labeled Show the Clock.**

5. **Click the Customize button.**

   The Customize Notifications dialog box appears, as shown in Figure 6-5. This box is where you can permanently hide any or all of the icons.

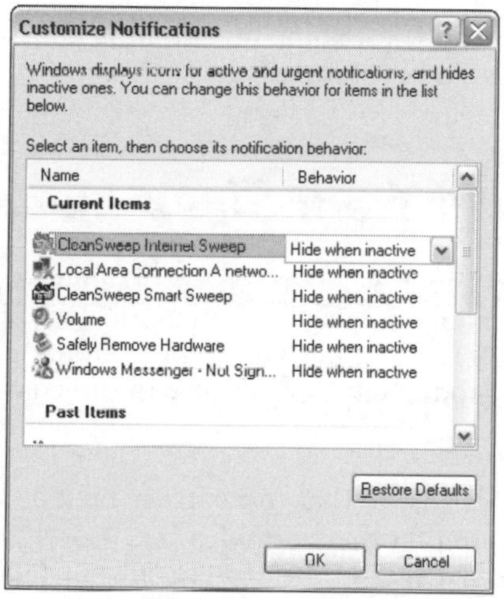

Figure 6-5:
Here's where you hide the icons in Windows XP.

6. **To hide an icon, click to select it.**

   This step displays a drop-down list in the Behavior column, as shown in Figure 6-5 (to the right of the CleanSweep Internet Sweep item, first on the list).

7. **From the drop-down list, choose the option labeled Always Hide.**

8. **Repeat Steps 6 and 7 for all icons on the list that you want hidden.**

9. **When you're done playing Easter Egg Hunt with the icons, click the OK button.**

10. **Click OK again to close the Taskbar and Start Menu Properties dialog box.**

Note that even with everything hidden, the notification area doesn't vanish completely. The chevron-thing (the Hide/Show arrow) on the left lip of the notification area still appears, which allows you to see the icons. But at least they're not "on stage" all the time.

Sleep Mode Poops Out, Hibernate Poops Out, We All Poop Out Now

Problems with Sleep mode (also known as Stand By) as well as Hibernation all stem from the same root: your computer's *power-management system*. That's a set of electronics that controls the computer's special low-power and power-saving modes of operation. For some reason, this hardware and software causes many PC users grief beyond despair.

The PC can't recover from Sleep mode

Some computers go to sleep and never wake up. The problem was so bad with Windows 95 that I recommended *not* using Sleep mode! But, since then, things have gotten better. Still, there are times when the computer just can't seem to wake up from Stand By mode. Rather than thump the computer on the head, there are a few things to try.

First, if your computer is a laptop, ensure that the battery light as well as the "moon" light are lit. These indicate that the computer has power and that it's still in Sleep mode, respectively. When either button is out, the laptop's battery has drained and, well, there's your problem! Plug the laptop into the wall, and you can use it again.

Second, determine whether this is a one-time event. Turn off the computer (refer to Chapter 2). When the computer comes on again, let it sit until Stand By mode comes back on. Then, see whether the same thing happens and the computer cannot revive itself. If so, see the section "Fixing the power-management software," a little later in this chapter.

If the problem with Stand By is a one-time thing, what happened, most likely, is that some program kicked the bucket during the sleep process. The problem is with that one program, not with Stand By mode itself or your computer's power-management hardware. (And, it's tough to determine which program walked the green mile, so just let it be.)

Third, when all else fails, just avoid using Stand By mode or just use Stand By on the computer's monitor instead. Leave the system and its hard drives on, but after a given interval, have the computer shut off the monitor for you.

"The Hibernation button is missing!"

This problem happens so often that I believe there's a Hibernation button convention somewhere and all the buttons leave their computers to attend it. Some thoughts:

✔ Hibernation is *not* available on every computer.

✔ Even when the Hibernation option is available, it must be enabled. This is done by using the Power Options icon in the Control Panel. Click the Hibernate tab and then put a check mark by the option labeled Enable Hibernation. Click OK to activate hibernation on your computer.

✔ The Hibernation option is *not* visible in the standard Turn Off Computer dialog box. To see it, you must press and hold the Shift key. By doing so, the Stand By button relabels itself to Hibernate. Then, you must click that button — all while pressing the Shift key — to get hibernation to work.

When the Hibernation button is missing, please review the preceding three points. Chances are that the second or third point is the solution you're looking for. Otherwise, keep reading in the next subsection to find out how you can update your computer's power management software.

Fixing the power-management software

Oddly enough, the power-management hardware in your computer isn't controlled from the Control Panel's Power Options icon. Nope, instead, you must use the Device Manager to locate your computer's power-management hardware, from which you can reinstall the driver that controls things. This process is tough, but it's often the necessary step you must take to fix your PC's power-management troubles. Obey these steps:

1. **Go visit the Control Panel.**

   You can get there from the Start button's menu.

2. **Open the System icon.**

   The System Properties dialog box appears.

3. **Click the Hardware tab.**

4. **Click the Device Manager button.**

   The Device Manager window appears, as shown in Figure 6-6.

5. **Open the item named System Devices.**

   It's toward the bottom of the list.

6. **Look for the power-management or ACPI item.**

   This is the tricky part; your PC's power-management system is uniquely named, so you have to search for it. In Figure 6-6, it's named VIA Tech Power Management Controller, though on most PCs it's named Microsoft ACPI-Compliant System. Regardless, the icon should have either Power Management or ACPI by its name.

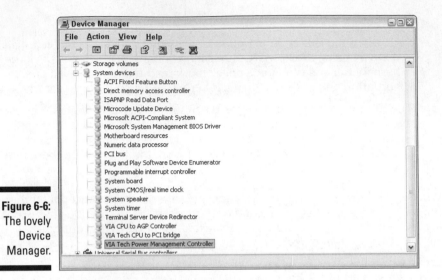

Figure 6-6:
The lovely
Device
Manager.

7. **Open the power-management item to display its Properties dialog box.**

8. **Click the Driver tab in the Properties dialog box.**

9. **Click the Update Driver button.**

10. **Obey the wizard to select a new driver.**

    Follow the instructions on the screen. If you need to connect to the Internet to visit the Windows Update site, do so.

11. **Click the Next button to work your way through the wizard, and answer questions as you go.**

12. **When the process is complete, restart your computer as indicated or follow whatever directions are given by the wizard.**

    Close any windows or dialog boxes that you have left hanging open.

Reinstalling the software should fix your power-management issues. If not, my next best advice is to visit your computer manufacturer or dealer's Web site and look for any updates or new software there. Only when nothing new can be found would I consider phoning up tech support for a solution. When you need to do that, refer to Chapter 5 in this book beforehand.

Oh, That Annoying Logon Dialog Box!

Must you log in to Windows? I'm afraid that the answer is "Yes" pretty much all the time. Sorry!

I once recommended removing or bypassing the Logon screen. In fact, if you're the only one using Windows XP and your account lacks a password, the Logon screen just doesn't appear. But, leaving your computer open that way is a major security risk, and I don't advise it.

The future of computing is password protected. You're better off getting used to entering passwords now than having to get into that habit later.

You Can't Open a File, or the Open With Fiasco

Some files were not meant to be opened. They're data files or support programs for other things you do on your computer. There's nothing wrong with poking around and trying to double-click every file you find. It's just that you had better be prepared to reset if anything new and wacky happens to your PC while you're poking around.

When you attempt to open an unknown file, you get the "I cannot open this file" dialog box, as shown in Figure 6-7. What do you do in this situation? Easy: Click the Cancel button.

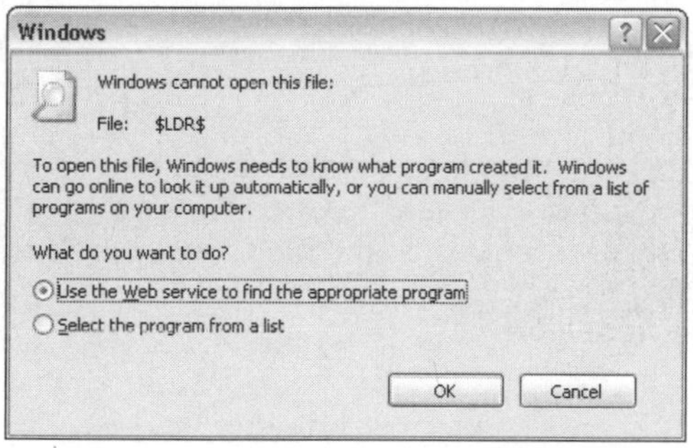

Figure 6-7:
Windows
XP is at
a loss.

> **Windows**
>
> Windows cannot open this file:
>
> File: LDR
>
> To open this file, Windows needs to know what program created it. Windows can go online to look it up automatically, or you can manually select from a list of programs on your computer.
>
> What do you want to do?
>
> ⦿ Use the Web service to find the appropriate program
> ○ Select the program from a list
>
> [OK] [Cancel]

Sure, you could have Windows venture out to the wilds of the Internet and search for *whatever*. Windows may find a program to open the file, so if you're curious, take a look. I have never done this myself. I either give up or, if someone e-mailed me the file, ask that person to send me the file again in a format my computer can read.

You definitely don't want to select a program from the list. If the icon can't be opened now, it can't be opened then either.

Common file formats your computer can read

Most of the time, I hear about file-opening programs because of strange e-mail attachments or files downloaded from the Internet. If you can't open a file, do what I do: Request that the person resend the file in a format your computer can read. Here are some of those common formats that just about any PC can read:

DOC: Generally, this is a "Document" file formation, though specifically most files ending with DOC are Microsoft Word files. Because Word is the most popular word processing program, many documents are saved and traded in this file format. (You can also open DOC files in the WordPad application.)

GIF: This common graphics file format can be viewed by the Paint program or Internet Explorer.

HTML: These documents are Web pages, which can be read by Internet Explorer. Just about any major application can save its documents in HTML format.

JPG: This is another common graphics file format.

PDF: This is the Adobe Acrobat file format. The P stands for Portable, which implies that you can read a PDF file on any computer. (DF is Document Format.) If your computer doesn't have the Adobe Acrobat Reader program, you can get it free at www.adobe.com/reader.

RTF: Using the rich text format for documents, any word processor can read these documents, which makes RTF even more common than HTML.

TXT: With plain-text documents, nothing gets simpler.

One handy trick to try in this situation is to right-click the file's icon rather than try to open it. When you do, you can access the Open With submenu, which can be handy for peering into the contents of some file types. Here's what you do:

1. **Right-click an icon.**

2. **Choose the Open With submenu.**

   The submenu displays a list of programs qualified to open the icon.

   Or, you can choose the Choose Program command to view a list of applications and select one to try to open the file.

This trick not only lets you specify which program to use for opening known files, but it also lets you experiment with opening unknown files without utterly lousing up your system.

Try opening unknown files by using the Notepad program. Notepad is designed to display pure text, so, for some text-based icons, it works very well. But, when all you see is gunk in Notepad, the file most likely needs to be opened by some other program.

That Wicked File Is Read-Only

Read-only is one of a handful of file *attributes* that can be applied to a file. In this case, the read-only attribute tells Windows that the file can be opened, examined, printed, and copied, but cannot be changed in any way — look, but don't touch, like the snake pit at the zoo.

Read-only files happen for two reasons. First, they're created that way. For example, any file on a CD-ROM disk is read-only, which it inherits from the read-only aspect of the CD-ROM drive (where the RO in ROM means Read Only). Second, you can change a file's read-only attribute at any time by using the file's Properties dialog box. That is also how you remove the Read-Only attribute from a file and restore it to normal.

Follow these steps:

1. **Right-click the file's icon.**

2. **Choose Properties from the pop-up menu.**

3. **Remove the check mark by the attribute labeled Read-Only.**

   See Figure 6-8, which shows the file's Properties dialog box for Windows XP, though it's similar to the older versions of Windows.

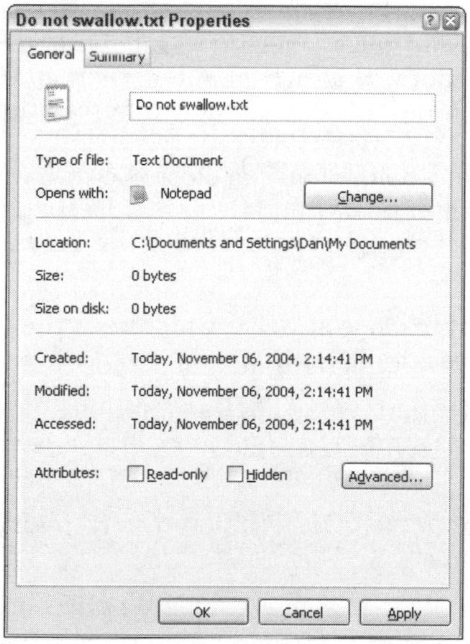

Figure 6-8: A file's Properties dialog box.

4. **Click OK.**

   The file is restored to non-read-only status.

The Microsoft Word read-only bug

Microsoft Word has a bug in it (although Microsoft doesn't call it a bug, I do). When you open a document created by another word processor, Word automatically makes that document read-only. It does this to ensure that you don't overwrite the original, non-Word document with a Word document. To overcome this bug, simply change the name of the document when you save it back to disk; use the File⇨Save As command and enter a new name as well as a new file type for saving the document.

Keep in mind that the read-only status may be set on a file for a reason. It's one of the few ways you can protect a file in Windows.

Full-Screen DOS Prompt

If you ever find yourself facing a computer that's showing an ugly text screen — not beautiful, graphical Windows — you have stumbled into The World of DOS. It's text, man — text!

DOS screens don't pop up as much as they used to. Still, it can happen. The first thing to try is pressing the Ctrl+Enter key combination. This keyboard command switches a DOS window from full screen to *windowed* mode, where DOS just looks like any other window (but uglier). After you're in windowed mode, you can close the DOS prompt window like any other window.

✔ You must quit DOS programs before you can close the DOS window. If not, a horrible error message appears and tells you just that. Even so, if the window is something you need to close, click the Yes button to terminate the DOS program.

✔ You can use your keyboard to close any DOS window: At the DOS prompt, type **EXIT** and press the Enter key.

✔ If you try pressing Alt+Enter and typing **EXIT** and nothing happens, somehow the computer was started in DOS mode. In that case, simply restart the computer; turn it off, wait, and then turn it on again.

✔ To restart the computer from the DOS prompt, press Ctrl+Alt+Delete (all three keys) simultaneously.

✔ If the computer appears stuck in DOS mode, type **WIN** and press the Enter key to run Windows.

"My computer always boots into DOS!"

Don't despair if your computer always boots into DOS. The problem can be fixed — well, unless you have an old DOS computer that doesn't even load Windows. But, if you have Windows 98 or Windows Me, you can easily fix the boots-into-DOS problem.

First, at the DOS prompt, type **WIN** to start Windows. After you're in Windows, run the Notepad program. Choose File⇨Open to display the Open dialog box.

In the bottom of the Open dialog box, choose All Files from the Files of Type drop-down list. Then, in the File name box, type **C:\MSDOS.SYS**. Type

that command exactly as I have written it here: C, colon, backslash, MSDOS, period, and SYS, and then click the Open button. This command opens a special boot file into Notepad.

In the file that appears on the screen, look for the line that reads BootGUI=0. That line is in the [Options] area. Change the 0 to a 1 so that it reads BootGUI=1. That's the command to start Windows rather than DOS.

Choose File⇨Save to save your change. Then quit Notepad. Restart the computer, and it boots into Windows rather than DOS.

Chapter 7

"Gosh! This Is Embarrassing!"

- -

In This Chapter

▶ Dealing with the Recent Documents list

▶ Erasing evidence from the history list

▶ Working around the AutoComplete feature

▶ Covering up nasty wallpaper

▶ Instantly hiding anything on the screen

- -

*N*othing makes you yearn for instant assistance like something unexpected and, well, *embarrassing!* This situation happens because the computer is programmed to indiscriminately remember just about everything you do. Remember that time you walked naked into the kitchen late at night and your insomniac great-aunt was sitting there? So does the computer.

Well, maybe it's not that bad. But, remember how handy it has been in the past for the computer to recall a file you just opened or to remember a Web page or someone you just sent e-mail to? That's computer convenience! Alas, the computer isn't discriminating with the stuff it remembers. Sometimes, places you didn't really intend to visit can pop up again — just like your aunt in the kitchen!

This chapter summarizes some of the many places where, well, "evidence" can be found that you have been somewhere shameful. Remember that the computer doesn't judge intent; no, it merely keeps track of your wanderings. If that concerns you, the tips and techniques presented in this chapter help you eliminate any potential cause for embarrassment.

✔ This chapter covers how to remove remnants of places you have been and files you have opened or saved, mostly from the Internet, but also from the daily operation of your computer.

✔ One of the best ways to prevent unwanted Internet filth from invading your PC is to use a tool such as NetNanny or CyberSitter. Visit www. netnanny.com/ or www.cybersitter.com/.

Deleting Recent Documents from the My Recent Documents Menu

The My Recent Documents submenu appears on the Start button's menu and lists all the files you have recently opened or viewed. Although this menu can be handy for opening any files you have recently worked on, it's also a severe security risk.

Do you really want to have a list of recently opened documents available? If you find yourself using the list, by all means, keep it. Otherwise, get rid of the dumb thing and cover your tracks, by following these steps:

1. **Right-click the Start button.**

2. **Choose Properties from the pop-up menu.**

   This step displays the Taskbar and Start Menu Properties dialog box, which you can also open through the Control Panel.

3. **Ensure that the Start Menu tab is selected.**

   Two Start menu options are in the dialog box: Start menu and Classic Start menu. The rest of these steps assume that you're using the Start menu option.

4. **Click the Customize button.**

   The Customize Start Menu dialog box wanders in.

5. **Click the Advanced tab.**

   This tab controls what you see and what you don't see on the Start button's menu, as shown in Figure 7-1.

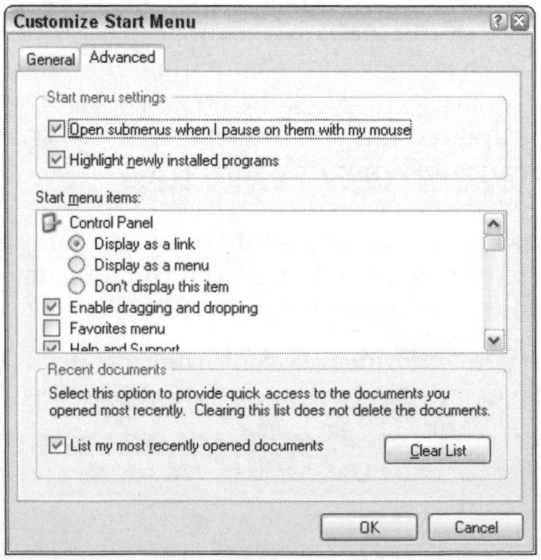

Figure 7-1:
Changing
the settings
for the
My Recent
Documents
menu.

6. **Click to remove the check mark by the option labeled List My Most Recently Opened Documents.**

   It's near the bottom of the dialog box. By completing this step, you remove the list.

   See the Clear List button? You can temporarily purge the My Recent Documents menu of all items by clicking the Clear List button. That doesn't do away with the menu, but it does remove the "evidence."

7. **Click OK to close the Customize Start Menu button.**

8. **Click OK to close the Taskbar and Start Menu Properties dialog box.**

   Now you can check the Start menu, and the My Recent Documents menu is gone.

And we all sing and dance a merry song of thanks.

Note that there's a difference between the My Recent Documents menu and the My Documents shortcut that may also appear on the Start menu. One is a shortcut to the My Documents folder. The other is a submenu that lists recently open documents.

Historically Speaking

Wherever you go on the Web, Internet Explorer (IE) makes a note of it, like some busybody neighbor or relative who must check up on you all the time. Internet Explorer notes which Web sites you visit and which pages you look at. At least it doesn't nag you about wearing a sweater. . . .

Supposedly, all this checking is done to make it easier to retrace your steps if you want to go back and visit someplace again. But it also serves as a trail of bread crumbs that just about anyone can follow to see what it is you look at on the Internet — obviously a potential source of embarrassment.

Clearing places from the history

To remove any Web site or specific Web page from the Internet Explorer history list, follow these steps:

1. **Click the History button in Internet Explorer.**

   The history list appears on the left side of the browser window, as shown in Figure 7-2. Web sites appear as folders. The pages you visit in the site appear as Web page icons beneath the folder, as shown in the figure.

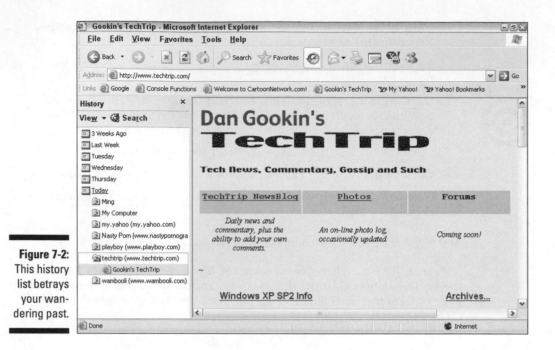

Figure 7-2:
This history list betrays your wandering past.

2. **Right-click any item you want to delete.**

3. **Choose Delete from the pop-up menu.**

4. **Click Yes in the warning dialog box if you're asked to confirm.**

   And the offending entry is gone.

Alas, the entry still may appear on the Address drop-down list. If so, try using the Clear List button, as described in the section "Deleting Recent Documents from the My Recent Documents Menu," earlier in this chapter.

✔ The Ctrl+H key combination can also be used to hide or show the history list.

✔ The number of days the history list keeps track of is initially set to 20. This value can be adjusted, as covered in the section "Disabling history altogether," just ahead in this chapter.

✔ Removing a history item isn't the same thing as removing an Internet cookie. For cookie information, see Chapter 18.

Clearing all the history

People who don't read history are doomed to repeat it. And, why not? Let's just go and make those same mistakes over and over. It builds character, or something like that.

When the entries on the history list appear to be overwhelming, consider zapping them all:

1. **Open the Control Panel's Internet Options icon.**

   Or, from Internet Explorer, choose Tools➪Internet Options. This step displays the Internet Options dialog box, as shown in Figure 7-3. On the General tab, you can control the history.

Figure 7-3:
You control history here.

2. **Click the Clear History button.**

   That removes everything.

Of course, if your spouse or computer partner is astute, they will have recognized that you zapped the history list. If so, be honest: Just tell them that things were in there that you would rather no one else see. Nothing wrong with that — it happens to everyone.

Disabling history altogether

If the history list is a complete and utter bother, just get rid of it: On the General tab in the Internet Options dialog box (refer to Figure 7-3), set the Days to Keep Pages in History option to 0. Click OK.

Although this technique eliminates history tracking for previous days, note that Internet Explorer still keeps track of the history *today.* So, if you have been somewhere today and you don't want anyone to know about it before midnight, you still have to manually delete the entries, as covered in the section "Clearing places from the history," earlier in this chapter.

Undoing the AutoComplete Nightmare

Remember that really smart-but-annoying person you once worked with? Whenever you started a sentence, he finished it for you. You would say "Let's go back to . . . ." and he would hurriedly say "The drawing board!" That saved you excess thinking time and tongue energy molecules, but frustrated your brain because you could never complete a sentence. I suppose that the fellow believed he was being handy. Call the chap Otto: Otto Kompleet.

In Windows, the AutoComplete feature is one of those nifty utilities that makes typing long, complex things — like Web page addresses — easier. What Windows does is to keep track of the places you have been and the addresses (and filenames) you have typed. When you start typing again, Windows automatically completes the address for you, by guessing what it is you want to type. Or, a drop-down list of alternative suggestions may appear.

Suppose that late one night Phil's wife wants to visit Mary's Boutique on the Internet. She starts typing `Marysbo`, and suddenly the Address bar fills with `Mary's Bondage and Discipline Dungeon`. Oops! It's time she had a talk with Phil!

Yes, AutoComplete can also be a source of embarrassment. Fortunately, you have several ways to deal with it, as covered in this section.

Turning off AutoComplete

When anything vexes you in Windows, the direct solution is usually to turn it off. Why not? Such features should be optional. On my computers, I find AutoComplete to be annoying; I'm startled when some other Web page spelling or suggestion comes up. No problem. AutoComplete can be turned off (or at least curtailed) by following these steps:

1. **Open the Control Panel's Internet Options icon.**
2. **Click the Content tab.**
3. **Click the AutoComplete button.**

   The AutoComplete Settings dialog box appears, as shown in Figure 7-4. Did you notice the two happy buttons labeled Clear?

4. **To turn off AutoComplete, uncheck everything.**

   Click. Click. Click. Click.

5. **Also click the Clear Forms and Clear Passwords buttons.**

   That removes anything stored in AutoComplete's memory. In fact, you can just perform this step (and Steps 7 and 8) to remove things stored in AutoComplete's memory.

Did you see the annoying message about the Clear History button? How hard would it have been for Microsoft to add a second Clear History button right there in the AutoComplete Settings dialog box? It was apparently too hard, so you must exercise your mouse-clicking muscles.

Figure 7-4:
Changing the Auto-Complete settings.

6. **Click OK.**

7. **Click the General tab.**

8. **Click the Clear History button.**

Now, everything is gone from AutoComplete.

Theoretically, this technique should work. No previous addresses or other information appear on the Address bar as you type. If something does, you can see the next section for a more direct and drastic solution to the problem.

✔ Using AutoComplete for Web addresses means that Windows remembers any address you have typed or the addresses of all Web pages you have visited, which can be recalled as you type new addresses.

✔ Using AutoComplete for forms means that any Web forms you complete that have similar fields (Name, E-mail Address, and Telephone, for example) are also filled in automatically as you visit various Web pages.

✔ Of course, the Forms option also covers entering information in search engines. If you have been searching for ladies' undergarments in extra-large gentlemen's sizes, that too appears if the Forms item is checked.

Removing an MRU list

MRU is Microsoft-spiel for Most Recently Used. This concept is the root of the drop-down list dilemma or the AutoComplete quandary. Those files or text you type are kept in various MRU lists and stored in a very dark and dank — and technical — place in Windows called the *Registry*.

Hopefully, the commands listed earlier in this chapter help you to get rid of the things you don't want on the various MRU lists. If not, you can venture into the Registry and manually delete things on your own. It's not that hard, but it does take a certain amount of intestinal fortitude:

1. **Click the Start button.**

2. **Choose Run.**

   The Run dialog box pops up.

   You can quickly summon the Run dialog box by pressing the Win+R key combination on your keyboard. (Win is the Windows key.)

3. **Type** REGEDIT **in the Open text box.**

4. **Click OK.**

   The Registry Editor shows up on the screen, as pictured in Figure 7-5. It looks — and works — like a Windows Explorer window. You open various folders to display more folders and eventually display the entries in the Registry itself.

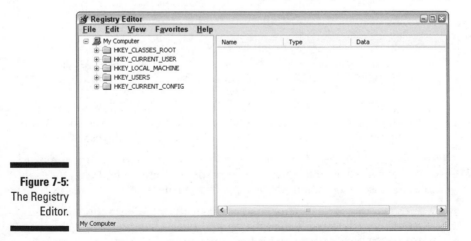

Figure 7-5:
The Registry
Editor.

To remove MRU items, you need to know where they are. This process involves being able to read a path to the MRU list and understanding which folders to open to get there. For example, here's the location where the addresses you type in Internet Explorer are stored:

```
HKEY_CURRENT_USER\Software\Microsoft\Internet Explorer\
            TypedURLs
```

Here's how to get there:

1. **Open the HKEY_CURRENT_USER folder.**

2. **Open the Software folder.**

3. **Open the Microsoft folder.**

4. **Open the Internet Explorer folder.**

5. **Open the TypedURLs folder.**

Refer to the path again. Note how each item in the path represents a folder to open. The folders are separated by backslash (\) characters. Now, look at the screen. You see the list of recently typed URLs or Web page addresses or anything you typed in the Address box. Figure 7-6 shows what it looks like on my screen, though it's a rather brief list because I just cleared my history.

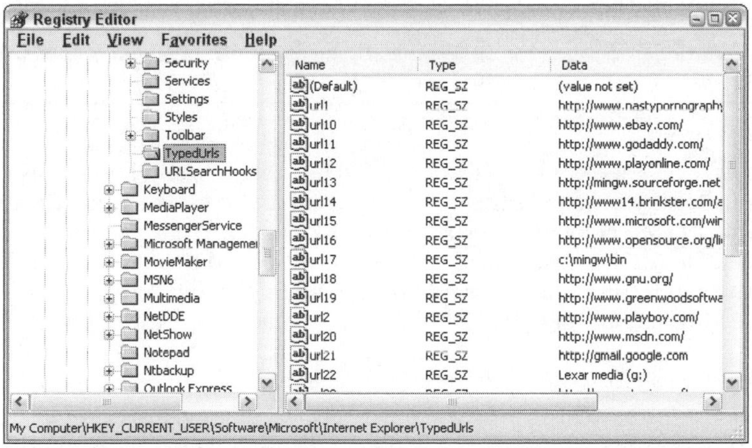

Figure 7-6:
Recently
typed Web
page
addresses.

To delete a specific entry, such as that offensive World Peace Web site, select it and press the Delete key. (Click the "ab" icon to select an entry.) Click the Yes button when you're asked whether you're sure that you want to delete the value. You're sure.

Table 7-1 lists a few other places in the Registry where you can find MRU lists. You can use them to go pluck out specific files that may be offending people — or stuff you just don't want other folks to know about.

Note that it's assumed that each location in Table 7-1 begins with HKEY_CURRENT_USER\Software.

Table 7-1	A Few MRU Lists in the Registry
Program	**List Location**
Excel	...\Microsoft\Office*version*\Excel\Recent Files
FrontPage	...\Microsoft\FrontPage\Explorer\FrontPage Explorer\Recent File List
Kodak Imaging	...\Kodak\Imaging\Recent File List
Media Player	...\Microsoft\MediaPlayer\Player\RecentFileList
Paint	...\Microsoft\Windows\CurrentVersion\Applets\Paint\Recent File List
Photoshop Elements	...\Adobe\Photoshop Elements*version*\Common\settings\Elements MRU
Run dialog box	...\Microsoft\Windows\CurrentVersion\Explorer\RunMRU
WordPad	...\Microsoft\Windows\CurrentVersion\Applets\Wordpad\Recent File List

If you don't see your application listed in Table 7-1 (and I don't have the space to list everything), use the Ctrl+F key combination to summon the Registry Editor's Find command. Search for a bit of text you have seen on the recently used file list. For example, if you have just opened the file NAUGHTY.DOC, you can search the Registry for that name. When you find it, you probably also find the MRU list for that application. If so, you can delete the entry manually.

Be sure to close the Registry Editor when you're done.

✔ Avoid the temptation to monkey with the Registry beyond my simple words of advice offered in this book.

✔ No, I can't recommend any other good book on the Windows Registry. I get this question often via e-mail, including requests that I write a Windows Registry book myself, but there really isn't that much to the Registry, and it can be a scary place if you're not careful.

✔ Set a system restore point before you do any messing around in the Registry (refer to Chapter 4).

Dealing with Nasty Wallpaper!

When you right-click an image on the Internet, you see on the pop-up menu the option Set As Background (or something similar). It turns the image into the desktop background, or wallpaper, which you can see when you use Windows. Sometimes, this is an accident. It need not be a nasty image, but whatever image it is, you probably want it off the desktop. Here's how:

1. **Right-click the desktop.**

2. **Choose Properties from the pop-up menu.**

   This step conjures up the Display Properties dialog box, which you can also get to through the Control Panel.

3. **Click the Desktop tab.**

   The Desktop tab is what sets an image, pattern, or straight color to use for the background or wallpaper. The current, offensive background image is previewed in the dialog box, as shown in Figure 7-7.

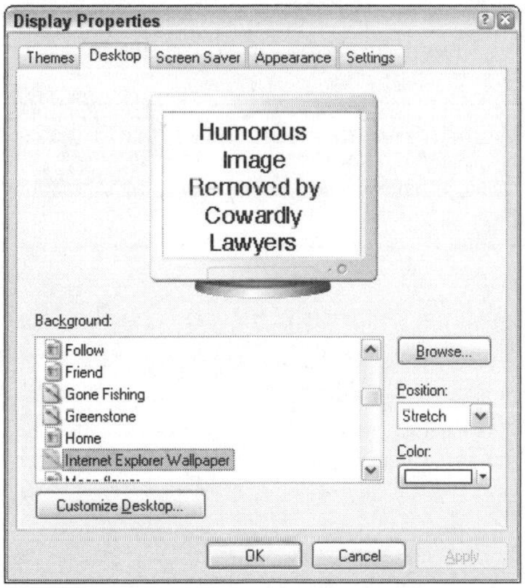

Figure 7-7:
Removing
an image
from the
desktop.

4. **Select a new background from the scrolling list.**

   Or, select None if you want a solid color.

5. **Click the Apply button.**

   The background on the desktop changes, by removing the old image and replacing it with a new one. That should fix the problem.

6. **Click OK to close the Display Properties dialog box.**

Generally speaking, these steps should fix whatever unwanted desktop images you have. To permanently remove the image, find the file and delete it.

Hiding Something on the Screen

I'm sure this never happens to you: You're looking at something diverse and interesting on the computer when someone else walks into the room. Do you panic? Do you freak out and yell at them? Or, do you quickly and stealthily know how to hide the entire contents of the screen?

Hopefully, you know the trick to instantly hide everything on the screen: Press the Win+M key combination, where Win is the Windows key. Win+M automatically *minimizes* every open window and leaves only the desktop displayed.

- ✔ Alas, you have no Win+M key equivalent if your computer's keyboard lacks a Windows key.

- ✔ The mouse equivalent for this command is to right-click the taskbar and choose Minimize All Windows from the pop-up menu. Alas, sometimes that's just too slow.

- ✔ Oh, you can always switch off the monitor, though that tends to arouse suspicion.

Chapter 8

Startup Problems

● ●

In This Chapter

▶ Understanding how the computer starts

▶ Dealing with immediate startup trouble

▶ Finding a missing operating system

▶ The joys of the boot menu

▶ The agony of the Startup menu

▶ Troubleshooting various startup messages

▶ Disabling those programs that start automatically

● ●

I t must take more oomph for a computer to get up in the morning than any human would know about. Consider the computer's electronic contemporaries: The television has no problem turning on. (Indeed, if there's a TV problem, it's not turning the thing off!) The toaster? Starts right up. VCR player? Works — sometimes even turns itself on when you shove in a tape. But, the computer? It must be a Herculean effort — a full-on electronic brawl — required to get the thing going.

The fact that the computer starts at all should be considered miraculous, especially considering the sheer number of things that go on in order to get the beast up and running. There's no reason for the delays, of course; because we tolerate a lengthy startup time on our computers, there's no rush for any manufacturer to speed up the process. Yet, for some reason, the delay is always long enough to build up some anxiety. Will the thing start? Why doesn't it start? And, what the heck does that message mean? All those issues are covered in this chapter.

How the Computer Starts

If you understand how the computer starts, you had better be able to pinpoint various problems that can occur during the startup process. This information isn't required reading, but it helps if you're familiar with what happens and where and how to be properly able to point the finger of blame.

Computer hardware is dumb. It needs software to tell it what to do. The problem, however, is that it's the hardware that starts up first. So, the hardware in a PC is geared toward immediately finding and loading an operating system so that the computer can become a useful tool and not a kingdom of confused characters searching for more instructions.

First: The first software the computer runs is encoded computer chips inside the computer's memory. Those chips are collectively referred to as the computer's *chipset*. The various chips tend to specific tasks, monitor things, and provide communications on a very low level. But, before all that happens, the chipset performs a special diagnostic test, called the Power-On Self Test, or POST. This test ensures that all the basic input/output devices (monitor and keyboard, for example) are working.

> **If it goes right:** Various copyright text appears on the screen.

> **What can go wrong?** When the POST fails, the computer either beeps several times or, if the monitor is working, an error message is displayed. Note that any error you get at this stage is always a hardware error.

Second: If the chipset is working properly, has passed the diagnostic, and found all the devices it was expecting, it attempts to find an operating system on one of the disk drives.

> **If it goes right:** The operating system takes over and continues starting up the computer.

> **What can go wrong?** If an operating system isn't found on any disk, a "Missing Operating System" error is displayed. Or, the text "Non-system disk" is displayed. This message is nasty.

Third: The operating system begins loading.

> **If it goes right:** You see the pretty Windows startup logo, or "splash screen."

> **What can go wrong?** Anything at this point can go wrong because software is in charge of the system. For example, in Windows a problem can be detected and you're thrust into the dreaded Safe mode. Or, Windows may detect new hardware and attempt to install it. Or . . . just about anything!

Fourth: The operating system loads other startup programs, such as device drivers, startup applications, antivirus utilities, the Task Scheduler, plus other programs you specify.

> **If it goes right:** Eventually, you're prompted to log in to Windows and start your merry Windows day.

What can go wrong? Lots and lots of things: You may find that you have missing devices or bad device drivers, an improperly uninstalled program can display various "missing file" or "missing DLL" error messages, and on and on.

Fifth, and finally: You can start using your computer.

> **If it goes right:** There is rejoicing throughout the land.
>
> **What can go wrong?** Everything.

It's important to know these steps because a different solution exists for the various problems that can occur as the steps progress. For example, a blank screen with a blinking cursor when you first turn on the computer means that even the chipset isn't working properly. That makes the solution relatively easy to find because you eliminate every other possibility.

- ✔ An older term for the computer's chipset was BIOS. However, the BIOS was originally one chip, and it did only one thing. Today's computers sport many chips, and together they comprise the computer's basic hardware. Together, the entire thing is called the *chipset.*

- ✔ BIOS stands for Basic Input/Output System.

- ✔ The chipset's instructions don't include loading the computer's operating system from disk. Instead, a program called a *boot loader* is found on the disk drive, and it's the boot loader that really loads the operating system.

- ✔ Boot loaders can often do more than merely load another operating system from disk. On some computers, the boot loader lets you select an operating system to start.

- ✔ System Commander, Partition Magic, or even the Linux program LILO are all examples of boot loaders that let you select an operating system to start.

Immediate Trouble

Nothing beats a novel that gets into the action right away or a film that begins in the middle of things with a chase scene (*Star Wars* comes to mind). It's the same with a computer: Nothing beats instant trouble. No sense in waiting for a long, dreary process to find out that something is wrong or missing. No, instant trouble is right there on the screen before you even have a chance to mangle the mouse.

On the downside, instant trouble is often the unfortunate sign of impending expensive repair or replacement. Not always, but often.

"I see nothing — just a blinking prompt!"

When the computer first starts, text should be displayed on the screen. Typically, you see a copyright notice. The computer make and model number may be displayed. (You may see a graphic image, but it's really a special text mode where the "characters" are bits of a larger image that are puzzle-pieced together on the screen.)

Traditionally, a memory count takes place when the computer first starts. You may see the counter tick away on some computers.

Depending on which hardware options are installed, you may see text regarding those options: hard drive, mouse, or video adapter, for example.

Eventually, the parade of text ends with a prompt to press a certain key — usually, Delete or F1 — to enter the computer's Setup program. You have about two beats of a lamb's tail to decide about that, and then automatically the computer's operating system is loaded, takes off, and displays that colorful, graphic Windows logo. That's the way it's supposed to happen.

When all you see is a blinking prompt, it means one of the following things:

Problem: A motherboard failure has occurred. Something is wrong with the motherboard — an electronics fault, no power, or some other type of corruption.

Solution: Take the computer into the dealer and have someone replace the motherboard. That can be expensive.

Problem: The computer is too hot. You can tell by feeling the case or checking to see whether the fans are spinning. A computer doesn't operate if its internal temperature is too hot.

Solution: Fix the fans. Some microprocessors have fans, and these can be replaced. Ensure that your dealer replaces only the microprocessor fan and not the entire microprocessor, which would be expensive. (However, if the dealer replaces the fan and the microprocessor is damaged, the microprocessor needs to be replaced as well.)

Problem: The hard drive has no operating system. This problem happens on those systems that show logos and not startup text. Occasionally, you may even see a "Missing Operating System" error.

Solution: See the section "The dreaded Missing Operating System message," a couple of sections from here.

✔ Some computers, such as eMachines, start with a graphic logo. You can change this in the computer's setup program so that you can see the startup text instead. That's a good option to choose if you're experiencing startup trouble.

✔ Make a note of which key combination starts the computer's Setup program. Text on the screen informs you of which key or key combination to press to enter this program. On most PCs, it's the Del or Delete key, F1, F2, Alt+S, or F10. Whatever the key, make a note of it, for example, in the manual that came with the computer or on this book's Cheat Sheet.

✔ Sometimes, cables come loose, which may lead you to believe that you have a major component failure, but it's just not the case. If you're bold enough, unplug the PC and venture into its case. Check to ensure that all the cables are properly connected and that all expansion cards are properly "seated" into their slots.

The nefarious Non-System Disk error message

The exact wording of the error message varies, but the cause is the same: You have left a nonbootable floppy disk in Drive A. The solution: Remove the disk and press the spacebar to continue booting from the hard drive.

✔ This error can also happen if you attempt to boot from a nonbootable CD. Same solution.

✔ If you get the CD error often or dislike the floppy drive error, you can fix it on most PCs. See the section "The computer stupidly starts from another drive," later in this chapter, for information on changing the boot order.

✔ If a hard drive produces this error, it means that the hard drive lacks an operating system. See the next section.

The dreaded Missing Operating System message

The most terrifying error message I have ever seen is "Missing Operating System." It's a hardware error message that comes from the chipset, though it could also be a boot loader message. Basically, it means that no operating system is on disk to load. Uh-oh.

There are many things you can do, however:

Boot from a bootable CD: For example, your computer may have come with a recovery disk, or you may have another bootable Windows CD. If so, try to start the computer with it. Again, this technique confirms that the computer is working fine; the problem may only be with the hard drive.

Use an emergency boot disk: Windows used to have a tool for making such a recovery disk, but because Windows XP is so huge, it doesn't fit on a floppy disk any more. Instead, you can still find emergency boot disks or CDs with some of your utility programs.

For example, Norton Utilities comes with an emergency boot disk that you can use to start the computer and, hopefully, make some repairs. Disk partitioning software also comes with emergency startup disks in case something goes wrong with that software. Finally, some third-party backup programs have boot disks you can use so that you can restore your computer system from a set of backup disks.

Reinstall your computer system: The final step, which is most drastic and terrible, is to merely start over and attempt a full system recovery. Most PCs come with a recovery CD, which you can use to reinstall basic system software and return your computer to the same state it was in when you took it out of the box.

I wish that I had better news on this error message. Generally speaking, the only way your operating system (Windows) can disappear and go for a powder is if you have somehow messed with it. This situation can happen if you attempt to modify or change the hard drive's partition tables, boot sector, or master boot record or, well, if you just up and delete all of Windows.

- ✔ Another culprit? Computer viruses. The Monkey virus can delete the FAT resource on a hard drive, which is the map that tells Windows where to find files. When the FAT is gone, so is the hard drive.

- ✔ Norton has a utility that may recover a hard drive if the FAT is damaged — but don't bet your data on it: Back up the hard drive and use antivirus software as a precaution.

- ✔ Hardware-wise, this problem may occur if the hard drive fails outright. However, that problem generates a BIOS error message on most systems when the hard drive fails to initialize.

- ✔ Does this stuff scare you? Then it's a good time to consider a backup strategy (see Chapter 25).

The computer stupidly starts from another drive

Starting the computer from a disk drive other than the hard drive isn't really trouble, though it can often be annoying and may lead to some surprise. Traditionally, the PC boots first from the floppy drive A, to check for the presence of a disk there and, if so, an operating system on that disk. Then, Drive C is checked.

Today's computers often check Drive A, the hard drive, and a CD-ROM drive. I have noticed that if I keep a CD-ROM in the drive, some of my test computers quiz me when they're started: "Do you want to boot from the CD?" or "Press any key to boot the CD." This option is valuable if anything happens to the hard drive.

If you would rather not mess with such messages, you can change the boot order. Most computers let you do this through their Setup programs: Read the screen when the computer first starts. Take note of which key (or keys) to press to enter the Setup program.

In the Setup program, look for boot information. You may see an option there to change the boot order, by specifying which disk drives you want the PC to check for an operating system and in which order.

Be sure to save your selection to the Setup program's memory if you make any changes.

- ✔ Not every PC's Setup program has boot options that let you change the order of which disk is checked for an operating system.

- ✔ I generally disable booting from Drive A on my computers; that way, I can be lazy and leave a disk in the drive, and it doesn't stop up my computer's boot process.

- ✔ If you have an emergency and you need to boot from a floppy or CD, you can rerun the Setup program and, once again, change the boot order. That way, you can use an emergency boot disk, if the need arises.

Dealing with the Boot Menu

It's entirely possible to have multiple operating systems on the same computer. For example, one test PC I have has Windows XP, Windows Me, Windows 3.1, DOS, and Linux all on the same system. This arrangement is accomplished through a software program I use, called System Commander, but it can also be done in Windows XP (and Windows 2000, though it's not specifically covered in this book).

When you have your system set up to boot into multiple operating systems, you see a boot menu appear as the computer starts. (On a computer with one operating system, you would see that sole operating system start.) You can then select from a list which operating system you want.

Normally, this choice is a good thing. After all, today's hard drives are roomy, and the ability to support several operating systems is entirely possible.

In Windows XP, the Boot menu feature is controlled from the Startup and Recovery dialog box, as shown in Figure 8-1.

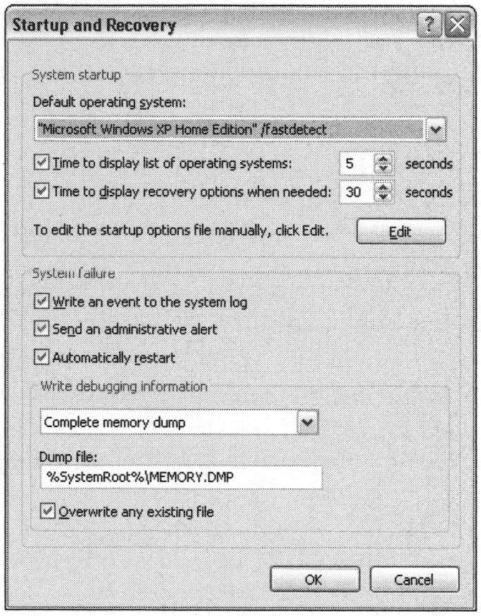

Figure 8-1:
Controlling
the boot
menu in
Windows
XP.

Here's how to display that dialog box:

1. **Right-click the My Computer icon on the desktop.**

2. **Choose the Properties command from the pop-up menu.**

   The System Properties dialog box appears.

3. **Click the Advanced tab.**

   Advanced doesn't imply anything dangerous or scary. I view it as a word Microsoft uses to throw in all the leftovers it couldn't stick in any other category.

4. **In the Startup and Recovery area, click the Settings button.**

   It's the lowest of the three Settings buttons in the dialog box. This step displays the Startup and Recovery dialog box, as shown in Figure 8-1.

The drop-down Default operating system list displays the available operating system on your computer. (At least, it displays the operating systems that Windows itself knows about.) This is where you choose which operating system you want to boot from automatically; for example, when you're away from your computer when it starts.

The Time to Display List of Operating Systems option tells Windows how many seconds to display the list before the default operating system is automatically chosen.

5. **To disable the menu, remove the check mark by the option Time to display List of Operating Systems.**

   This way, Windows always boots into the operating system you have selected.

6. **Click OK when you're done making changes to this dialog box.**

Again, the list of operating systems appears only if you have installed multiple versions of Windows on a PC and Windows itself is managing those operating systems.

> ✔ If you're using another system to control which operating system starts, such as System Commander or the Linux LILO program, you have to check its documentation for the various options and settings.
>
> ✔ Now would certainly be a good time for a hot, soft peanut butter cookie.

Getting at the Windows Advanced Options Menu (Startup Menu)

Not to confuse you or anything, but your computer has a third startup menu. In addition to the Setup menu and Boot menu, there's also the Windows Advanced Options menu. Here's a rundown:

Setup menu: This is part of the computer's Setup program, and it appears when you press a certain key when the computer starts. The Setup menu, or Setup program, is used to configure your computer's hardware.

Boot menu: This menu appears courtesy of the boot loader. The menu allows you to select an operating system to start, but only when more than one operating system is installed in the computer. Or, if you have configured the Windows XP Recovery Console, the Boot menu also displays that option.

Windows Advanced Options menu: Also known as the Startup menu, this menu is used for troubleshooting your computer's startup woes. It's generated by Windows itself, so this is the last of the three startup menus available. You see it only if you know the trick.

The trick? Why, the F8 key! To see the Windows Advanced Options menu, press the F8 key immediately after you hear the computer beep or you see the menu to select an operating system or you see the "Starting Windows" message on the screen. If you're paranoid, just keep pressing the F8 key until you see the Windows Advanced Options menu, a sample of which is shown in Figure 8-2.

Figure 8-2:
The
Windows
Advanced
Options
menu, or
Startup
menu.

```
Windows Advanced Options Menu
Please select an option:

   Safe Mode
   Safe Mode with Networking
   Safe Mode with Command Prompt

   Enable Boot Logging
   Enable VGA Mode
   Last Known Good Configuration (your most recent settings that worked)
   Directory Services Restore Mode (Windows domain controllers only)
   Debugging Mode
   Disable automatic restart on system failure

   Start Windows Normally
   Reboot
   Return to OS Choices Menu

Use the up and down arrow keys to move the highlight to your choice.
```

REMEMBER

You have to be quick! If you're too late, you don't see the Windows Advanced Options Menu.

The Windows Advanced Options menu typically displays one or more of the following items, depending on your version of Windows and which options are installed:

✔ **Safe mode:** The computer is started, but Windows doesn't load any specific hardware drivers. Please see Chapter 24 for all the details and reasons why.

✔ **Safe mode with networking:** This option is the same as Safe mode, but with networking abilities enabled so that you can use the network and, possibly, restore a network backup or download updated files from a server.

✔ **Safe mode with command prompt:** The computer is started in DOS mode in Windows and uses only basic configuration files. Note that this is the only DOS mode, or command prompt, startup option available to Windows XP.

✔ **Enable boot logging:** A text file is created as the computer starts, listing which programs or processes start and whether they're successful. The file is named NTBTLOG.TXT, found in the Windows folder. You can use the file to pinpoint problems the computer may have when starting, though the information there is decipherable only by highly trained tech-support people or Vulcans.

✔ **Enable VGA mode:** Select this option if you're having video troubles in Windows. The option looks similar to Safe mode, but unlike in Safe mode, the rest of the computer starts up normally (only the video driver is disabled). That way, you can fix a video problem and still have the rest of your computer in working order.

✔ **Last known good configuration:** This option uses a type of System Restore "on the fly" to return the computer to a state where it last started properly. This option is good to choose if you're unable to start the computer to run System Restore after some upgrade. Alas, unlike a real System Restore, this option doesn't fix or uninstall bad drivers or missing files. (You need to run System Restore in Safe mode for that to happen.)

✔ **Directory services restore mode:** You can happily avoid using this option.

✔ **Debugging mode:** This option is used to check for problems on one computer using a second computer connected via a serial cable. Both this and the preceding selections are advanced options most likely used by people in white lab coats and thick glasses who are best equipped to deal with such things.

✔ **Disable automatic restart on system failure:** This option helps you avoid the endless-loop situation when Windows automatically restarts on a hardware failure. In such a situation, the computer forever starts up and restarts. Selecting this option ends the madness.

✔ **Start Windows normally:** Just continue loading Windows as though you didn't press F8 to see the Startup menu.

✔ **Reboot:** Restart the computer.

✔ **Return to OS choices menu:** On computers that have multiple Windows operating systems (OSs) installed, this option returns you to the operating system selection menu (or the boot menu, as covered in the preceding section).

Make your choice based on your troubleshooting needs. Various sections elsewhere in this book recommend choices and options to take for this menu.

✔ On some computers, you can press and hold the Ctrl key rather than the F8 key.

✔ If you see the Please Select an Operating System to Start menu (the Boot menu), you have to press the F8 key again to get at the Startup menu.

✔ Any additional options not mentioned in the preceding list are generally advanced configuration items. Mess with such options only when directed to do so by a support technician.

✔ Believe it or not, the Windows Advanced Options menu doesn't appear, nor does the F8 key work, when you boot your computer into another operating system, such as Linux.

✔ If the computer starts in Safe mode no matter what, see Chapter 24 for more information.

✔ The Automatic Restart on System Failure problem has supposedly been licked by Microsoft. Reportedly, no option is available in Windows itself to turn on that feature, yet the menu option remains, most likely for old time's sake.

Hunting Down Mystery Startup Messages

Suppose that your computer starts as it normally does. However, along its tired journey, some oddball messages pop up. It's stuff you have never seen! Is Windows causing the message? Is the message something to be concerned with? And, most importantly, how do you get rid of the dumb message?

For some reason, Selective Startup is on

Selective Startup is a debugging tool set by the System Configuration Utility (MSCONFIG). Here's how to turn it off:

1. **From the Start menu, choose the Run command.**

   The keyboard shortcut here is Win+R.

2. **In the Run dialog box, type** MSCONFIG **and click the OK button.**

   The System Configuration Utility dialog box appears, as shown in Figure 8-3.

3. **Choose the option labeled Normal Startup – Load All Device Drivers and Services.**

4. **Click the OK button.**

Windows may beg you to restart the computer after making this change. Do so.

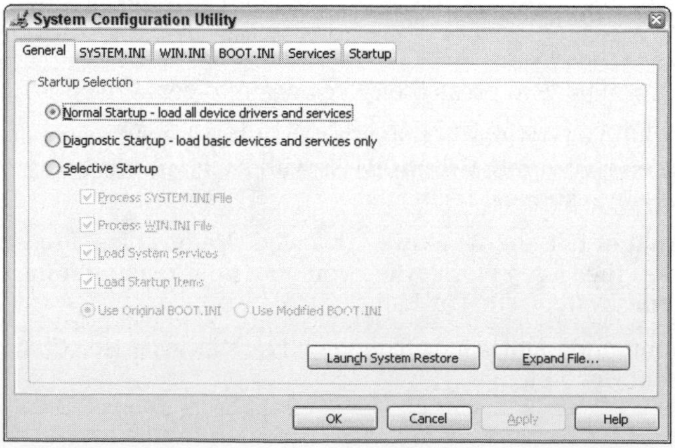

Figure 8-3:
The System
Configura-
tion Utility
(MSCONFIG).

System Configuration Utility

General | SYSTEM.INI | WIN.INI | BOOT.INI | Services | Startup

Startup Selection

○ Normal Startup - load all device drivers and services

○ Diagnostic Startup - load basic devices and services only

○ Selective Startup

   ☑ Process SYSTEM.INI File

   ☑ Process WIN.INI File

   ☑ Load System Services

   ☑ Load Startup Items

   ○ Use Original BOOT.INI   ○ Use Modified BOOT.INI

[Launch System Restore]   [Expand File...]

[OK]   [Cancel]   [Apply]   [Help]

If this technique still doesn't work, check the BOOT.INI tab in the System Configuration Utility. Repeat Steps 1 and 2 in the preceding steps and then click the BOOT.INI tab, as shown in Figure 8-4. Ensure that the /SAFEBOOT option isn't checked. Indeed, ensure that *none* of the options is checked. Then, click the OK button.

See Chapter 24 for information on the System Configuration utility.

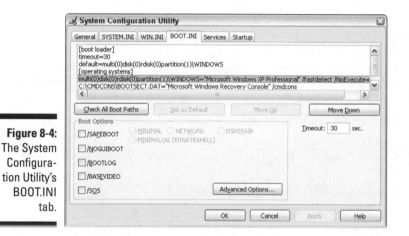

Figure 8-4:
The System
Configura-
tion Utility's
BOOT.INI
tab.

The missing DLL or VxD file mystery

A typical nontext message that crawls under your skin appears in a dialog box. Windows announces to you that a DLL or VxD or some sort of file is missing or doesn't exist. As with most text screen error messages, this one means that something wasn't installed or was uninstalled properly. The idea is to find which idiotic program is displaying the message and squelch it.

The System Configuration Utility is the best tool for tracking down the causes of unknown messages. Follow these steps to employ it and eliminate the annoying error message:

1. **Write down as much as you can about the message.**

   If the missing file has a name, write it down. If another program is mentioned, write it down.

2. **Search for the file in question.**

   See Chapter 9 for information on finding files. You know the file's name; it was displayed in the warning dialog box. Now you need to check to see whether the file exists. If you can find it, note in which folder it lives.

3. Start the System Configuration utility.

Refer to Steps 1 and 2 in the preceding section.

Your job now is to try to find the program associated with the bum startup program. It may be started directly or run when another program starts.

The name of the folder in which the missing file exists can be your clue to which program "owns" the file.

4. First, check the Startup tab.

Scroll through the list of programs and see whether you can find the "bad" one in there.

If you find the bad program listed, remove the check mark. This step prevents that program from starting and the error message from being displayed.

5. Second, check the Win.ini tab.

WIN.INI is an older Windows initialization file, used before Windows 95 introduced the concept of the Windows Registry, yet it's still a source of trouble.

6. Look for and open the `[windows]` **folder.**

If the folder isn't there, you're done; skip to Step 8.

7. Look for the `run=` **or** `load=` **entries.**

Those two entries are used to specify startup programs, such as

```
load=ptsnoop.exe
```

If either one lists your program, uncheck that entry to remove the program and the error message.

8. Close the System Configuration Utility when you're done.

These steps should help you eliminate the programs that cause most of the annoying "missing DLL" file messages. If not, you can also choose Programs⇨ Startup to see whether the errant program appears on that menu. See the following section.

> ✔ Missing DLL/VxD file messages appear right after installing or uninstalling a program. If you just installed a program and you get the message, try installing the program again. If that doesn't work, phone the developer and have someone there fix the error.

> ✔ See the Microsoft Knowledge Base on the Internet for information regarding missing DLL files for Windows. Visit `http://support.microsoft.com/` and select your version of Windows. Search for the DLL or VxD file's name, and any information about the file appears in the search results, along with information on how to fix any problems. (Also refer to Chapter 5.)

TECHNICAL STUFF

"What's a DLL file?"

The DLL file is one of the most regrettable mistakes made by the people who originally created Windows. The idea seemed worthwhile and wholesome: Much of computer programming involves the redundant rewriting of a few common routines. For example, most applications use the Open, Save, Print, and several other dialog boxes. Rather than re-create that programming code over and over, the wise programmers at Microsoft decided to save everyone time and bother. So, they created the Dynamically Linked Library (DLL) file concept.

A DLL file contains common routines to be used by all programs. For example, the COMMDLG.DLL file contains the programming needed to use the Open, Save, Print, and other common dialog (COMMDLG) boxes. Other DLL files were created so that programmers could link into them and everyone could share all the same code and be happy and go on to live lives of religious and spiritual fulfillment.

Alas, the DLL solution became a problem in itself because just about everyone figured out how to make better DLL files. There were conflicts! There was competition! There was hoohaw! And eventually the simple solution turned out to be a gigantic pain in the rear. I have heard a rumor that the next version of Windows will do away with DLL files. If so, there will be much rejoicing.

Stopping Things from Automatically Starting

Windows can stick programs in three places to start them automatically. The first two are covered in the preceding section; the System Configuration Utility's Startup tab lists programs that Windows itself automatically starts for you. The [windows] section of the old WIN.INI file could also be used to secretly start programs, though that's exceedingly rare for Windows XP.

For you, a mere mortal user, you have the Startup folder on the Start button's Programs menu: After clicking the Start button, choose All Programs⇨Startup. The menu you see, similar to what's shown in Figure 8-5, lists a bunch of programs designed to start automatically whenever the computer starts — a nifty thing to have.

Well, it's nifty until a program is in there that you don't want to start automatically. In that case, I recommend either deleting the program or moving it to a NotStartup folder.

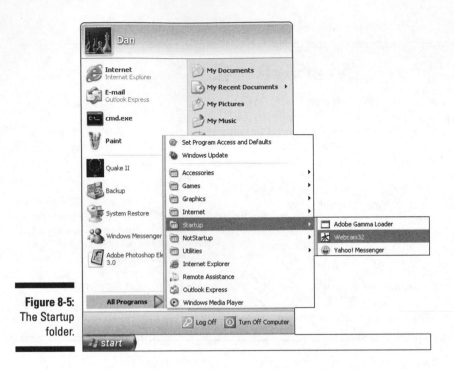

Figure 8-5:
The Startup
folder.

Deleting a program from the Startup folder

To delete the program, right-click its entry on the Startup menu. Choose Delete from the pop-up menu, and the program is gone.

✔ Only a shortcut icon is deleted. The program isn't removed from the hard drive. (To remove a program, you must uninstall it.)

✔ If you make a mistake, press Ctrl+Z right away, and your deleted menu item is yanked back.

Be aware that Windows XP has many Startup folders. Just because you have deleted the file from one account doesn't automatically delete it from every user's account.

To remove the unwanted startup program from everyone's account, follow these steps:

1. **Right-click the Start button.**

2. **Choose Open All Users from the pop-up shortcut menu.**

   A window appears that displays program shortcuts and folders common to all user accounts on your computer.

3. **Open the Programs folder.**

4. **Open the Startup folder.**

5. **Remove the unwanted programs.**

   Click to select a program's icon and then press the Delete key on your computer's keyboard.

6. **Close the window when you're done.**

Creating a NotStartup folder

Better than deleting a Startup menu item is disabling the program from starting. You do that by moving the menu item from the Startup folder to a special folder you create, called NotStartup. Such a folder is shown in Figure 8-5 (just below the Startup folder).

Here's how to create your own NotStartup folder:

1. **Right-click the Start button.**

2. **Choose the Open command from the pop-up menu.**

   This step opens a window into the Start button's menu folder. That's where folders appear as submenus and shortcut icons appear as menu commands. It's sneaky, but also a very good way to edit the Start menu.

3. **Open the Programs folder.**

   You see menu items (shortcut icons) and menus (folders), including the Startup folder.

4. **Choose File⇨New⇨Folder from the menu.**

   The new folder appears highlighted in the window.

5. Type NotStartup as the folder's new name.

   If this step doesn't work, reselect the New Folder icon by clicking it once with the mouse. Press the F2 key, and then you can rename the folder.

   The NotStartup folder is now a new menu off the main All Programs menu. You can pop up the Start button and look at the menu to confirm this, if you like. Or, you can continue by moving those items you want disabled from the Startup folder to the NotStartup folder.

6. **Open the Startup folder.**

7. **Click to select the program that you don't want to run when the computer starts.**

   If it's more than one program, press the Ctrl key as you click the mouse. This step lets you select more than one icon.

8. **Choose Edit⇨Cut from the menu.**

9. **Click the Up button to return to the main Programs folder.**

10. **Open the NotStartup folder.**

11. **Choose Edit⇨Paste.**

   The shortcut icons are moved — and disabled from starting up every time Windows starts.

12. **Close the Programs window.**

The beauty of this system is that you can easily reenable the programs by moving them from the NotStartup folder back to the Startup folder. Nothing is ever lost.

And now, the bad news: In Windows XP, there's more than one Programs folder. If you want to make this change for all accounts on your computer, you have to repeat the preceding steps. But, in Step 2, choose Open All Users rather than the Open command. Then, repeat all the steps as written. That operation builds the NotStartup folder for everyone to use.

Don't bother peppering me with questions about why Windows XP has two sets of folders for everything! That's trouble I would rather not shoot in this chapter.

Where else do startup programs lurk?

The Startup folder is obviously not the only place Windows tucks programs that automatically start. No, Windows is pretty sneaky about knowing where to hide programs that can start — and it has quite a few of them.

The place to disable these programs is the System Configuration Utility, which is covered throughout this chapter as well as in Chapter 24. What the System Configuration utility shows you is merely information that exists deep within the Windows Registry. One such place is the devious Run entry.

Before messing with the devious Run entry, first run System Restore to set a restore point. That's in case you really screw up; the restore point gives you a chance to undo anything major (refer to Chapter 4). Then, follow these steps:

1. **Choose the Run command from the Start menu, or press the Win+R keyboard combination.**

   The Run dialog box appears.

2. **Type REGEDIT and click the OK button.**

   The ominous Registry Editor program comes forth. (Cue the scary music and howling-wolf sound effects.)

3. **Open the HKEY_LOCAL_MACHINE key.**

4. **Open the Software folder.**

5. **Open the Microsoft folder.**

6. **Open the Windows folder.**

7. **Open the CurrentVersion folder.**

8. **Finally, open the Run folder.**

   The contents of the Run folder appear on the right side of the window, as shown in Figure 8-6. Each of those items, flagged with an "ab" icon, is the name of a supersecret startup item.

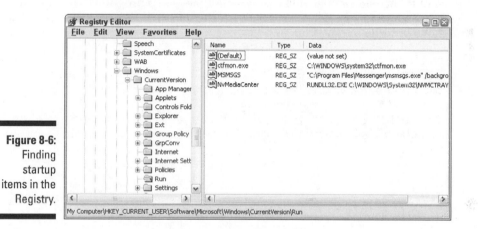

Figure 8-6:
Finding
startup
items in the
Registry.

9. **Remove unwanted items.**

   To remove a startup item, click it with your mouse. After the item is selected, press the Delete key on your keyboard to remove that item. Do this only if you really want to remove the item! Some of those startup items are programs that your computer needs and you want. Be careful!

10. **Close the Registry Editor when your desires of wanton destruction are quenched.**

Many of the items listed in the Run area of the Registry are also found on the Startup tab in the System Configuration Utility. Try removing them in that program first before descending into the Registry.

Sometimes, even this type of drastic file removal doesn't work! Specifically, in the case of spyware, you may find that programs you remove — even in the Registry — come back to life to haunt you. In that case, you must use anti-spyware software to fully and properly remove the annoying program. See Chapter 24.

Mystery startup programs from beyond

The total number of programs and processes running in your computer can be viewed by using the Task Manager window. To summon the Task Manager, press Ctrl+Alt+Delete.

The Task Manager's Applications tab lists all running programs in your computer, similar to what's shown on the taskbar. But, the truth is that many dozens of programs are running in your computer at one time. To see the log, click the Processes tab.

Figure 8-7 shows the Processes tab in the Task Manager window. There are 34 of them, each an individual program or piece of a program that is busily doing something in Windows. This begs the question "Where the heck did all those programs come from?"

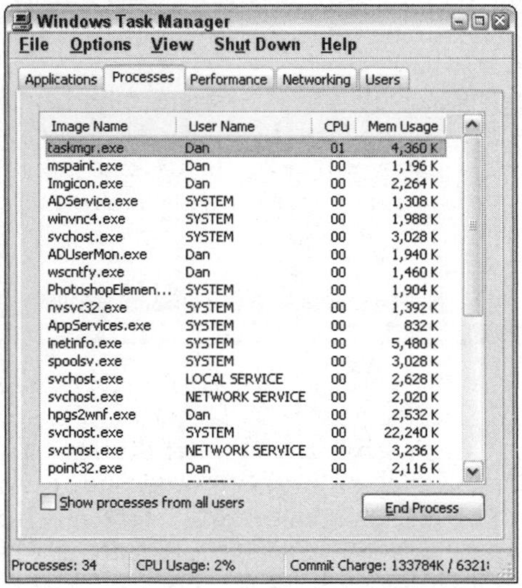

Figure 8-7: Processes running in your computer.

The processes listed in the Task Manager aren't really traditional programs in the sense that you run them the way you run other programs in Windows. In fact, you may notice that many of the processes are run by a single program called SVCHOST.EXE. That's a general service program that runs all sorts of servers and software assistants inside Windows.

Notice that curious End Process button, which makes it seem like a normal and regular thing to select and end various processes. It's not. Although it's true that some processes could be viruses and that not all the processes running are necessary, randomly killing off a process isn't advisable.

✔ If you want to shut down an unwanted process, refer to Chapter 21 for the proper techniques to go about doing so.

✔ For more information on what the items in the Image Name column mean, see the appendix in this book.

Disabling a window that appears every time you start the computer

Occasionally, I get e-mail from a reader who is bugged beyond tolerance for a silly old folder window that appears each and every time the computer starts. There it is! There it is again!

Folks, Windows is *designed* to redisplay any windows you had open the last time you shut down. So, if you quit Windows but leave a My Documents window open (or even minimized as a button on the taskbar), don't be surprised when that same window appears (open) when you restart Windows. It's supposed to happen that way!

✔ If you don't want a window to appear when Windows restarts, close it before you shut down Windows.

✔ There's an oddball chance that the Windows Explorer program may have been installed in the Startup folder. Windows Explorer (EXPLORER.EXE) is the name of the program that displays folder windows on the screen. When a copy of that program is in the Startup folder, or any of the various spots used to start programs when Windows starts, that may also be producing the phantom folder on startup. This situation, however, is extremely rare.

✔ The open folder may be a remnant of a recently uninstalled program, or from some other operation that was somehow botched. Remember that things go awry in a computer because something has changed. Review your PC's recent changes to perhaps locate the problem's source.

"My PC Annoyingly Phones the Internet Every Time It Starts!"

Many programs have the urge to contact the Microsoft mothership, or any of a number of motherships, every time the computer starts. This is entirely normal, though to most folks it's kind of surprising to find the computer using the modem every time Windows starts.

Some programs, such as antivirus utilities, may dial in to the Internet to obtain updates when your computer first starts.

Some programs dial in to the Internet to complete the installation process. For example, if you have recently installed a Microsoft mouse, it wants to confirm with Microsoft various configuration information as a final step in the setup process.

Again, all these things are normal. My only beef is that the program should be forthright about its intentions. A dialog box should appear and tell you, "This program needs to contact the Internet for important update information." Alas, few of these surprise programs do so.

✔ Should you let the program dial in? It's up to you. I have toyed with the Microsoft mouse program long enough that it finally gave up.

✔ Watch out for those registration programs that run fresh after you install new software or hardware. You don't have to register on the Internet if you don't want to.

✔ Obviously, if you have a broadband (always-on) Internet connection, this situation happens to you too, but you don't really notice it as much as the dial-up Internet users do.

Chapter 9

Finding Lost Files and Things

• •

In This Chapter

▶ Looking for lost files

▶ Finding a file you had yesterday

▶ Scanning for a file by its contents

▶ Locating a missing shortcut

▶ Recovering a missing menu on the Start menu

▶ Getting your Internet passwords back

▶ Remembering your Windows passwords

• •

*Y*ou would think that a Roman coin, one that's about 2,000 years old, would cost more than $10. At one time, it did! But that was before folks all over Europe started using inexpensive metal detectors. They discovered, buried there in the ground for hundreds of years, jars and jars of ancient money — so much so that finding a Roman coin today is easier than finding an American coin of just 200 years ago.

Finding things is important. The guy who buried his coins 2,000 years ago was being smart about saving his money, but hasty about remembering where he put the treasure. Saving files on your PC works much in the same way. You can look up. You can look down. You can trod all over the hard drive with a pickax and shovel. Eventually, you just find yourself with a yard full of holes — unless you get the proper tool (a metal detector) to find the coins you're looking for. In Windows, that tool is the Search command.

Finding and Searching

In the top drawer of the Windows treasure chest is a wonderfully powerful file-finding command. It's fast. It's convenient. It's always correct. If only it were easy to use, most of this chapter would be unnecessary. Alas.

Why do your files get up and go?

Files disappear for two reasons: You forgot where you put the file, or the file was deleted. Yeah, this is one of those few cases where it *really* could be your fault! Unless you believe in the File-Deleting Fairy. . . .

In the case of file downloads from the Internet, sometimes the files never appear. That's because you're supposed to *save* the download to disk, not *open* the download — but that's a sorrowful woe for another chapter.

The quick Search command

In a hurry? You can use tricks to immediately search for stuff. Two key commands come to mind:

- ✔ **Win+F:** Press the Windows key plus the F key to summon the Search Results window.

- ✔ **F3:** Press the F3 key to bring up the Search Results window — but this technique works only when no other windows are open or you're viewing a folder window.

Either of these keys displays a Search Results window, which looks like a regular file folder window, but with the Search Companion panel off to the left, as shown in Figure 9-1.

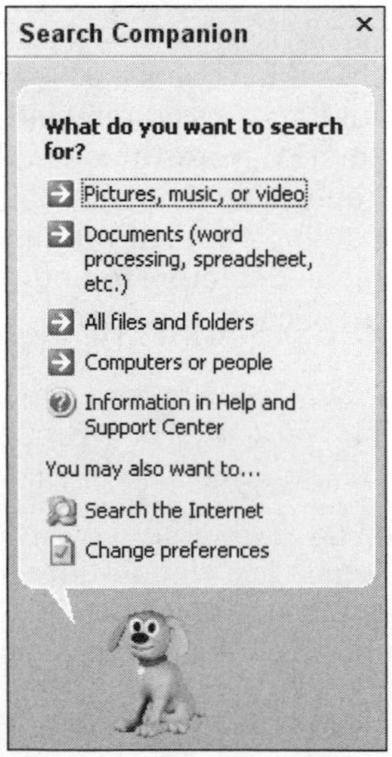

Figure 9-1:
The Search
Companion
panel.

Search Companion

What do you want to search for?

Pictures, music, or video

Documents (word processing, spreadsheet, etc.)

All files and folders

Computers or people

Information in Help and Support Center

You may also want to...

Search the Internet

Change preferences

You can also summon the Search Companion panel in any folder window by clicking the Search button. The keyboard shortcut here is Ctrl+E.

The next few sections assume that you have the Search panel ready to go and look for stuff.

🖝 Configure the Search Results window so that Details view is showing: Choose View⇨Details from the menu. That's the best way to sift through the results.

🖝 See the dog in Figure 9-1? Don't let its pleasant nature lead you to believe that it's accommodating.

🖝 Nope, there's no way to get rid of the dog. Yeah. I know how you feel: You slogged through (more than) four years of college and then three years of law school. You paid $3,000 to get the computer of your dreams for your law office. And there you are, trying to do some good and a silly, insipid, animated puppy is trying to help you out. Don't let the clients see it; the world doesn't need *another* lawyer joke.

🖝 The F3 key may not always summon the Search Results window. In some applications, the F3 key has other functions. (That's why it's called a *function* key.)

Searching for something you created or downloaded today or yesterday

I tend to lose things immediately, so first I try to search for files created in the past day or so. Hopefully, one of them is the one that's missing.

Toss all that fun and graphic frivolity of the Search Companion out the window, my friend. The best way to find files is to get at the raw controls. Heed these steps in the Search Companion panel:

1. **Choose All Files and Folders.**

2. **Choose My Computer from the Look In drop-down list.**

   You want to ensure that Windows looks everywhere for your file, though if you're certain that it's in the My Documents folder or on Drive C, choose those options instead; that makes the search go a wee bit faster.

 3. **Click the downward-pointing chevron by the option When Was It Modified?**

4. **Choose Specify Dates.**

   You must be specific — today or even yesterday!

   5. Choose Created Date from the drop-down list.

   6. Type yesterday's date in the From field.

   The date shown is today's date, so modify the day (and month, if needed) to reflect yesterday.

   The To field contains today's date, so it need not be changed.

   7. Click the Search button.

   Files flow into the window (see Figure 9-2), each one of them created today or yesterday. Hopefully, you don't see too many; Figure 9-2 says that 89 files were found. Golly.

   8. If you know the approximate time you created the file, click the Date Modified heading.

   Scroll through the list to seek out files created during the approximate time you were downloading. That should find you the file you want.

   You can also use the Size column to locate the file if you can remember about how big it was. For some reason, I remember how large download files are (probably because of the time it takes to receive them).

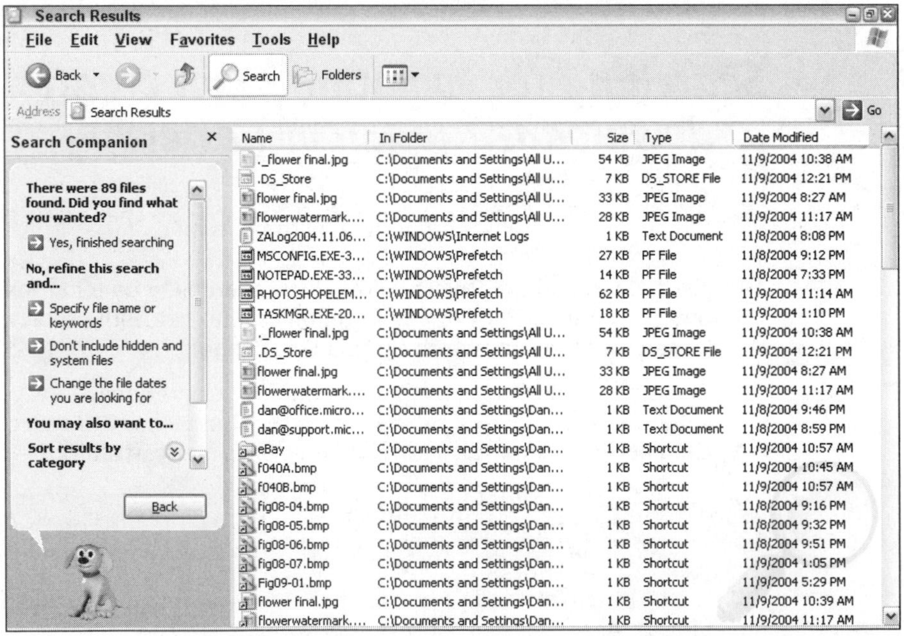

Figure 9-2: Search results.

If you found the file, great! Right-click its icon and choose Send To⇨My Documents from the pop-up menu. That action moves the icon to the My Documents folder — perhaps not the best place for the file, but at least a place where you can see it! Close the Search Results window, and then you can move the file from the My Documents folder to wherever you feel would be a better place for it.

If the search results came up with disappointing results, maybe the file just wasn't saved to disk. That happens. You can try modifying the dates to search: Specify a date earlier than yesterday, for example, and then try again.

Files you download from the Internet must be *saved* to disk. Choose the Save button, not the Open button, when you're downloading files.

Searching for something when you know only the file's contents

The more you know about a file, the easier it is to find. For example, I knew I had an Excel spreadsheet that documented my recent travel expenses. I forgot the name of the file, but I remembered that it was an Excel spreadsheet and that it had the phrase "not including hookers" in it. That certainly makes finding the file easier.

- ✔ Alas, on the downside, when you have Windows search each file for a chunk of text, the searches can last forever. So, when you do need to search for a bit of text, please try to specify as much additional information as possible: filename (or part of it), program that created the file or file type, size, or date or approximate date, for example.

- ✔ The Search command can locate documents only by text, not by any other information. Graphics files, for example, cannot be searched, even if the graphics image is a text picture.

- ✔ Be sure to specify the My Documents folder and check to ensure that subfolders are being searched. Rarely is it necessary to search *everywhere* on the hard drive for a document containing a bit of text.

As you would expect, Windows buries the option for finding text in a document. I suppose that hiding that option was done in the name of making things easier, but I doubt it.

To find a file based on a bit of text, follow these steps:

1. **Bring up the Search Companion panel, as described earlier.**

   If you have just finished one search, click the Back button in the Search Companion panel to start over with a new search.

2. **Choose the item labeled Documents (word processing or spreadsheet, for example).**

   Only documents contain text. All the other choices are for system files or files that contain things far scarier than plain text.

3. **Click the item labeled Use Advanced Search Options.**

   This item is found in the bottom of the next panel that appears.

4. **Type your text into the box labeled A Word or Phrase in the Document.**

   You may need to use the scroll bar in the Search Companion panel to find and use this option.

   Type the text as you remember it. Don't worry about proper uppercase or lowercase right now; Windows is smart enough to find any matching text — even stuff that's remotely close.

5. **Click the Search button.**

   Windows scurries off to hunt down the file.

If the file you want isn't listed in the results, choose one of the additional options in the Search Companion to help refine your search. The more information you can specify, the more successful (and brief) the results.

How to find a found file's folder

After you find the wayward file, you most likely want to open up the folder it lives in, either to scold the file or to properly cut and paste it back into a more appropriate folder.

When Windows finds a file, it lists the file's folder information right by the file's icon. This information is best seen in Details view, as I recommend earlier in this chapter. (Choose View⇨Details in the Search Results window.) But, listing a file's folder information can be vague or confusing. There has to be a better way to open that folder . . . .

Ta-da! Presenting the better way: Right-click the file's icon. That displays a pop-up menu, from which you can choose the command Open Containing Folder. That opens the folder containing the found file, with the file's icon highlighted, or selected, inside the window. See? Computers really do make life easier!

"Wow! This Search command is awesome! Is there anything it cannot find?"

The Search command is good for locating files anywhere on your computer system, in any disk drive. Except — the Search command *does not* look inside the Recycle Bin.

Files inside the Recycle Bin are considered deleted, even though they aren't really gone forever. Even so, the Search command doesn't look in the Recycle Bin for lost files. (Refer to Chapter 4 for more information on finding files in the Recycle Bin.)

The Search command does, however, scan through compressed folder, or zip file archives. Those files must be freed from their archive prison to be useful, but Search locates them.

Recovering Other Lost Things

Most places that deal with the public have a lost-and-found department. With computers, there must also be a Hopelessly Lost and Never Found department. When the Search command comes up empty, you can try my suggestions from this section to see about recovering files in more obtuse and creative ways.

- ✔ Don't forget the Undo key, Ctrl+Z! If something just disappears, try Ctrl+Z to see whether you can call it back.
- ✔ Sometimes, you just have to accept things: When a file is gone, it's gone. Pity.

"The shortcut points to nowhere!"

Shortcuts are handy copies of a file, but without all the extra bulk. File lite: Same great taste, but only a few bytes of hard drive space. I probably don't need to justify creating a shortcut here because you already have one and, well, its original file has gone bye-bye.

When you see the Missing Shortcut dialog box, as shown in Figure 9-3, don't panic! Windows begins a minisession of the Search command and tries to locate the mislaid original file.

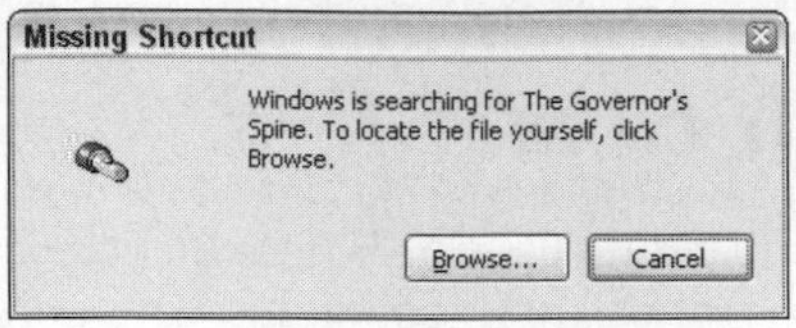

Figure 9-3:
Uh-oh.
Shortcut
points to no
man's land.

Most of the time, the search is successful. Windows finds the original file and asks whether you want to redirect the shortcut to that file. If so, a tearful reunion ensues. Sometimes, however, the search results may show similar files, but nothing that really works. In that case, too bad.

Finally, if the original file is truly gone and nothing similar remains, you see a dialog box, as shown in Figure 9-4. Click the Delete It button; the shortcut points nowhere.

Figure 9-4:
It's time to
give up
finding the
original.

✔ If you renamed or moved the original file, click that Browse button in the Missing Shortcut dialog box (refer to Figure 9-3). Then, repoint the short-cut icon back at the original by using the Browse dialog box. This advice assumes, of course, that you know where the original was moved.

✔ Windows is smart enough to recognize when you rename or move an original file so that all the shortcuts are updated. Or, at least that's what's promised in the brochure.

✔ Windows isn't smart enough to delete shortcuts when you delete their original files.

✔ Don't forget to look in the Recycle Bin for the original! If you find it, restore the deleted file, and your shortcut works again.

Who knows what evil lurks in the hearts of files? The Shortcut knows!

Shortcut icons remember who owns them. You can discover this information as well, even if the original file has long since left for more digital pastures: Right-click the shortcut icon. Choose the Properties command from the pop-up menu. The shortcut's Properties icon appears, as shown in the following figure. There, you can divine lots of information about the shortcut.

The Target box lists the original file's full pathname. That's where Windows expects to find the original. Don't worry about hunting it down; just click the Find Target button and that folder is opened for you. This technique doesn't work if the original was deleted; you end up with the same dialog boxes as shown in Figures 9-3 and 9-4. However, it does give you a good idea about where the original file belonged.

Shortcut to Do not swallow.txt Properties

General | Shortcut

Shortcut to Do not swallow.txt

Target type:	Text Document
Target location:	My Documents
Target:	ettings\Dan\My Documents\Do not swallow.txt"
Start in:	"C:\Documents and Settings\Dan\My Document:
Shortcut key:	None
Run:	Normal window
Comment:	

Find Target... | Change Icon... | Advanced...

OK | Cancel | Apply

"The whatever-submenu on the Start menu is missing!"

This tragedy happens immediately after user enlightenment; you suddenly discover that you can, indeed, edit and tidy up that bloated, messy Start menu! And so you go at it: pruning, grafting, creating, destroying. But when you're done, you discover that some submenu is missing. It's gone!

Or, you may just start using the computer one day and discover that some menu or menu item is missing from the Start menu.

The official tech-support response for this situation is as follows:

Tough!

Sadly, if you remove a chunk of the Start menu, it's gone. If you catch yourself right away, you can press Ctrl+Z, the Undo command, to get that menu back. But, beyond that, you're just stuck out of luck.

✔ If you catch yourself accidentally moving a menu with the mouse, immediately press Ctrl+Z to undo it. Otherwise, you have to look for the menu and carefully drag it back by using the mouse.

✔ If the menu was deleted, look in the Recycle Bin for it.

✔ On rare occasions, you may need to reinstall a Windows component to get a certain menu back. For example, the Games menu may disappear if all the Windows games have been removed. To reinstall the games, use the Add/Remove Programs icon in the Control Panel. Refer to the section in Chapter 4 about bringing back bits of Windows.

✔ To turn off personalized menus in most Office 2000 applications (Word and Excel, for example), choose Tools⇨Customize. In the Customize dialog box, click the Options tab. Then, remove the check mark next to the option labeled Menus Show Recently Used Commands First. Click Close.

✔ For Office XP (Word 2002 or Excel 2002, for example), choose Tools⇨ Customize to display the Customize dialog box. Click the Options tab and put a check mark by the item Always Show Full Menus.

Forgotten Passwords

The best way to remember your passwords is to *write them down!* The obviously dumb thing to do is write them down on a sticky note, titled "Passwords," and paste that note to the side of your monitor. That's silly.

It's better to write all the passwords down and put them in your office's fire safe or between the covers of *Upgrading and Repairing PCs* or some other book that no one else reads.

Another fine place to hide passwords is in your daybook or on a calendar. Jotting a password down on a page or date looks innocent and random, but only you make the connection between that bit of text and your password.

Beyond that help, there may be times when you just downright forget a password. It's missing! Where did it go! Think back to before the tequila binge last weekend. Then mull over this section.

What's a good password?

The best password is cryptic, containing a mixture of letters and numbers, and also something that you can easily remember. The experts suggest creating a password composed of two common yet unrelated words that are connected by a number. For example:

smart9dodo

hillarious1funeral

annoying5wealth

delicious77fungus

Even better is to capitalize one or more letter. In fact, some Internet sites and office networks require that you have a password *more* than six characters long with a combination of numbers and upper- and lowercase letters.

Isn't this crazy? No! Security is important. As you start doing more online, you appreciate the added value of having a hard-to-crack password. The only better thing you can do is to frequently change your good password. The experts recommend doing so at least four times a year.

Missing Internet passwords

Because you're most likely automatically logged in to the Internet, chances are that when you really need to know your password, such as when you're setting up a new e-mail program, you won't remember it.

I keep all my ISP's records in a locked file cabinet. When I forget what my original Internet password is, I just open the file cabinet and look it up. Unless you have planned ahead like that, the only other solution is to phone your ISP and request the password. They may tell you the password over the phone, or they may e-mail you the password. (Of the two, I would prefer to hear the password spelled out over the phone.)

Immediately after getting the lost password, use your ISP's configuration Web page to change your password to something else. Like other organizations, ISPs may not hire the most trustworthy people. Therefore, it's a good idea to immediately change your password after it has been recovered.

Missing Web page passwords

More and more Web sites have passwords used to protect your account and verify your identity. It's not recommended that you use the same dang doodle password for all those Web sites (though many folks do). When you use multiple passwords, it's easy to forget them. Another flaw is that you can configure your Web browser to automatically type your password, which means that, after a while, you forget it.

Most Web sites have a feature where your password is mailed to you if you forget it. Take whatever steps necessary to have the Web page send you the forgotten password. Then, wait and in a few minutes or so the password should arrive in your e-mail inbox.

Web sites may also employ a password hint. The hint is text you type that, hopefully, reminds you of your password. For example, if your password is the number and street of the house you grew up in, the hint may be "Address of first house." That's a good hint because it reminds *you* of the password, but doesn't let others know what that address could be.

Using password recovery in Windows

The saying goes that if you forget your password in Windows, you're screwed. Microsoft can't help you. I can't help you. Gurus on the Internet can't help you. Some even laugh at you. I have heard rumors of password-cracking programs, but my guess is that those things are really viruses in disguise (also known as Trojan horses). What's a human to do?

First, you can add a hint to your password prompt in Windows. Follow these steps:

1. **Open the Control Panel.**

2. **Open the User Accounts icon.**

3. **Click to select your account.**

4. **Click the item titled Change My Password.**

   You use the next screen, as shown in Figure 9-5, to enter a new password, and also enter the password hint.

5. **Fill in the blanks on the screen.**

   Type your old password and then the new password twice. To keep the same password, type it three times. Then type the password hint, which should help clue you in to what the password is, if you forget it.

   Don't make the password hint the same as the password! That's like taping your house key to the front door — or leaving it in the lock!

To see the password hint, click the blue question mark button when you see the graphical Windows logon screen, as shown in Figure 9-6. This option isn't available in the other, traditional logon screen.

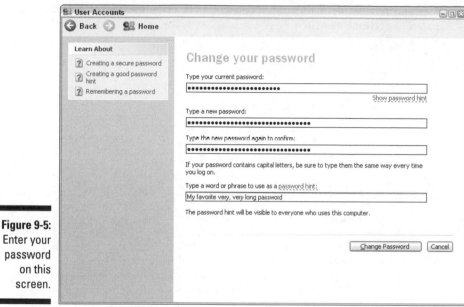

Figure 9-5:
Enter your
password
on this
screen.

Figure 9-6:
Click the
blue
question
mark to see
your
password
hint.

Second, after creating the hint, you can make a Password Reset disk. This disk can always be used to unlock your computer whenever you forget a password. But, like with a house key, you must put the disk in a safe place or else any nimrod can get into your computer.

Here's how to create the Password Reset disk:

1. **Open the Control Panel.**

2. **Open the User Accounts icon.**

3. **Click to select your account.**

4. **In the Related Tasks panel (on the left), click the item titled Prevent a Forgotten Password.**

   This step runs the Forgotten Password Wizard.

5. **Obey the wizard's instructions!**

   Follow along as the wizard helps you create the Password Reset disk; click the Next button as necessary.

   You need a floppy disk or any other type of removable media (but not a CD-R) to use as the Password Reset disk.

   The wizard doesn't erase the disk!

6. **Click the Finish button when you're done with the wizard.**

The Password Reset disk has been created; remove it from the drive and properly label it. Or, don't properly label it, but label it so that you can identify it and others may not. (I mean, it wouldn't be very secure to label the disk Password Reset and leave it lying around for anyone to use.)

To use the disk, simply try to log in to Windows *without* typing your password. When you do, you're asked whether you want to use the Password Reset disk. Just follow the instructions to do so.

The administrator's passwords

The *administrator* is the main account in Windows XP. It plays a heavier role in Windows XP Professional than it does in Windows XP Home, but in both versions of Windows the administrator's account remains the primary user account for the computer.

Unlike your own account, the administrator's account is used only when modifying or repairing your computer. In fact, you may not even see the administrator's account on the logon screen unless you're starting your computer in Safe mode.

If you have never set a specific administrator's password, try using your own account's password. That probably will work. Otherwise, if you have forgotten the administrator's password, there's nothing you can do, short of reinstalling Windows on your computer.

That's a lie: There are things you can do. Primarily, you must restart your computer by using either a special DOS boot disk or a Linux CD. Special hacker software is then used to read information from the hard drive that helps crack the password, but these techniques require advanced knowledge of computers *and* they often damage the computer. My advice: Use the Password Reset disk as described in the preceding subsection. Do it now.

Chapter 10

Sounds Like Trouble

· ·

In This Chapter

▶ Troubleshooting the no-sound problem

▶ Setting up your sound scheme

▶ Things too loud!

▶ Things too soft!

▶ F-f-f-fixing the stuttering sound

· ·

*E*arly computers were mute. In fact, the "bell" the computer rang was on the teletype machine, not inside the computer itself. When the micro-computer first came out in the late 1970s, it had a speaker — much cheaper than installing a bell. The hobbyists of that era soon discovered that the speaker could be programmed to make all sorts of noise.

Sound has evolved to become an indispensable part of computing. The com-puter talks, sings, plays music, and does a number of other interesting audio things — all of which you miss when the sound system stifles itself. Because sound has evolved in the PC (it was sort of a happenstance thing), the root of the sound problem could lie in a number of places: the CD-ROM drive, sound adapter, speakers, or software, for example. This chapter helps you narrow down the options and get your PC bleeping again.

✔ Refer to Chapter 8 for information on beeps (or no beep) you may hear when the computer first starts.

✔ Indeed, sound has evolved on the PC. The original IBM PC had a speaker that could beep or play simple songs. The Tandy 1000 computer intro-duced an integrated sound card into its PC design in 1986. When CD-ROMs became a part of the PC's hardware inventory, external speakers became the requirement. Then, along came the Web in 1996 or so with *streaming audio*. And, in 1999? MP3 files. Sound has come a long way.

✔ The ASCII code for the bell is ^G (Control-G). The ASCII code for page eject is ^L (Control-L). A common college prank of the 1970s had sopho-more computer science majors concocting a program that sent an infinite number of ^G^L commands to the system printer, usually at 2 a.m. Ha-ha. On today's computers, you can still hear the bell: Open a DOS prompt window and type **ECHO** and a space and then press Ctrl+G. Press the Enter key. *BEEP!*

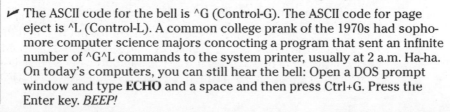

It Is the Sound of Silence

Sound is so much a part of the computing experience that we miss it when it's gone. So, a frantic search begins! There's no specific place to start looking, so obey the steps in this section in order and, hopefully, one of them will lead to a noisy solution.

- ✔ As with most immediate boo-boos, try restarting Windows to see whether that gets the sound back.
- ✔ Don't forget the System Restore command! When you hear (or don't hear) sound trouble, immediately attempt a System Restore to go back to a louder time.

Checking the speakers

The sound trail starts at either side of your head, with your ears. Not to make light of excess cerumen build-up, but do ensure that your ears are clear of debris. That's the first step. Next, check your PC's speakers.

Check the speaker connections. Here's that patch of ground where your computer becomes a stereo system. The question: Are your speakers properly plugged in — plugged into the computer; plugged into each other; plugged into a subwoofer; and plugged into the power source? Use the diagram in Figure 10-1 to help you check things. (If you think that the figure is ugly, wait until you see all the cables behind the PC!)

From the computer, the sound goes out the speaker jack, which may also be labeled Line Out or Phones (as in headphones). This is where the speakers plug in.

On the back of the speaker, the wire goes into an input jack, though most speakers have this wire permanently attached.

Another wire goes from one speaker to the other. In Figure 10-1, the Left Out wire goes to the input jack on the left speaker.

Finally, speakers need power, so a power cable goes from the main speaker (the one on the right in Figure 10-1) to a power source.

If you have a subwoofer, the nightmare gets worse: Sound must go from the speakers to the subwoofer, and the subwoofer must be powered as well.

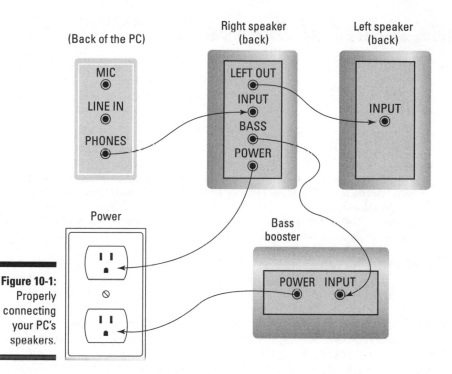

(Back of the PC)

Right speaker
(back)

Left speaker
(back)

MIC

LINE IN

PHONES

LEFT OUT

INPUT

BASS

POWER

INPUT

Power

Bass
booster

POWER   INPUT

Figure 10-1:
Properly
connecting
your PC's
speakers.

✔ If your PC has a DVD player, check to see whether it also has a DVD player expansion card. If so, plug your speakers into that card and not into the regular sound jacks! Turn your PC around and look for the DVD expansion card, which should have speaker jacks as well as an S-Video connector (plus other connectors). Plug your speaker into the speaker jack on that card.

✔ Make sure that everything is plugged in snugly!

✔ Subwoofers are also called bass boosters.

✔ As you're facing the monitor, the "right" speaker is the one that sits on the right side of the monitor. The "left" speaker is the one sitting on the left side. This arrangement can be confusing because when you work on the speakers, you're often working behind your computer, where left and right are backward.

✔ The speakers plug into the speaker jack.

✔ The speaker jack may also be labeled with a symbol, one that usually has an arrow pointing away from it.

✔ Newer systems have color-coded audio jacks. The speaker jack is typically coded lime green.

✔ Figure 10-1 shows the right speaker as the main one, though the left speaker may be the main one on some models.

✔ In some situations, the subwoofer is the main speaker, and it connects directly to the PC. Then the left and right speakers connect to the subwoofer.

✔ Yeah, it's nuts.

✔ I hate to mention it, but you can often "test" the speakers by touching the input plug — the one that plugs into the computer — to the computer's case. If the speakers are okay, you hear a slight hum as you do that, which is the sound of the speakers picking up the computer's electric field. I'm sure that audiophiles would cringe at the thought, but it works.

Any knobs on the speakers? Some speakers have volume control knobs. Are they up? How about a power knob? Is the speaker on?

Are the speakers getting power? Yes, this is a speaker-connection issue, but note that some speakers use batteries as their source of power. Be sure to check the batteries.

Or, to hell with batteries! Go get a power converter for your speakers. They should have a little power plug that the converter can plug into. Listed somewhere on the speaker are its power requirements, which you should note and then go to the electronics store to get the proper converter.

Are the speakers getting enough oomph? If the speakers make noise, but only feebly, check the volume control, which is covered later in this chapter.

If the volume is all the way up, however, what's most likely happening is that the sound is unamplified. Check your PC's rump to see whether it has another hole for the speakers to plug into.

If none of these steps works, try running the speakers through a subwoofer. Or, if they're running through a subwoofer, ensure that the subwoofer is on!

If nothing seems to help, get a new set of speakers.

Checking the master volume control

So, the speakers work, huh? Maybe it's the computer itself to blame? Check to see whether Windows has muted the situation:

1. **Click the Start button.**

2. **Choose Run.**

   The Run dialog box unfurls. You can also bring it forth by using the Win+R keyboard shortcut.

3. **Type** SNDVOL32 **into the box.**

4. **Click OK.**

This step brings up the Play Control window, as shown in Figure 10-2.

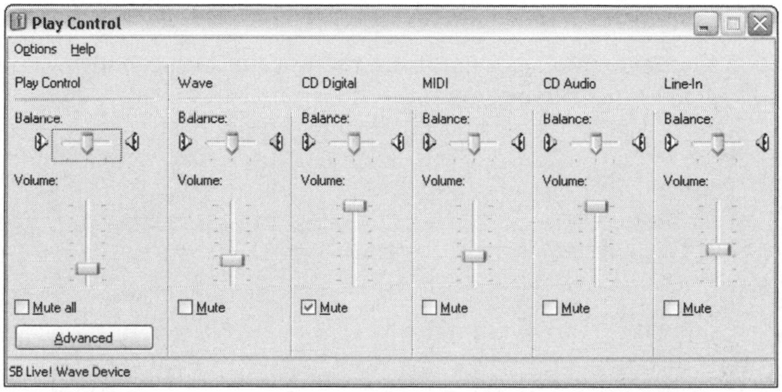

Figure 10-2:
The Play
Control
program.

So? Is anything muted? Check the Mute options, such as the CD Digital item shown in Figure 10-2.

Is any specific volume turned down? If so, adjust the volume slider higher.

Test-play a sound: Choose Help⇨About Volume Control from the menu. An About dialog box appears. Now, try to click the Play Control window. The computer should beep when you try to do this because the About window is on top of the other one. That's the easiest way to test the sound.

Click the OK button to close the About dialog box.

Adjust the sound levels as necessary and then close the Play Control dialog box when you're done playing with it.

Last stop: The Device Manager

Now you're getting your elbows dirty. You need to summon the Device Manager and examine the Sound, Video, and Game Controllers option. Follow these steps:

1. **Open the System icon in the Control Panel.**

2. **Click the Hardware tab in the System Properties dialog box.**

3. **Click the Device Manager button.**

   The Device Manager's window appears.

4. Open the item titled Sound, Video, and Game Controllers.

There, you see a list of anything having to do with sound in your computer, as shown in Figure 10-3.

If you notice immediately a yellow circle flagging a particular device, something is definitely wrong: Double-click to open the flagged device and follow the information you see in that dialog box.

If the Device Manager's seas are rather calm, you can always poke around.

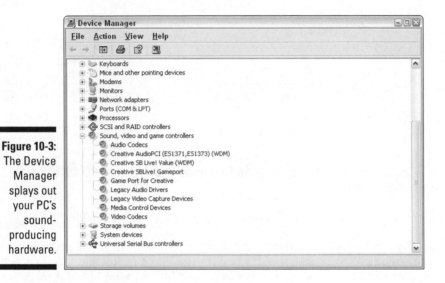

Figure 10-3: The Device Manager splays out your PC's sound-producing hardware.

5. Open the item for your computer's sound card.

This is the tricky part: The name isn't that obvious. In Figure 10-3, it's Creative AudioPCI *blah blah blah,* though a few other entries appear as likely candidates. Don't worry if you get this wrong the first time; you're just poking around.

When you're successful, you see a Properties dialog box for your computer's sound system.

6. Click the Driver tab.

Even if you have no problems, sometimes it works like a charm to replace or update the *driver* — the software that controls your computer's sound system. Clicking the Update Driver button does this, as shown in Figure 10-4, though I recommend choosing that option only if nothing has helped thus far.

The Update Driver button runs a wizard that helps you locate or install a new driver for your sound system. Hopefully, that technique fixes the problem.

7. Close all open windows when you're done troubleshooting.

Creative AudioPCI (ES1371,ES1373) (WDM) Properties

General | Properties | Driver | Details | Resources

Creative AudioPCI (ES1371,ES1373) (WDM)

Driver Provider: Microsoft
Driver Date: 7/1/2001
Driver Version: 5.1.2535.0
Digital Signer: Microsoft Windows Publisher

[Driver Details...]   To view details about the driver files.

[Update Driver...]   To update the driver for this device.

[Roll Back Driver]   If the device fails after updating the driver, roll back to the previously installed driver.

[Uninstall]   To uninstall the driver (Advanced).

[OK]   [Cancel]

Figure 10-4:
Use the Update Driver button to replace your PC's sound device software.

Anything else to check as far as sound goes?

If you have read through all the previous sections in this chapter, you have completely shot all the potential trouble that could exist in your PC's sound system, from top to bottom. If the problem hasn't been solved, return to the speakers and start over again.

- ✔ For solutions to problems with playing a music CD, see the section in Chapter 15 about CD-ROM catastrophes.

- ✔ If your problem is with playing a specific audio file, consider that the file may be corrupted — or you may not have the proper software to play that file.

Sounds to Scheme Over

As long as the sound software and hardware are, well, "sound," you can do a variety of things with sounds in Windows. It's all controlled from the Control Panel, through the Sounds and Audio Devices icon.

Figure 10-5 shows the Sounds tab in the Sounds and Audio Devices Properties dialog box. You see a scrolling list of events to which you can assign sounds in Windows.

For example, to play a specific sound when you get new mail, you scroll through the list and find the New Mail Notification event. Click to select that event, and the selected sound file appears in the dialog box. Click the Play button to hear the sound or use the Browse button to pluck out a new sound.

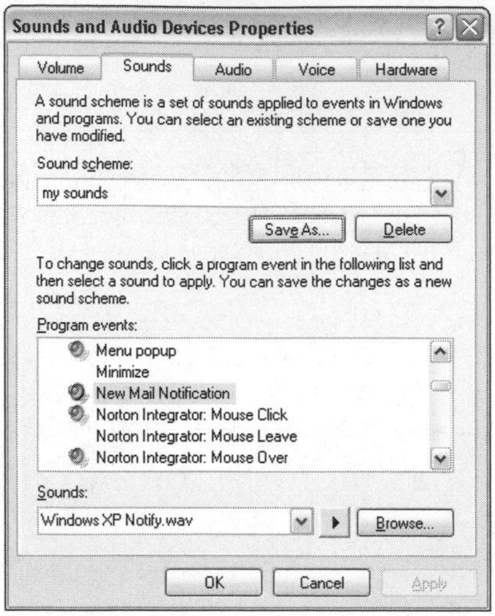

Figure 10-5:
Controlling
your
computer's
sounds.

If you go through the trouble of assigning your own, unique sounds to events, do yourself a favor and save them to disk as a theme:

1. **Click the Save As button.**

2. **Enter a name for your sound scheme.**

   Be Microsofty and call it My Sound Scheme.

3. **Click the OK button.**

   Now, that scheme shows up on the list. Your stuff is saved!

If anything ever happens to your sounds, such as someone else messes with them, you can instantly restore all of them at one time by choosing your sound scheme from the drop-down list.

✔ If you don't save your sounds as a scheme, you have to individually restore each and every sound on the list.

✔ Check out some of the other available sound schemes, one of which may only require subtle modification to become your personal sound scheme.

Other Sound Weirdness

You know what sounds weird? Lots of things! Read this section for some sound weirdness cures and tonics.

"Sound gets suddenly loud!"

Holy smokes! That was loud!

When the computer suddenly grows thunderous on you, check the usual suspects: the volume control in the system tray/notification area, volume knobs on the speakers, and even the master volume control.

Then, check the program you're running. Some games make their own sounds, which means that the sound setting must be made in that game independently of Windows. See the game's options or settings to see whether you can reset the sound level to something your neighbors would be more comfortable with.

The microphone gets muted

When using a microphone with a computer, you run into a potential problem: The microphone may pick up the sound coming from the speakers. The result is *feedback,* which can morph from a soft echo to a loud, piercing squeal!

To prevent feedback, you mute the microphone. The problem is that some programs do that for you! The solution, unfortunately, is to use the master volume control — keep that window open — so that you can unmute the mic when you need it.

- ✔ You can also write to the software developer and ask that person to include a nonmuting or unmute option for future releases of the program.
- ✔ Another nifty option is a microphone with an on-off switch on it so that you can "hardware-mute" the thing.
- ✔ Refer to the section "Checking the master volume control," earlier in this chapter, for more information.

Annoying MIDI files play on Web pages or in e-mail

This is my own personal rant: I dislike sudden music coming from Web pages or even e-mail. The music isn't in the form of WAV files. It's in the form of MIDI files, which are files played over the computer's internal synthesizer. I love turning that option off so that the unexpected music doesn't startle me.

To turn off MIDI music for your computer, mute the MIDI column in the master volume control, as shown in Figure 10-2. Or, if you prefer to hear the music, but not as loudly, just slip that volume slider down a tad. There.

- ✔ The MIDI column may be labeled SW Synth on some computers. That stands for *software synth*esizer, which is essentially the same thing.

- ✔ If you don't see the MIDI column, choose Options⇨Properties in the Play Control window. Scroll through the list to find the MIDI option and check it. Click OK.

- ✔ MIDI sounds differ from WAV files just as sheet music differs from buying a CD. WAV files are recorded (or generated) sounds. MIDI files just tell the computer's internal synthesizer to play various notes or instruments for certain durations.

- ✔ And now you know that your computer has an internal synthesizer.

That stuttering sound

This problem is a puzzling one, but one I have experienced myself: The sound playback seems choppy, or the sounds themselves stutter rather than play smoothly. Alas, I have no specific solution, although it's definitely a problem.

On my computer, I discovered that if I move the mouse while sound is playing, the sound gets interrupted. The reason was a conflict between the mouse software and the sound software; the sound "hardware" was really a software emulator that pretended to be hardware. The solution was to upgrade to a "real" sound card and disable the cheap motherboard sound.

To disable your computer's onboard sound, run the Setup program when the PC first starts. On one of the menus, you can find an option to disable the onboard sound system. When there's no option to disable the sound system in the computer's Setup program, you can use the Device Manager. Follow the steps in the preceding section. After Step 4, choose the Disable option from the Device Usage drop-down list, at the bottom of the General tab in the Properties dialog box. Click OK to disable the onboard sound.

Then, install a third-party sound expansion card, or use one of those new external USB sound systems. That should fix the stuttering.

Chapter 11

The Mystery of System Resources (and Memory Leaks)

● ●

In This Chapter

▶ Discovering the PC's resources (or lack thereof)

▶ Monitoring resources

▶ Understanding memory leaks

▶ Plugging a memory leak

▶ Improving on dwindling resources

▶ Removing, disabling, and minding PC resources

● ●

*F*ew can argue that computers are not technical. They're — very technical! Swirling around any computer is a maelstrom of technical terms and jargon. Windows helps insulate you from such lingo so that you can use your computer all day and never worry about the *stack* or the *heap* or any of several dozen various *buffers*. But, one technical term pops up more than others: That's *resource*.

Because there's an error message that goes something like "Resources are low," many people find themselves obsessing over resources. Logically, if resources are low, you must endeavor to fill them up again. That's when the trouble starts — so much trouble that I have devoted this entire chapter to help you troubleshoot and solve the low-resource quandary.

What Are System Resources?

After boiling the term *system resource* for several hours, to vent off all the steam and impurities, what you're left with is plain old memory. RAM. System resources are simply one way your computer uses memory. The resources part is what Windows uses the memory for: windows, icons, fonts, graphics, and other pieces parts.

As you use Windows, it consumes resources. When you have several windows open on the screen, they devour resources. Using lots of fonts? There go the resources!

Some programs are real resource hogs. Microsoft Word is one. When Word runs, it sets aside memory for oodles of resources — whether it needs them or not.

Bottom line: When you run lots of programs, you use lots of resources. When those resources get low, some programs may not be able to run. The quick solution is to simply close a few programs and try again. Or, restarting Windows often flushes out all the resources and lets you run the program.

Monitoring resources

In older versions of Windows, the System Monitor program was used to check up on resources and see how much of them were left and what Windows was using. In Windows XP, the System Monitor program has vanished, but you can still check on resources. Here's how:

1. **Open the Control Panel.**

2. **Open the Administrative Tools icon.**

   This step opens the Administrative Tools window, which is like another Control Panel, but one that contains advanced toys for you to use to seriously mess up your computer.

3. **Open the Performance icon.**

   The Performance window opens, which displays a graphical chart of how Windows is using some of the computer's resources, as shown in Figure 11-1.

   In Figure 11-1, and most likely on your screen, the Performance window is monitoring three resources: memory, disk usage, and microprocessor usage. These are shown on the bottom of the window, each associated with colors: yellow for Memory; blue for Physical Disk, and green for Processor.

   Try opening a few windows or popping up the Start menu to see how that affects the graph being drawn — a real-life example of how resources are used in windows.

4. **Click the Add button to monitor additional resources.**

   Or, you can use the Ctrl+I keyboard shortcut. The Add Counters dialog box appears, as shown in Figure 11-2.

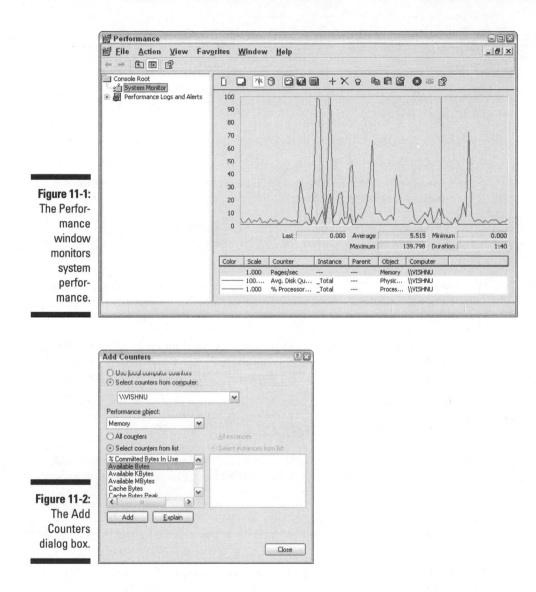

Figure 11-1:
The Performance window monitors system performance.

Figure 11-2:
The Add Counters dialog box.

5. Select resources to monitor in the Add Counters dialog box.

The Add Counters dialog box allows you to select which resources and stuff to monitor. You select the resource from the drop-down list labeled Performance Object. Then, select individual aspects of that resource from the counters list, or just click All Counters to see everything.

Use the Explain button in the Add Counters dialog box to understand what each item represents, though often the explanations are really cryptic and designed only for the Vulcans or the Krell.

6. **Click the Add button to add the specified resource.**

   For example, to further monitor memory usage, select Memory from the Performance Object drop-down list and then select Available Bytes from the counters list. Click the Add button. This action adds that item to the System Monitor. (You may have to move the Add Counters dialog box out of the way to see it.)

7. **Close the Add Counters dialog box when you're done.**

   Click the Close button.

8. **Close the Performance window, as well as any other open windows, when you're done gawking.**

There's really nothing you can do in the Performance window other than look. But, when you know what to look for, you can easily spot problems and pinpoint solutions.

For example, if running one particular program causes all resources to suddenly dwindle, you know that there's a great demand for resources in that program.

Suppose that when you quit a certain program, you notice that the resources are not reduced, meaning that the program isn't releasing resources as it quits. This is known as a *memory leak,* and it's covered later in this chapter.

Perusing performance

Another place in Windows where you can monitor performance is the Task Manager, which is a little easier to get at than the Performance window.

Specifically, the Performance tab in the Task Manager's window is home to a quick summary of key resource information in Windows, as shown in Figure 11-3. Granted, it's not as exciting or as interactive as the Performance window (refer to Figure 11-1), but it does boil down the information to the bare essentials.

The top chart monitors microprocessor (CPU) usage, similar to one of those Boop machines that monitors heart patients in a hospital (though the Task Manager does not go "boop"). This line represents the same information as the Processor line in the Performance window.

The lower chart in the Task Manager/Performance window (refer to Figure 11-3) shows page file usage, which tells you how often and how much stuff is being written to or read from virtual memory. Increased activity here could show signs of memory trouble.

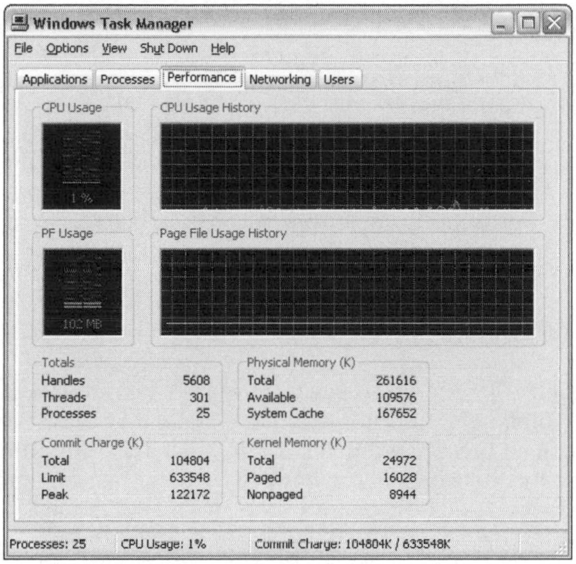

Figure 11-3:
The Task
Manager
monitors
your PC's
perfor-
mance.

Below the two scrolling graphs are four areas of text information that look really impressive, but I have no idea what it could all mean or what's really vital to watch. No, the real solution to the memory leak problem lies on the Task Manager's Processes tab, which is covered in the next section.

- ✔ *Virtual memory* is disk storage used to supplement regular memory, or RAM.

- ✔ If you want to see the CPU usage jump, open a few windows or play a sound.

"Omigosh! My performance meter just suddenly and randomly spiked!"

Yeah, it does that. You can sit there and watch your PC's performance graph do *nothing,* and then suddenly it peaks up and is *very* active. But then, it returns back to where it was.

No, nothing is wrong. This behavior is entirely normal for a computer. If you click the Processes tab in the Windows Task Manager (refer to Figure 11-4, a little later in this chapter), you see dozens of programs all running at once in your computer. A performance spike simply means that one of those programs went about doing its task and occupied the PC's microprocessor for a wee amount of time. That goes on all the time. It doesn't mean that your computer has a virus or a worm; it's just standard operations.

Leaky Memory

One thing the performance meters and various charts and gauges can help you fix is a *memory leak.* This is a nasty problem that some programs have where your computer's resources are gradually or rapidly consumed, leaving you with a slow or sluggish computer or a system that shuts down at odd or inconvenient times. Fortunately, memory leaks can be fixed.

What's a memory leak?

I remember a gag letter I wrote in to one of those Q&A computer columns in the newspaper: "I think my computer may have a memory leak. Should I put down a towel?" Ha-ha. I have heard jokesters telling naïve computer owners to tape over the ports and holes in the back of a PC so that a memory leak doesn't happen. Ha-ha.

Leak is perhaps the wrong term. A better description is *hole,* or a place where memory is poured in and never returns. And the hole grows larger and hungrier — like children, but without that cuteness thing. Despite my better descriptions, the leak jargon is still widely used.

A memory leak means one of two things. First, it could be a program that is simply dead in memory. Windows cannot remove the program, so it just ropes off that memory so that other programs don't touch it. The memory is "occupied," but not being used; therefore, it's wasted. The solution is to restart the computer to free the dead memory, which is why you see the warning message that tells you to restart Windows after a program has crashed.

The second type of memory leak is nasty. It happens when a program continues to use memory and cannot be stopped. For example, you close a program, yet some small part of it remains in memory and consumes more of it. Over time, the program uses up all the memory in the computer and everything stops. That's a true memory leak, and you can discover it by observing a dwindling number of resources over time with no apparent cause.

The cure for the memory leak is to kill the program that's consuming memory. Hopefully, that frees up the used memory. If not, the only other cure is not to run that program in the first place.

Tracking down a memory leak

Memory leaks are easily spotted on the Task Manager's Processes tab. That tab lists not only the major applications, but also every dang doodle program, or process, the computer is running. Figure 11-4 shows a sample.

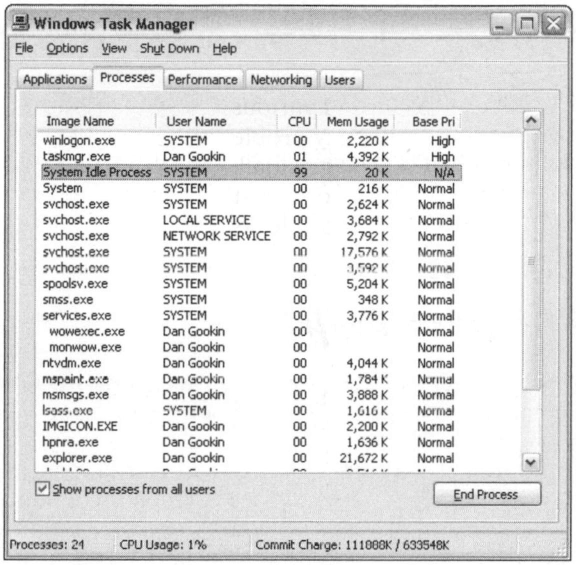

Figure 11-4:
Checking for
leaks of the
memory
kind.

Memory leaks are spotted on the list by noting a program that shows growing values in the CPU or Mem Usage columns. For example, if the Windows Explorer program is crashing, you may notice that the Explorer.Exe Image Name (program) on the list is using 25 percent CPU time, which suddenly ticks up to 26 and then 27, yet you're not doing anything on your computer.

To halt a process gone awry, click to select it and then click the End Process button. You're asked to confirm; click the Yes button. Then, when you have control over your system again, restart Windows.

- ✔ If a program is running intensively, it shows a high value in the CPU column. That's normal. It's only when a program uses more CPU time than seems logical that you have a problem.

- ✔ Yes, the System Idle Process is busy when the system is idle.

- ✔ Be sure to reset after ending a process! If you don't, remnants of the process may interfere with the computer's operation and lead to other crashes.

- ✔ I have caught only one memory leak and fixed it in this manner (which is more a credit to Windows than to me). The computer was being sluggish, so I looked at the processes and noticed one hogging lots of CPU time. Ending that process instantly made the computer peppy again. Still, I did restart Windows, just to be sure.

Things You Can Do to Improve Resources

Rather than strive to improve your dismal resources situation, you should do some healthy things to improve your computer's overall performance. There's a link between resources and performance: Improving one improves the other.

Your system will never have 100 percent free resources

Before discovering how to improve resources, understand this minor bit of wisdom: *Your system will never have 100 percent free sources.*

To run Windows, you *must* use system resources. In fact, the only time you could possibly have 100 percent free resources is when the computer is turned off. Otherwise, something is always going on in the computer, which consumes the resources.

Number-one strategy: Add more RAM!

Resources equal memory! Adding more memory to your computer fixes many low-resource problems.

- A great place to purchase memory online is www.crucial.com. It's not the cheapest, but the memory is high quality, the Web site is excellent, and the support is outstanding. I recommend the site and use it myself.

- Windows XP really needs about 256MB of memory to do well. However, 512MB or more is even better.

Remove excess fonts

Sure, you can have 10,000 fonts installed, but that definitely drains resources and slows things down, to boot. The solution: Install only those fonts you regularly use.

For the rest of the fonts, either keep them on the CD-ROM they came in or create an Excess Fonts folder, which you can store in the My Documents folder. Just move into that folder the fonts you seldom use; move them as you would cut and paste any file.

Don't move system fonts out of the Fonts folder. Windows needs these fonts, and if you copy them out, the computer doesn't display information properly.

What's this virtual memory thing?

One key item that slows down all Windows computers is their virtual memory. Having nothing to do with virtue, *virtual memory* is simply disk storage used to bolster physical memory, or the RAM, in your computer.

When your computer has lots of RAM, virtual memory isn't a problem. But, when memory is low, all that disk swapping can slow things down. The solution is to add more RAM, but you may also be able help the situation out a bit by adjusting the virtual memory setting.

To get at the virtual memory settings, open the Control Panel's System icon. Click the Advanced tab. Click the Settings button in the Performance area. This action summons the Performance options dialog box. Click the Advanced tab, and then click the Change button in the Virtual Memory area. At long last, you arrive at the Virtual Memory dialog box, shown nearby.

The best option to select is the one labeled System Managed Size. But, if you're having lots of paging problems and general sluggishness, you may consider a manual setting that is much

higher. Situations like this one are rare in Windows XP, mostly because the system-managed size is fairly smart. So, apply wisdom when you're making your selection.

Be sure to properly close all open dialog boxes and windows when you're done fiddling.

- System fonts are flagged with an *A* icon in the Fonts folder.

- You can get to the Fonts folder from the Control Panel; open the Fonts icon.

- Also avoid moving the following fonts, which are often used by Web pages:

  - Arial

  - Comic Sans MS

  - Tahoma

  - Times New Roman

  - Trebuchet

  - Verdana

Disable unneeded background programs

Background programs — such as antivirus utilities, disk optimizers, animated desktops, and Active Desktop items — also consume resources. If resources are low, consider disabling or halting such programs.

  ✔ Refer to the section in Chapter 8 about stopping programs from automatically starting for more information on disabling programs.

  ✔ Also refer to the appendix to find information about running processes, and which ones you need or can do away with.

Mind what you install; uninstall what you don't use

If you're like me, you occasionally download and install programs from the Internet just to see what they do. If so, great. But, be mindful to uninstall the program if you don't use it.

All installed programs use resources. By uninstalling the program, you free up those resources. So, occasionally scour your Program Files folder as well as the Add/Remove Programs icon in the Control Panel. Look for programs you no longer intend to use and uninstall them.

Uninstall the programs! Don't succumb to the urge to simply delete them. That strategy is wrong and causes big heaps of trouble later.

I recommend the CleanSweep utility, from the Norton people. It's perhaps the best tool you can use to completely uninstall older programs.

Chapter 12

The Slow PC

*O*ne welcome feature in a new computer is its speed; new computers are notably faster than the ones they replace. The speed difference is attributed to technology, of course. Replacing a tired old Pentium III computer with a Pentium 4, for example, makes everything run faster — or at least seem to.

The problem with a slow PC isn't that technology is brushing by. That's more of a fact than a problem. No, the true slow PC is sluggish for a number of reasons, some of which definitely can be helped, as discussed in this chapter.

> ✔ See Chapter 17 for information on improving slow Internet connections.
>
> ✔ I recommend drinking coffee for slow mornings or to help your own brain maintain speed during long meetings. I don't recommend coffee for your computer.

Slow Is Relative

Computers aren't designed to be slow. In fact, if you were to peer into a tiny window and observe the microprocessor, you would discover that it spends most of its time doing *nothing*. It waits. That's because most things the computer does aren't that speed intensive.

When you word-process, the computer spends electronic epochs waiting for you to type the next letter — even if you're a fast typist. And, no matter how fast your Internet connection, the computer is literally twiddling its thumbs while waiting for the next byte of data to stroll in.

There are intensive operations, of course: Any time you manipulate graphics, you're making the computer do some real work. Even the fastest computers have to wait while images are rendered. And, some mathematical calculations cause the microprocessor to fire all its burners. Even then, for the most part, the computer sits and hums.

- ✔ It's because the computer sits and waits that you find things like barking dogs or tap-dancing wizards to amuse you while you type in your word processor.

- ✔ Speed apparently isn't a true issue when it comes to computer performance. Developers could make software go even faster than it does now, but there's little demand for it. Also, increasing program speed would mean that the programs would take longer to develop, so as long as people don't mind waiting, developers have no incentive to make things faster.

Why things can get slow (and what you can do about it)

Your computer can slow down for a number of reasons, almost too many to mention. Slothfulness boils down to one of the causes listed in this section:

Malfunctioning hardware: The hard drive may be on its last legs, in which case it has to read and reread information because of errors. That adds overhead.

Corrupted programs: Most sudden slowness is caused by some corrupt program, which may be tainted on the disk or somehow become besmirched in memory. In any event, the program's response time dwindles, which affects overall PC speed.

Viruses: Computer viruses can also slow things down, either by corrupting existing files or consuming resources in memory or on the hard drive, or they may just be designed to slow down your computer.

Most of the time, some corrupt program brings the computer down and crawling on its knees. Fix or eliminate that program, and the problem goes away. Typically, recovering speed is simply as easy as restarting Windows.

Please be patient! Yes, restarting Windows probably fixes the situation. But, give the slow computer its due. Obey the rules! Shut down like you normally do, even if it seems to take longer. Give the computer a chance before you impatiently punch the power switch or defiantly unplug the sucker.

- Corrupt programs may be spotted by their memory leaks. Refer to Chapter 11.

- Refer to Chapter 2 for information on restarting Windows, the penicillin to cure most PC ills.

- Sluggish hardware needs to be fixed or replaced. Alas, there's no easy way to spot sluggish hardware, which tends to get slower over time.

- Some third-party utilities, such as Norton, have various disk-diagnosing programs that can indicate pending hard drive doom.

- Also check with the Microsoft Knowledge Base on the Web to see whether the slowness can be attributed to any known flaws in Windows or other Microsoft products: `http://support.microsoft.com/`.

- Little-known fact: A hard drive can misread data on a disk up to three times before it reports an error. The operating system itself can tolerate as many as five errors of this type before it reports a problem with the drive.

Any way to speed things up?

The old joke went that you could double your computer's speed by plugging it into a 240-volt socket. I actually got e-mail from a man who believed this to be true and wanted to know where he could get a power adapter. Of course, following through would have resulted in a blown-up power supply.

Computers do some things fast and some things slow. Aside from getting a newer computer, you can do only a handful of legitimate things to improve overall performance:

- Eliminate what you don't need. Uninstall programs you don't use.

- Review your startup programs, as covered in Chapter 8. Ensure that utilities you don't need are disabled and not using RAM or disk space.

- Install more RAM. Computers can always use more RAM.

- Check for viruses.

- Keep an eye out for memory leaks.

- Defragment (especially good for older drives).

In your applications, try to avoid using lots of fonts or pasting images into a word processor until the text editing is done. Word processors, such as Microsoft Word, really slow down when you add graphics into the mix. Write your text first and then add images.

For image editing as well as other demanding applications, try not to run other programs at the same time. That conserves resources and gives more power to the programs that demand it.

Above all, try to avoid software fixes that claim to speed up your computer. Although some of them may subtly tweak resources and give you better performance, most of the ones I have encountered are shams. These programs seldom perform as promised and end up turning your PC into a billboard for endless advertisements or porn.

- ✔ I don't recommend upgrading the microprocessor as a solution to a slow PC. Older PCs that could theoretically benefit from a newer CPU are typically not compatible with the new microprocessors. And, the replacement CPUs you can get often don't give you the same bang for the buck as a better upgrade, such as more RAM or a second hard drive.

- ✔ Also refer to Chapter 11, on system resources. Low resources can also cause a system to run slowly.

- ✔ See Chapter 23 for more information on defragmenting a hard drive.

- ✔ Internally, the computer uses only 5 or 12 volts to run things, so doubling the input voltage from 120 to 240 volts — even if you could — wouldn't improve your speed situation.

Some Slow Q&A

Anyone who has used a PC for any length of time has encountered the slow PC. After initial disbelief, you probably act like I do and seriously wonder whether a black hole is nearby and slowing down the entire space-time continuum.

Do you slam your keyboard into the desktop? I have tried it. Doesn't work.

And, yes, a few times I just flipped off the power to the UPS because the computer was taking geological time to restart. I know. Naughty me, but sometimes the stupid device wears my patience paper-thin.

Q: It's suddenly slow, and it wasn't like that yesterday!

Sudden slow is good. Sudden slow means that some program has twisted itself into a confusing garden of electronic salad. A simple reset fixes this problem.

In Windows XP, try checking the Task Manager's Processes tab to see whether you can find the process hog and kill it off. At least that method tells you which program was running amok, if only for future reference. Refer to Chapter 11.

I have noticed that some USB devices may fly south and attempt to take other USB devices with them. For example, the scanner may be on the fritz, and so the USB keyboard no longer responds quickly. Consider disconnecting (from the computer) the USB devices that you're not using and see whether that improves the situation.

Q: The computer is just always slow.

Remember that speed is relative. Or, as it was put to me long ago by a friend with a much better computer: You never know how crappy your system is until you sit down at a better one.

- Buy more RAM!
- Consider running fewer programs.
- Also consider using a thorough disk drive analysis utility, such as Norton Utilities, to see whether the hard drive is becoming too errorprone. If so, consider replacing the hard drive.

Q: The computer gets slower the longer I leave it on.

This is definitely a sign of a memory leak. The best way to track this one down is as follows:

- **First, don't run any software.** Just let the computer sit and stew. Note whether it's getting slow. If so, it's Windows itself that's slow, one of the supersecret startup programs (refer to Chapter 8) or perhaps a virus that's causing the problem.
- **Second, run your programs one at a time.** Pause. Note whether that particular program is causing the computer to slow down. If not, restart the computer and run your next program. Run them one at a time to search for the culprit.

When you find the program that's slowing down the computer, check with the developer to see whether it has any information about causes or fixes. Refer to Chapter 5 for more information on tech support.

Q: The computer has gotten slower and slower in recent weeks.

This problem is most likely caused by some nasty programs infiltrating your computer, such as a virus or worm or spyware. These programs consume resources and run without your knowledge, so it isn't readily obvious what's to blame for the slowdown.

See Chapter 24 for information on tools to fight viruses and spyware.

Another problem may be hardware-oriented. A full hard drive can slow down a computer. To check the hard drive's capacity, follow these steps:

1. **Open the My Computer icon on the desktop.**

2. **Right-click the hard drive you want to examine.**

3. **Choose Properties from the pop-up menu.**

   On the General tab, you see a graphical pie chart showing you the amount of disk space used versus what's remaining, as shown in Figure 12-1. When only a little pie is left, you've got disk woes!

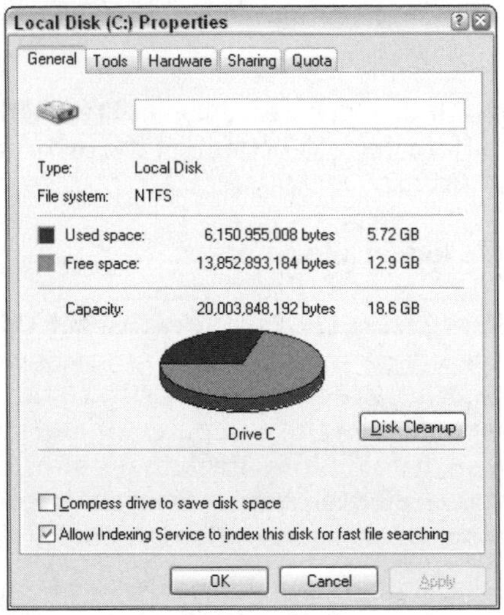

Figure 12-1:
The famous disk pie.

4. **Close the Properties dialog box as well as the My Computer window.**

Refer to Chapter 23 for more information on what you can do to help remedy a full hard drive.

Slowness can also just be a sign of "tired RAM" or an older computer in general. It's time to buy a new one.

Q: The computer's clock is slower than normal time.

Yes. Computers make lousy clocks. The clock in your typical PC is off anywhere from several seconds to a few minutes at the end of each day, depending on what you do with the computer. This is normal.

In Windows XP, you can configure the computer to automatically set the time: In the Control Panel, open the Date and Time icon to display the Date and Time Properties dialog box. Then, click the Internet Time tab to see something that looks like Figure 12-2.

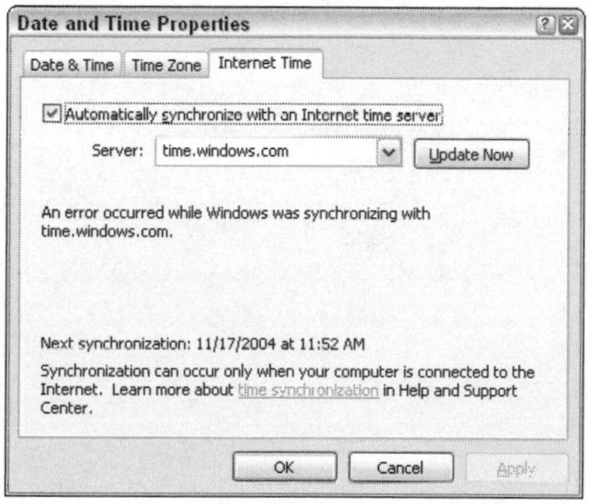

Figure 12-2: Keeping the clock current in Windows XP.

To synchronize your PC's clock with a live time server, click the Update Now button. (You must put a check mark by the option Automatically Synchronize with an Internet Time Server for that button to work.) Click OK when you're done.

- The best atomic and Internet clock utilities can be set to automatically dial or connect at specific times every day, which keeps the clock very current.

- If your computer is on a local-area network, check with your network administrator about time servers you can use to keep the PC's clock accurate.

Chapter 13

Keyboard, Mouse, and Monitor Dilemmas

. . . .

In This Chapter

▶ Knowing whether to blame the peripheral or the PC

▶ Controlling the keyboard

▶ Fixing mouse troubles

▶ Dealing with monitor troubles (hardware only)

▶ Cleaning stuff

. . . .

*W*hat do the keyboard, monitor, and mouse all have in common? Anyone? Anyone?

Yes! They comprise the PC's basic input and output, the old I/O. Remember those songs you used to sing in computer camp? Well, perhaps not. In any case, the keyboard is the primary way *you* (the human) communicate with the computer. Supplementing that, of course, is the mouse. And, the computer communicates back to you by using text or images displayed on the monitor.

Without a keyboard, mouse, or monitor, your computer would have to communicate with you via its flashing lights or beeping speaker. You (the human) could always kick the computer, but that has rarely been an effective communications technique.

Therefore, all three of these devices — keyboard, mouse, and monitor — have similar troubleshooting issues, problems, and resolutions: Hence, this combined chapter.

> ✔ This book assumes that you are human or, if visiting from elsewhere, that you're assuming human form.
>
> ✔ In 1978, a divider was installed beneath the table to prevent the world chess champion Anatoly Karpov and the challenger Viktor Korchnoi from kicking each other during the match.

The Best Way to Tell Whose Fault It Is

When it comes to the keyboard, mouse, or monitor, a common question pops up: Is the device itself or the computer to blame? For example, is your mouse itself wacky, or is it the mouse port or the motherboard or mouse software? The easy way to find out is to *swap it out*.

First, turn off the computer.

Second, remove the device that's causing trouble — the keyboard or mouse or monitor. Set it aside.

Third, install a working replacement device. It can be a keyboard, mouse, or monitor from another computer or a friend's computer. Ensure that you know the device is working properly.

Fourth, turn on the computer and see whether the device works. If the swapped-in component works just fine, you have solved your problem: Replace the keyboard, mouse, or monitor with something that works.

- ✔ Keyboards and mice are relatively inexpensive to replace.

- ✔ Before replacing, see other sections in this chapter for some potential solutions to keyboard and mouse problems.

- ✔ You can try having your monitor fixed, especially if it's a high-end model. Most TV repair places can fix computer monitors.

- ✔ Never try to fix the monitor yourself, even if you have the proper footwear. Monitors and PC power supplies are two things you should never disassemble or otherwise mess with.

- ✔ Or — what the heck? — toss that old CRT monitor and get yourself a fancy new LCD monitor.

- ✔ There's no need to turn off the computer if your mouse or keyboard (or even the monitor) is a USB device. You can plug or unplug any USB device without damaging the computer.

- ✔ Never plug a mouse or keyboard into the standard mouse or keyboard port when the PC is on. Doing so can damage the keyboard, mouse, or computer.

- ✔ You can plug a monitor in or out from a working computer. I have done it a few times. But I feel better about turning the thing off whenever I attach or detach any hardware.

Keyboard Kraziness

Keyboards don't have the run-amok potential of other computer peripherals. I think that the reason they stay so well-behaved is that they know how cheap replacement models are. So, unless your hands weigh 75 pounds each, your computer's keyboard will most likely outlive just about anything else on the computer.

- ✔ A simple reset should cure most keyboard strangeness, such as one key producing another key's character.

- ✔ Keyboard-mapping and macro programs are available, such as QuicKeys, from CE Software, Inc. (www.cesoft.com/). You can use them to customize keyboard behavior as well as assign lots of text or complex commands to simple key combinations.

The keyboard's Control Panel home

Any messing or adjusting of the keyboard is done in the Control Panel by opening the Keyboard icon (see Figure 13-1). This area is where you adjust things such as the keyboard's repeat delay and repeat rate.

- ✔ The *repeat delay* is how long you have to hold a key down before its character is repeated.

- ✔ The *repeat rate* is how quickly the character is repeated.

Figure 13-1: The official keyboard-messing location.

Keyboard Properties

Speed | Hardware

Character repeat

Repeat delay:
Long _____ Short

Repeat rate:
Slow _____ Fast

Click here and hold down a key to test repeat rate:

Cursor blink rate
None _____ Fast

OK | Cancel | Apply

According to Figure 13-1, pressing and holding the P key down after a short delay quickly prints a bunch of *P*s: pppppppppppppppppppppppppp. (Supposedly, that's how kitty cats do it.)

The language problem

You can configure your keyboard to mimic the behavior of foreign language keyboards. For example, in France, they have keys on the keyboard for the ç and Ç keys. In the United Kingdom, Shift+3 produces the £ character rather than #. And many foreign language keyboard layouts have "dead keys," which are used for diacritical marks, such as ü or á, or are just not used for anything.

 All this foreign language nonsense is controlled through the Control Panel's Regional and Language Options icon. If you suspect that your keyboard is misbehaving in a strange, foreign manner, check its language.

Open the Control Panel's Regional and Language Options icon. Click the Languages tab, and then click the Details button. You see the Text Services and Input Languages dialog box, beautifully depicted in Figure 13-2.

Figure 13-2:
Here's where you add foreign language keyboard layouts.

Choose the keyboard layout you want to use from the Default Input Language drop-down list.

To add new layouts, use the Add button.

Click OK to close the various dialog boxes after you have made your choices.

The Language toolbar then appears on the taskbar, which is how you control the various languages and keyboard layouts, as shown in Figure 13-3. You can click the language button (labeled EN in Figure 13-3) to switch between languages and layouts.

Figure 13-3:
The
Language
bar and
pop-up
menu.

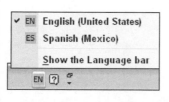

When the Language bar is visible, you can use the keyboard's left Shift+Alt keyboard combination to switch languages and layouts. You notice that the two-letter button changes each time you press left Shift+Alt. For example, it changes from EN (English) to ES (Spanish).

Mouse Mayhem

I once wrote "You need a mouse to use Windows." Well, you kinda do. I have discovered that many things done with a mouse — especially with regard to clicking menus and buttons — can be done faster with keyboard shortcuts. But, that's another story. If the mouse doesn't work, I would bet that you would rather keep using the mouse as opposed to train yourself how to use keyboard shortcuts, whether they're faster or not.

Give me mouse control!

Most common mouse options (speed, pointer appearance, and special effects, for example) are set by using the Mouse icon in the Control Panel. Alas, the options and settings and their locations vary depending on which type of mouse you have, so some poking around in the Mouse Properties dialog box (see Figure 13-4) may be required in order for you to discover which settings need adjustment.

  ✔ If you have trouble seeing the mouse, select a new mouse pointer from the Mouse Properties dialog box. The Pointers tab is the place to look.

  ✔ The mouse can be made left-handed, if you like. Refer to either the Buttons or General tab for the details.

  ✔ For more mouse configuration information, refer to my book, *PCs For Dummies* (Wiley Publishing, Inc.).

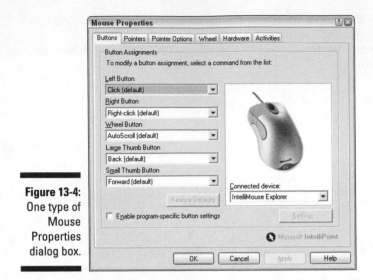

Figure 13-4:
One type of
Mouse
Properties
dialog box.

Common mouse maladies and cures

Most mouse mishaps can be cured with a simple restart of Windows. Why does the mouse go nuts? I don't know. But whenever my mouse pointer is missing or the mouse freezes or just acts plain weird, restarting Windows solves the problem.

If you have a USB mouse, unplugging the USB connection and plugging it in again sometimes wakes the mouse back up.

If restarting doesn't work, check the Device Manager, which displays any conflicts and offers some fixes or suggestions. Here's what to do:

1. **Open the Control Panel.**

2. **Open the System icon.**

3. **Click the Hardware tab.**

4. **Click the Device Manager button.**

   The Device Manager window lists all your PC's hardware, as shown in Figure 13-5. The item labeled Mice and Other Pointing Devices contains information about your computer's mouse.

5. **Open the item named Mice and Other Pointing Devices.**

   You see beneath that item an entry for every mouse or pointing device installed on your computer. (Yes, you can have more than one.)

   The first thing to notice here is whether the mouse hardware is flagged with a yellow circle and exclamation point. If so, the hardware has definitely gone haywire; continue with Step 6 to see what specifically is wrong.

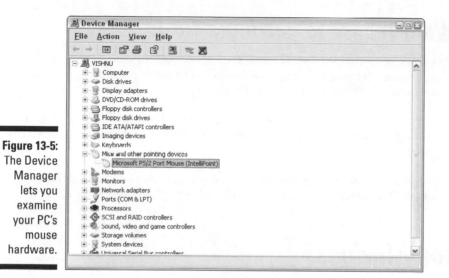

Figure 13-5:
The Device
Manager
lets you
examine
your PC's
mouse
hardware.

6. **Open your mouse's hardware entry to see its Properties dialog box.**

   The Mouse's Properties dialog box appears. Any known trouble is listed in the Device status area. You can also use the Troubleshoot button on the General tab to help diagnose mouse maladies.

   If you need to change the mouse's device driver, click the Driver tab and then click the Update Driver button. Heed the wizard's instructions to properly reinstall or update the mouse driver.

7. **Close the Properties dialog box, Device Manager, and other open windows when you're done.**

In my travels, rarely have I had to install any specific mouse device drivers. It's really Windows itself that controls the mouse. The only reason to reinstall or update a mouse driver would be to use any special, nonstandard features on the mouse, such as extra buttons or "Internet" buttons.

Oh, and those wacky nonstandard mice — including the infamous 3D flying mouse — they need their own software to do their tricks.

✔ Mouse pointer jumping around? Hard to control? See "Cleaning the mouse," later in this chapter.

✔ Your laptop's mouse is typically a touchpad. Yes, you can install an external mouse on your laptop, in which case it sports *two* pointing devices.

✔ You can find software for the various breeds of the Microsoft mouse at the Microsoft download center, at www.microsoft.com/downloads/.

✔ Logitech mouse support is on the Web at www.logitech.com/.

Your mouse is getting s-l-o-w

Mice can slow down if they're dirty. Consider cleaning your mouse, as discussed later in this chapter. A more common cause is simply age. Old mice slow down. They get crappy. They break. Kaput.

If the mouse is older than about four years (sometimes not even that old) and it's getting frustratingly slow, replace it. Buy a new mouse. That fixes the problem.

Beyond fixing the slow mouse problem, nothing is more satisfying than repeatedly pounding the mouse into the table with an aggressive fist.

Monitor Madness

Monitors are possibly the most peaceful of computer peripherals. Unless, of course, you're watching a science fiction TV show from the 1960s. In that case, the monitor is most likely the thing that explodes whenever the computer becomes confused. But that's mere fiction! Ha-ha.

Monitors don't explode. They implode. And, that's only the CRT (cathode ray tube) type of monitor. LCD monitors don't explode or implode. But, the CRT monitor's glass encloses a vacuum. If you poke a hole in the monitor's glass — *thwoop!* — implosion. I don't feel that I need to devote any space here to troubleshooting that problem.

Beyond the rare CRT implosion, your monitor rarely, if ever, screws up. No, it's the *image* on the screen that bugs you most of the time. Those problems are covered in Chapter 6, in the section about the display being stuck in dumb mode. For now, here's a small assortment of monitor hardware problems:

The monitor buzzes or hums. Monitors buzz and hum naturally. Loud humming can be a problem, however. If the humming distracts you from doing your work, repair or replace the monitor.

Connections get loose. If the image is missing or appears in all one color or "weak," check the monitor cable. Ensure that one end is snugly plugged into the monitor and that the other end is snugly plugged into the PC.

The image is distorted. This could be a sign of interference from some other electronic device. Strong magnetic fields can distort the image on a monitor. If the monitor is exposed for long periods, the magnets damage the monitor permanently. To fix this problem, move the monitor away from whatever is causing the interference.

The image gets fuzzy. Monitors lose their crispness over time. The sure sign of an old monitor is a fuzzy image. If the image doesn't improve the longer the monitor stays on, retire the monitor and get another.

Another way to fix a fuzzy, flickering, or generally frazzled monitor is to adjust the refresh rate. You can use the buttons on the front of the monitor or change the screen's resolution or number of colors.

The monitor is only half of your PC's graphical equation. The other half is the graphics adapter or hardware inside the PC's console. If the monitor checks out okay but the image is still ga-ga, suspect the graphics adapter. You can tell by trying out another monitor on your computer. (*Remember:* Swap out to test!) If the other monitor is ga-ga, you know that the graphics adapter hardware needs replacing. You may want to have a technician or your dealer swap you in a newer, better graphics adapter.

A Time to Clean

Another thing that the keyboard, mouse, and monitor have in common is that they're easy to clean. And — boy! — is that ever necessary. I have been using the same keyboard for almost 14 years now. Although the robust sucker has lasted me through five different computers, it's just filthy! Time to clean:

- The best way to keep your stuff clean is *not to eat in front of your computer*. I know that's a hard admonishment to keep. (I'm typing this with one hand as I dig into a bowl of peanuts with the other.)

- Also, if you sneeze, cover your mouth and nose so that nothing ends up on the screen.

- Smoking? Bad for the computer. And you.

- Keep cats away from computers. Computer mice attract cat hair, and it eventually screws up the mice. Cat hair also loves to stick to the monitor.

- Yes, I *like* my keyboard. I have two more just like it for when this one breaks. It's an IBM keyboard from the early 1990s. Metal. Heavy. Full action. Hearty click noise.

Yes, you can clean your keyboard

They're hard to find, but when you see one of those tiny keyboard vacuum cleaners, get it! It deftly sucks the dirt, crud, hair, and potato chip chunks from the inner crevices of your keyboard.

One good way to clean the keyboard: Flip it over and give it a good, vigorous "You've been naughty" shake. Have a whisk broom and dustpan handy to dispose of the results of this action.

Another good way to clean between the keys of your keyboard is with a blast of air. No, don't let Uncle Dale use his air compressor. Instead, go to an office supply store and get a can of compressed air. A few shots help blow all that *stuff* out of the keyboard.

To clean the key caps, use an old toothbrush — or if you're angry with your spouse, use their toothbrush — and some household cleaner, like 409 or Fantastik. It you can stand the smell, ammonia is perhaps the best key cap cleaner. Put the cleaner on the toothbrush and then brush away at the key caps. Don't use much liquid because it drips into the keyboard's guts.

Finally, in a last desperate step, you can give your keyboard a bath. For example, if you spill orange soda pop into the keyboard, try to save matters by bathing the keyboard. First, turn off the computer. Second, unplug the keyboard. Third, immerse it in some warm, soapy water. Let it sit for a spell. Then remove the keyboard and let it drain. Keep it out overnight so that it's utterly dry when you reconnect it. If it doesn't work, that's okay; at least you gave it your best shot. Buy a new keyboard.

Cleaning the mouse

Mice pick up crud from your desktop or mouse pad and, boy, does that really gum up the works!

For a traditional mouse, remove the ball from its belly to clean it. A cover twists off so that you can remove the ball. Rub the ball with a damp cloth, though the real filth is on the rollers that detect the ball's movement.

To carefully clean the rollers, get an X-Acto knife and a pair of tweezers. Carefully scrape the gunk away from the rollers by using the X-Acto knife. The gunk generally comes off in large chunks, which you can then extract using the tweezers. Replace the ball when you're done cleaning.

Optical mice get dirty too! To clean them, use a pair of tweezers to pull out the hair and gunk in the optical mouse's "eyehole." In fact, any time an optical mouse gets weird on you, flip it over and clean the eyehole. Chances are that a strand of hair is wreaking havoc with the LED sensor.

✔ While you're at it, clean your mousepad as well as the mouse. Use a stiff brush to clean the cloth pads. Or, heck, just toss the old pad out and get a new one.

✔ If cleaning doesn't help, get a new mouse.

Cleaning your monitor

The only part of the monitor worthy of cleanliness is the screen — the part where information is displayed. Sure, you could clean the monitor's housing, but rarely have I seen that done, nor is it even necessary (unless you opt to clean off that dandelion-like effect all those yellow sticky notes have).

Start by spraying some window cleaner on a soft cloth. Then, use the cloth to gently wipe the sneeze globs and bits of bean dip from the front of the monitor. This action works for both glass and LCD monitors, though you should be especially gentle on LCD monitors because they really do have liquid inside them.

- Never spray cleaning solution directly on the screen.

- It helps to have a nice, bright yet plain image on the screen while you clean. I open up the Paint program and fill the screen with a nice, white palette so that I can see all the gunk on the monitor.

- For cleaning LCD monitors, I recommend a substance called Klear Screen, from Meridrew Enterprises (www.klearscreen.com).

- On the other hand, dust disappears unless you turn the monitor off. If you're just doing a good dust job, turn the monitor off and you see all that "pixel dust."

Chapter 14

Printer Problems

Though a printer is considered part of the basic computer system, it's really a device all unto itself, complete with its own assortment of demons and vices. This is one reason that printers are always packaged separately, unlike some computers where the monitor or keyboard may be integrated into the console. You see, because it's a separate device, it's far easier to fling an unruly printer out of a high window. I believe that was part of the original design, and it's good to see that after 25 years of personal computing, the separate printer unit remains a standard today.

Printer problems can come in many areas, so it's one of the tougher things to troubleshoot. The problem could be in Windows, your application, the printer's cable, or the silly printer itself. This chapter helps you narrow down the potential culprits and then shoot the appropriate trouble.

So Is It the Printer?

You can easily tell whether the problem is with the printer or the software you're using: Does the problem happen when you print from the one program or from all of them?

If every program has the same printer problem, it's a printer problem, with either the printer hardware or the printer software (the driver). If it's only one program that can't print, the problem is with that particular piece of software. Contact that software developer — ignore its vain attempts to shuttle you off to the printer manufacturer — and get the problem solved.

Your best friend, Print Preview

When the printer acts up or the hard copy looks strange, don't blame the printer first! Double-check to see that the printer isn't just blindly obeying your orders by using the application's Print Preview command, File⇨Print Preview.

How does the document look in Print Preview? How are the colors? The margins? The fonts?

If the screw-up is visible in the Print Preview window, blame yourself or the application. If Print Preview looks like you intended, blame the printer driver or the printer itself. Read on!

- *Hard copy* is another term for the stuff that comes out of the printer — printed information as opposed to information on the screen.

- The Print Preview command has a companion toolbar button in many applications.

- Not every program has a Print Preview command.

It helps to know this painful information on how printing works

Printing happens in a PC like this: You give the command to print, Ctrl+P. That tells the application to print the document. But, it's not the application itself that does the printing. Instead, instructions are passed along to something called the printer driver.

The *printer driver* is a part of the operating system, installed when you first set up Windows. The driver's job is to control the printer, by telling it what to print. So, although some things — document content, margins, colors, and styles, for example — are controlled by your application, it's the printer driver common to all of Windows that's really in charge of the printing job.

As the printer driver takes over, a wee little "printer guy" icon shows up in the system tray/notification area (on the right end of the taskbar).

The printer driver's job is to talk directly with the printer and send it the proper instructions that tell it to print what you want. Hopefully, if all goes well, your stuff gets put down on paper and you become O So Very Happy with the results.

After the document is printed, the printer driver goes back to sleep and the wee printer-guy icon disappears from the system tray/notification area.

Problems? They can occur anywhere along the line. Having a general idea of how the process works, however, can help you pinpoint who or what is to blame.

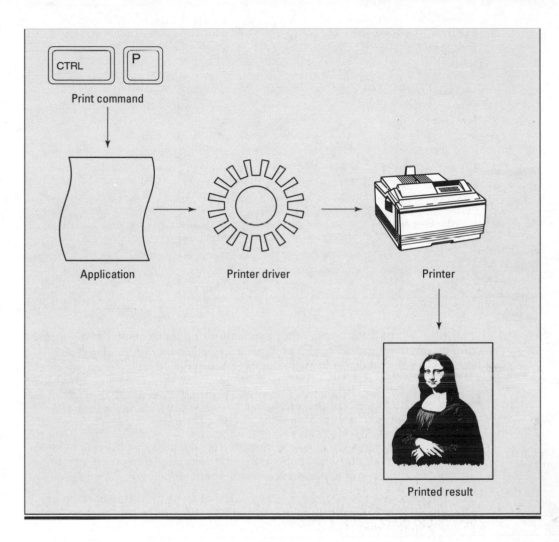

✔ Graphics applications in particular seem to lack a Print Preview command. That's because the graphics image you see on the screen is supposed to be identical to the one that's printed.

Controlling the printer from your application

The printer, like all hardware, is dumb all by itself. It needs your carefully guided instructions to tell it what and how to print. That's the job of the Print dialog box, but also the Page Setup dialog box in most applications.

Figure 14-1 shows the Page Setup dialog box for the Paint application in Windows.

The Page Setup dialog box in other applications contains similar commands, though often more of them and perhaps organized a bit differently. Typically, you can set the following items in the Page Setup dialog box:

- **Margins:** These define the area where printing takes place. Most printers require a minimum half-inch margin, either ½ or ¼ inch, inset from the edge of the paper.

- **Paper size:** Most often, you print on letter-size paper, but this spot is where you tell both the application and the printer that you're printing on another size of paper, such as legal or envelope.

- **Paper source:** Some printers have different trays for different sizes of paper. Or, if the paper is manually fed into the printer, that's where you set that option.

- **Orientation:** You have only two choices: normal, which is called *Portrait* orientation, or long-ways, which is called *Landscape* orientation.

- **Layout options:** These settings can include options for binding, centering the page, scaling the image (larger or smaller), headers, footers, and multiple pages per sheet.

Not every application has a Page Setup dialog box. In some applications, the only control you have over printing is with the Print dialog box, a sample of which is shown in Figure 14-2.

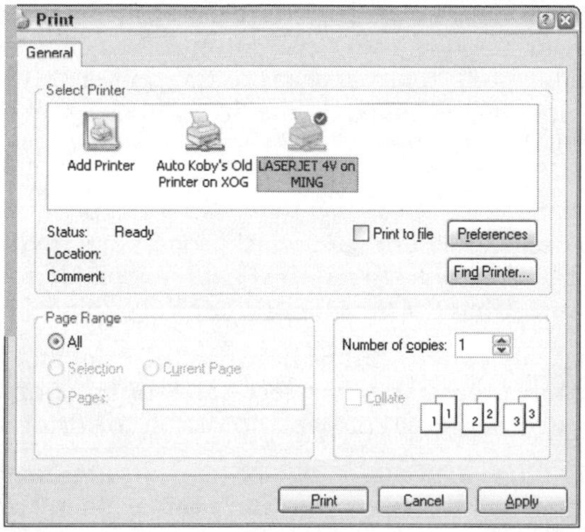

Figure 14-2:
Options in
the Print
dialog box.

Yes, you find additional printing options here:

✔ **Select a printer:** Windows affords you the luxury of using one of any number of computers, either directly connected to your PC or via a network. It's in the Print dialog box that you choose which printer you want to print on.

✔ **Configure the printer:** The Print dialog box is a part of Windows, but it typically contains extra tabs or an Advanced, Properties, or Preferences button (refer to Figure 14-2) that lets you set custom printing options, such as graphics resolution, color settings, printer language, and other often trivial settings.

✔ **Choose the pages to print:** Normally, you print all the pages, though the Print dialog box lets you select a single page, individual pages, or ranges of pages to print.

✔ **Select the number of copies:** You can also print multiple copies of the same document. When I create my annual Christmas letter, I specify several dozen copies to print, one for everyone on the list.

✔ **Collation and other options:** Each Print dialog box is different, with different options and settings depending on the printer or application. An option common to many of them is *collation,* which prints multiple copies either one page at a time (seven Page 1s followed by seven Page 2s) or in sets (Pages 1 through 5 and then another set of Pages 1–5). Another option is printing in reverse order, which is nice if the copies come out of the printer face-up.

The Page Setup and Print dialog boxes are two places you can use to configure your printer from your application. Of course, after you click the Print button (in the Print dialog box), control passes to the printer driver. So, any problems from that point on are blamed on the driver itself or on the printer, as covered in the rest of this chapter.

✔ Setting the page margins isn't the same thing as setting paragraph margins inside a word processor. Refer to your word processor's Help system for more margin information, or just read the best book on Microsoft Word ever written, my own *Word For Dummies* (Wiley Publishing, Inc.).

✔ Yes, many applications switch options between the Print and Page Setup dialog boxes. In some programs, you select paper orientation in the Page Setup dialog box; in other programs, you do that in the Print dialog box.

✔ Selecting a printer other than the *default,* or main, printer may affect the outside margins on a page. If so, you have to print again, by returning to the Page Setup dialog box to fix your margins.

✔ Acquaint yourself with some of your printer's more esoteric options. If additional tabs are in the Print dialog box or if you see a Properties or Preferences button there, click it to peruse those extra options.

✔ Be especially observant of the location where you can turn color printing on or off for a color printer. For example, the printer chosen in Figure 14-2 is a color printer, yet the option for printing in color isn't apparent in the dialog box. Therefore, the option must lie elsewhere, such as behind that Preferences button.

✔ Some applications may also have a Document Setup or Page Setup command on the File menu. You can find additional page-configuration items in that dialog box.

✔ Which dialog box has priority? The Print dialog box does. Any changes you make there directly affect the printer. Oftentimes, however, some coordination is required between the Page Setup and Print dialog boxes. For example, if you're printing in Landscape mode, you need to tell both the application (via the Page Setup dialog box) and the printer (via the Print dialog box) to print in that mode and on that paper.

Envelope printing tips

The best way to print an envelope is to use a program that's designed to print envelopes! After all, a specialist knows more about their specialty than the jack-of-all-trades. For example, the Envelope printing tool in Microsoft Word is a great way to print envelopes. But, printing an envelope on the fly in something like WordPad takes skill and, well, knowledge of the following pointers:

✔ Know that an envelope is merely a specialized type of paper. Specifically, in the USA, envelopes are known as number 10 or Envelope #10. If you choose that type of "paper" in the Page Setup dialog box, your document automatically formats itself to envelope dimensions.

✔ Use the Print Preview command to see how the envelope paper is oriented on the page. You want to ensure that this orientation matches how the envelope is fed into the printer.

✔ Use the program's margin settings (the paragraph margins, not the page margins) to set the locations for the address and return address.

✔ Use Print Preview again to determine that you have placed the address and return address in the proper position and orientation.

✔ Pay special attention to how the printer eats envelopes (which side is "up" and how the text gets positioned, for example).

✔ Print a test envelope first. Better still, mark which end of the envelope went into the printer first and which side of the envelope was "up." That way, you can confirm that the envelope was inserted in the proper orientation.

Where the Printer Stuff Hides in Windows

To properly futz with a printer in Windows, you need to know where these printer things are and what they do:

✔ The Printers and Faxes folder
✔ Your printer's window
✔ The little printer guy

Each one has something to do with printing, as described in this section.

Finding the Printers and Faxes folder

The Printers and Faxes folder is where Windows stores information about all the printers connected to your computer, either directly or indirectly. This folder is where you can add new printers, though in Windows, printers on your computer network are added automatically. It's also the location for any fax modems you may have on your computer, considering how faxing works a lot like printing.

To open the Printers and Faxes folder, open the Printers and Faxes icon in the Control Panel. You may also be able to find this item on the main Start button menu panel thing. Either way, the Printers and Faxes folder you see looks similar to Figure 14-3.

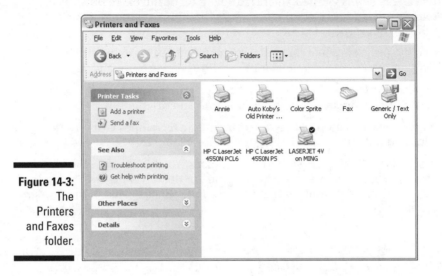

Figure 14-3:
The
Printers
and Faxes
folder.

You can do several things in the Printers and Faxes folder as far as trouble-shooting is concerned:

✔ **Click the Troubleshoot printing link to run a Windows troubleshooter for your printer.** This item is found in the See Also task pane, on the left side of the Printers and Faxes window.

✔ **Open your printer's Properties dialog box: Right-click your printer's icon and choose Properties from the pop-up menu.** This method is good for adjusting and tweaking the printer. You can also print a test page from the dialog box.

✔ **Instantly halt printing by right-clicking your printer icon and choosing Pause Printing from the pop-up menu.** See the section "Halting a printer run amok," later in this chapter, for more information.

✔ **Delete and reinstall a printer: Click to select an icon and then choose File⇨Delete from the menu.** That command removes the printer. You can then use item labeled Add a Printer Task to reinstall that same printer. Often times, this technique fixes printer driver problems.

✔ **Choose which printer you want to use as your main, or default, printer.** Just click the printer to select it and choose File⇨Set as Default Printer from the menu. The default printer has a white-on-black check mark by its icon, as shown in Figure 14-3.

Your printer's window

When you print, you can open your printer's icon in the Printers window to view the progress of the documents being printed. The documents appear there, in the order you printed them, marching off to the printer one by one while you move on to do something else.

Figure 14-4 shows a printer window, though no documents are listed in it — my printer is too fast to list any. So, just pretend.

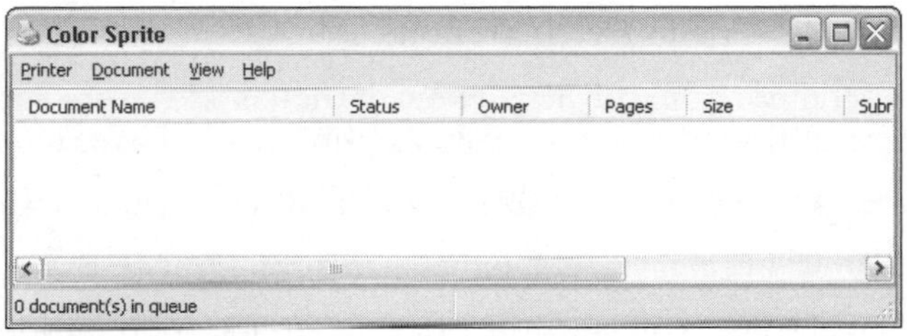

Figure 14-4:
The ever-busy printer window.

- The items waiting to be printed are called print *jobs*.

- The printer's window is primarily a place where you can change the order of the print jobs. Make this change by simply dragging one document above another.

- You can also remove jobs from the list by selecting the job and choosing Document⇨Cancel from the menu. Also see the section "Halting a printer run amok," later in this chapter.

Little printer guy

You never really need to keep an eye on the Printers folder while you print. Whenever something is printing (or, to be technical, whenever the printer driver is sending information to the printer), a printer icon appears in the system tray/notification area. You can double-click that icon to instantly open your printer's window and review the documents waiting to be printed.

The little printer guy goes away when the last byte of data has been sent to the printer.

And Then, the Printer Goes Wacky

Printers are dutiful little creatures, handily going about their work without care or notice . . . until they screw up. Then the printer can become the most hated piece of office equipment in the building. Vile creatures. Cruel and unkind. And, stubborn? I don't care how fancy the display is on your printer, when it's acting stupid, it has nothing useful to say.

General troubleshooting advice

The first thing to try when the printer goes haywire is a printing trouble-shooter. This is the Microsoft Q&A way to help track down most printer problems. Follow these steps:

1. **Open the Printers and Faxes window.**

   You can get there from the Start menu, if there's a Printers and Faxes item there, or from the Control Panel's Printers and Faxes icon.

2. **Choose the link labeled Troubleshoot Printing in the See Also panel.**

   Note that this link can be seen only when a printer icon is *not* selected.

   By clicking the link, you start the Printing Troubleshooter, which is part of the Windows Help and Support Center, as shown in Figure 14-5.

3. **Answer the questions by selecting the proper response from the list.**

   The first question, as shown in Figure 14-5, is "What problem are you having?" This wording was chosen over the alternative, "What the hell is wrong with you?" and the overly insensitive "Go away!" phraseology.

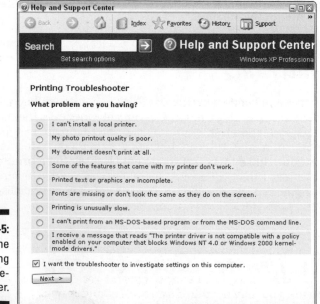

Figure 14-5: The Printing Trouble-shooter.

4. **Work your way through the troubleshooter and answer the questions as best as you can; click the Next button after making a selection.**

   Some of the time, this step works.

Eventually, the troubleshooter either leads you to the promised land or you get stuck in a "Duh, gee, I don't know" type of loop. In that case, you need some more active troubleshooting. Keep on reading in this chapter.

- ✔ Also check to see whether your printer came with any self-diagnostic software or utilities or its own troubleshooter-like program.

- ✔ If you need to reinstall a printer driver, the easiest way to do that is to delete your printer from the Printers folder and then add it again.

- ✔ You may want to check with your printer manufacturer's Web page to see whether it has any updated printer drivers. Refer to Chapter 5 for more information on finding those Web pages.

Things to check when the printer isn't printing

Ah, the usual suspects: Check all the cables. One cable must plug between your computer and the printer — both ends must be snug. The other cable plugs between your printer and the wall socket. Snug. Snug. Snug.

Is the printer turned on?

Is the printer *selected?* Some printers have the ability to be powered up, but deselected or taken offline. You typically push a Select or On-line button to ensure that the printer isn't ignoring the computer. (This option is on high-end printers, mostly.)

Do you have a device between your printer and the computer, such as an external disk drive or CD-R or scanner? These printer-port devices must be turned on for the printer to print.

Ensure that you have chosen the proper printer from the list in the Print dialog box. I once sent three copies of a document to a printer in another office before I figured out that I had the wrong printer selected and *that* was the reason nothing was printing on my own printer.

Also check the printer's display or panel for errors. Some low-end printers simply blink their lights if they have a paper jam or low-ink problem.

The computer network must be up and running for you to print on a network printer. Sometimes, you may need to turn your computer off and on again for it to "find" the network printer. You also need to check the computer's firewall software to ensure that it's allowed to print on the network printer. (You may need assistance from your network manager to help set that up.)

There are lines or blanks on the page

Two types of problems appear, both of which are native to inkjet-type printers. The first problem is the lines that appear on the page, such as a smeary line or smudge down the length of the page. The second problem is lines of text or an image where "bands" of information are missing. For example, only the top and bottom parts of each line of text are printed, and there's a white line down the middle.

In either case, the smeary smudge or the blank lines, the solution is to clean the inkjet's printer nozzles. This isn't something you do with Mr. Clean and a scrub brush. Instead, you need to look in the printer's manual, or sometimes just under the lid or cover, to find the instructions for cleaning the nozzles or printer heads.

On my Epson inkjet printer, I need to press the ink droplet button and hold it for two seconds to clean the print nozzles. After I release the button, the printer grinds and grunts for about 12 seconds. After that, printing the same page over again yields much better results.

Do not remove the ink cartridges and attempt to manually clean them yourself. The result is a terrible mess, plus the expense of having to purchase new ink cartridges.

The "weird text atop the page" problem

Printers that print strange text across the top of the first page, or ugly text on every page, have a driver problem. Most likely, the wrong printer driver was installed when the printer was set up, such as 401B when you really need a 401A — like that.

The easiest way to change or update printer drivers is to reinstall the printer. Obey these steps:

1. **Open the Printers and Faxes window.**

   Instructions for doing this step are found throughout this chapter.

2. **Click to select your printer's icon.**

3. **Choose File➪Delete from the menu.**

   Click the Yes button if you're asked to confirm your choice. Poof! The printer is gone. Well, its *driver* is gone. The physical printer doesn't disappear.

4. **Choose File⇨Add Printer from the menu.**

   The Add Printer Wizard appears.

5. **Obey the wizard to reinstall your printer.**

   You need to know the printer's make and model and some other details, which you fill in as the wizard quizzes you.

6. **Keep following the directions and clicking the Next button as necessary.**

   Eventually, you're done and the printer is reinstalled.

The key is to be sure that you properly select your printer from the manufacturer and model list presented in the Add Printer Wizard. It's when you don't do that, or you make a "best guess," that you end up with printing problems.

Consider checking with the printer manufacturer's Web site to see whether it has updated printer files or even a printer setup utility you can download and use.

- ✔ When the problem is a network printer connected to a specific computer, you must update the driver on that computer, not on your own computer.

- ✔ If the weird text appears only when you print from one application, it's the application's doing and not the printer driver's.

- ✔ Use the File⇨Print Preview command to ensure that it's not the application itself that's producing the weird characters.

- ✔ If the characters at the top of the page appear to have their heads cut off, your page's top margin is set too high; use the Page Setup dialog box to increase the top margin.

The color is all wrong (too pink, too blue, too green, and so on)

Adjusting the color of printer output is an obsession with some people. But, this type of error doesn't involve the subtleties between PMS 133 and PMS 140. If the color is wrong, such as too green or not enough red, your printer is probably low on one type of ink.

- ✔ Sadly, unless you have a printer with separate ink cartridges, you have to replace the entire three-color ink cartridge when only one color gets low. I know: It's a rip-off. But the printer was cheap, wasn't it?

- ✔ PMS is an acronym for the Pantone Matching System, a set of numbers matched to specific colors. PMS is used by graphics professionals to ensure that their printed results are exactly the color they want.

✔ You can try checking the Print dialog box for an Advanced, Properties, or Preferences button and see whether you find controls there for manipulating the color. Most of the time, a discolored image is the sign of low ink.

"My black-and-white image prints dark blue"

Most color printers come with a three-color ink cartridge and then a single black ink cartridge. Their controls can also switch so that you can use only the black cartridge, which is the case if you're printing a black-and-white or grayscale image. Simply tell the Print dialog box that you want to use only the black ink.

✔ The color doesn't have to be dark blue. It could be dark green or dark red or any tone other than black.

✔ Some older, cheaper inkjet printers lack the black ink cartridge altogether. They create "black" the same way little kids do: by mixing all the other colors together. Obviously, with this type of printer, obtaining a true black tone would be fairly impossible.

Halting a printer run amok

I have done this tons of times: You print and then . . . you realize that you want to take it back and stop printing at once! Here's what you do:

1. **Scream "Stop, you jerk!"**

   This step doesn't really help, but it sure *feels* good.

2. **Double-click the printer icon in the system tray/notification area.**

   This step is the fastest way to open your printer's window and cancel the document being printed.

   If you don't see the little printer guy, all the information has been sent to the printer and is now living inside the printer's memory. Skip to Step 6.

3. **Locate on the list the document you want to halt.**

   The one at the top of the list is the one that's "printing."

4. **Select the document and choose Document⇨Cancel from the menu.**

5. **Wait until the document disappears from the list.**

   After it's gone, you notice that the printer is still printing. That's because most printers have internal memory in which to store several pages of a document. And, yes, the printer continues to print. Oh, gads!

6. **Turn off the printer.**

   Yes, this is a mean thing to do. But, it works. It stops the printer from printing, and it erases the document in the printer's memory. It doesn't harm the printer, though it may make some inky spots with some low-end inkjet-style printers.

7. **Turn the printer on again.**

   As long as you purge all the printing documents from your printer's window (refer to Step 4), nothing else is printed.

8. **Eject the page from the printer.**

   This step removes the last bit of the document that was printing and prepares the printer to print again.

These steps are your only hope if you run off and print something you want to cancel. Well, that — or you can stop at Step 4 and just wait for the printer to spew out two or three more pages. (I had to halt my printer once when I realized that it was printing 300 pages of random text. Ugh.)

A reader has told me that some printers now come with Print Job Cancel buttons on them, or on a menu you can access from the printer's control console. Consider yourself blessed if your printer sports such a feature. Press that button or access the menu to cancel printing, which should be your first (and only) step.

Printer Maintenance Chores

Printers run relatively maintenance free, which is amazing considering how many moving parts are inside. The only regular maintenance you need to perform on the printer is the routine changing of the ink cartridges or toner.

If you have a nice inkjet printer, which means that you paid more than $300 for it, I recommend buying brand-name or approved replacement ink cartridges. The reason is that these high-end printers rely on the high-end cartridges to help keep the inkjet nozzles clean.

If you have a cheaper printer, you can save some money by using those ink cartridge refilling syringes that are advertised on TV and sold in office supply stores. They work just fine and aren't really that messy, but the ink is of a lower quality, so you don't want to use them in a high-end inkjet printer.

For laser printers, you can get a few extra sheets out of the thing by "rocking" the toner cartridge when the first Toner Low warning comes. Simply remove the toner from the machine and rock it from left to right gently in your hands. This technique somehow redistributes the toxic "inkstuff" so that you can print a while longer before you have to shell out beaucoup bucks for another toner cartridge.

As far as jams go, simply clear them as best you can. Printer jams happen because the paper is damaged, too thin, or too thick. If the paper is too old, it may contain moisture that can make a laser printer grunt.

In my travels, I have discovered few printers that can print on paper stock heavier than 25 pounds. One printer could do it, but it was a laser printer where the paper passed in a straight line from the front to the back of the printer. Other printers, where the paper scrolls up and down and back and forth, cannot handle thick paper stock, which jams and causes you undue delay and stress.

We could all use a little less stress.

Chapter 15

Dealing with Disk Disaster

· ·

In This Chapter

▶ Determining whether a hard drive is in trouble

▶ Dealing with a failing hard drive

▶ Troubleshooting CD-ROM drives

▶ Messing with the autoplay feature

▶ Figuring out floppy disk dilemmas

· ·

*P*erhaps nothing else in a computer can induce that frozen pang of dread better than a disk error. *Disks* are where you store your stuff. Disk errors mean that, potentially, you may lose your stuff. Even when my first PC's feeble 63-watt power supply blew up (blue smoke and all), I was merely surprised. Then I laughed, "Ha! Ha!" I knew that my data was still safe on the hard drive.

Many types of disks dwell in the typical PC. The most important type is the hard drive, which is where the operating system lives, where your applications live, and where your stuff lives. Obviously, its care is important, but you probably have other disks as well: CDs, DVDs, and floppies. I cover them all here in this rather beefy chapter on dealing with disk disaster.

Note: You should also refer to Part III of this book, which deals with preventive maintenance, backup, and other disk tools.

Smells Like Hard Drive Trouble

Securely spinning in the bosom of your typical PC, the hard drive is expected to last anywhere from four to five years. After that time, the hard drive begins to call it a day, errors increase, and things move slower. That's expected. Anything wrong before that is not only unexpected, but unwelcome as well.

Hard drive, hard disk — what's the diff?

The terms hard drive and hard disk are fairly interchangeable, and I'm sure that nerds at cocktail parties would argue the differences down to the tiniest micron. But, that's a moot point.

The *hard drive* is a chunk of electronics about the size of a thick paperback book (though the size does vary). That unit contains several spinning disks, all stacked on the same spindle and all of which store data on both sides. That whole thing is a hard drive, but for technical reasons, refer to it as a physical drive. Most PCs can have two or more physical drives installed internally and as many external physical drives as you can afford.

As far as the operating system is concerned, a physical hard drive can be one or more *logical*

drives. You can *partition* the physical drive inside your computer into two logical drives: C and D. So, one physical disk can be one or more logical disk drives.

You can find lots of technical folderol having to do with disk drives, partitioning, and such, but my point is that when a single physical hard drive goes, it can bring down one or more of the logical drives as well. Conversely, a corrupt file on a logical drive may not affect any other logical drives on the same physical drive.

So, the terms hard drive and hard disk aren't really important, although it helps to know that a physical hard drive can be divided into logical hard drives.

"A hard drive is missing!"

Whoops! How did the hard drive escape?

Your first option, as usual, is to restart the computer to see whether the missing hard drive can be found. That generally fixes the problem.

If the hard drive is an external model, ensure that it's properly connected and getting power. I have noted that some external USB or IEEE 1340 (FireWire) drives must be attached directly to the computer console for them to work.

If you're certain that the hard drive is a second physical drive inside the console, turn off the computer and open up the console to see whether it's still properly connected. Or, if that makes you uneasy, consider having your dealer do it.

Sometimes, the hard drive icon may be hidden in the My Computer window; choose View➪List to change the way the drives are displayed. That reveals any icons hiding behind other icons.

If you boot with a floppy disk, or start an older version of Windows, you cannot access any high-capacity hard drives. The drives appear to be missing, but it's merely that the older software cannot recognize the drive as a real disk drive and not a slice of cheese. The solution here is to start the computer normally.

✔ External drives must receive power. Some external drives must be turned on *before* the computer starts so that they're recognized.

✔ *Daisy-chaining* some types of drives (connecting two or more drives, one after the other) may render the last drive invisible to the operating system.

✔ USB and IEEE 1340 drives must be plugged into a powered hub, either the computer's console or a hub that plugs into the wall for power. If plugging the drive into the hub doesn't work, plug it directly into the computer console.

Hard drive failure warning signs

Most of the time, hard drives let you know well before they die. If your computer were a novel, the hard drive death scene would go on for pages and pages. That's good news — well, good news about impending bad news.

You may see several signs of impending hard drive doom. They may come in this order, in any order, or all at once, or only one may occur:

First sign: An increasing number of errors and bad sectors occur. As you run your programs, you may see access or read errors or the infamous Blue Screen of Death. Or, when you run Check Disk or other disk utilities, errors may be reported. At first, they're fixed — which is great. But as time rolls on, the number and frequency of errors increase.

Second sign: Drive performance suffers. Disk access becomes sluggish. Defragmenting the drive doesn't help.

Third sign: The drive becomes louder and louder. I caught one recent and rather sudden drive failure because I noticed a clicking sound as the drive was accessing data. The clicking got louder over the next hour, and immediately I backed up the entire drive. Good thing too because the next morning, the hard drive was dead.

Other sounds include an increasing whistling or grinding noise that may diminish over time, but still is a sign that the drive may be on its last leg.

- ✔ The monitor, too, can make a loud, annoying noise when it's starting to go berserk. Refer to Chapter 13 for information on how to tell whether it's the monitor, and not the hard drive, that's hurting your ears.

- ✔ See Chapter 23 for more information on Check Disk.

- ✔ Hard drives also tend to die when you turn the computer on, so if you suspect trouble — by all means! — leave the computer on until you can do a backup.

What to do when you suspect trouble

Whenever you suspect trouble, *immediately* you should back up your data. If you have a backup program, run it at once!

If you don't have a backup, but have a second physical hard drive, back up the data to that second hard drive; just copy all your important files over to the drive. But, it must be a separate physical drive, such as an external disk drive or a disk drive on another computer on the network. Don't back up to another logical drive (or partition) on the same physical drive.

Hands down, you have to replace the defective drive. You're buying, at minimum, your computer a second hard drive. If possible, try to get an internal hard drive. Have your dealer set it up as the main hard drive, and have that person reconfigure the existing hard drive as the second hard drive. Then, you can copy information from the old hard drive to the new hard drive and eventually dispense with the old one.

If the drive is deceased, is its data dead as well?

Sometimes, the information on the hard drive goes with the hardware, and sometimes the information on the hard drive is still intact. That is why it's best to copy that stuff from the failing hard drive while you have the chance. If the hard drive goes, however, it's still possible to recover your data. Possible, but *expensive.*

Various outfits in most major cities specialize in disk disaster data recovery. Most of these places can take an old hard drive and, as long as you didn't blast the thing with a shotgun, fully recover all the data and either place it on a CD-ROM or a new hard drive or print it all for you.

Although this sounds like a wonderful service, data recovery is *very* expensive. It's primarily used for large companies or the government or other situations where the files are critical and no other backup exists. If your stuff is precious to you, *back up your hard drive,* as covered in Chapter 25. Save the data recovery job for those few places that can afford it.

Know your CD-ROM drive letter

If you're going to be working with your CD-ROM, and especially if you end up phoning tech support, you need to know which drive letter belongs to your CD-ROM drive. This PC puzzle is one that most users haven't yet solved.

In most documentation, the CD-ROM drive letter is referred to as Drive D. That's because Drive D is the CD-ROM (or DVD) drive in about 70 percent of the computers sold. Drive C is the one and only hard drive. Drive D, the next letter, belongs to the CD. But that's not always the case.

If you have a hard drive D, the CD-ROM drive letter may be E.

If you're a clever user and have reassigned your CD-ROM drive letter, it could be any letter of the alphabet, up to Z! On two of my computers, the CD-ROM is drive letter R. So, how can you tell?

Open the My Computer icon on the desktop. Choose View⇨Details from the menu. You see your computer's disk drives organized as shown in the nearby figure. Look in the Type column for any CD-ROM Disc or Compact Disc entries. That's your CD-ROM drive. Note which letter it is, such as F in the figure. (Drive D is a DVD drive, though you cannot tell from the My Computer window.)

✔ Under no circumstances should you expect or accept someone's offer to fix the drive. No, just replace the defective drive. It's not worth the cost or trouble to fix the drive.

✔ See Chapter 25 for information on backing up a hard drive.

✔ It helps to get a second, larger hard drive in any computer. The cost isn't that much.

✔ Yes, you can add a second hard drive yourself, but it's often a real pain. Hard drives must be configured as master and slave, which can be confusing — especially if you get two drives from different manufacturers. No, unless you consider yourself experienced at this sort of thing, have your dealer do it.

CD-ROM Catastrophes!

Since the mid-1990s or so, the CD-ROM drive is a standard feature on every PC. Almost all new software comes on CDs, and with the addition of CD-R/RW and DVD drives, these removable, shiny media are a valued and trusted part of any PC system.

And, like anything else in the computer, they can go kaput at the most ugly of times.

The all-purpose, do-or-die, tried-and-true CD-ROM troubleshooter

When the CD drive doesn't read a disc, play music, or do anything, you can follow these steps to effectively troubleshoot the drive:

1. **Push the eject button on the drive.**

   What should happen: If the tray slides out or the disc spits out (depending on the type of drive), you can be absolutely certain that the drive is getting power.

   If nothing happens: The drive is dead. There are two things you can do: First, you can (if you know your screws and nuts) turn off the computer and check the drive connections to see whether they're loose. If they're all snug, do the second option: Replace the drive with one that works.

2. **Insert a music disc.**

   The computer is smart enough to know that you play music discs when they're inserted. Notice that most CD-ROM drives even have a headphone jack and volume control. You use them to hear whether the music CD is playing.

What should happen: You hear the music play over the headphones. This means that the drive is working and what's missing is the connection between the drive and the motherboard (for data) or the connection between the drive and your PC's sound card (for music).

If nothing happens: The drive is dead, or the connections are loose. You can check the connections, and that may fix the problem. If not, replace the drive.

3. **Insert a cleaning disc.**

Go to Radio Shack or Wal-Mart or wherever and pick up a CD drive cleaning disc. This disc buffs out the laser lens and possibly fixes a CD drive that skips or reads data intermittently.

What should happen: The drive suddenly works again.

If nothing happens: It's time to get a new drive.

That's pretty much it for troubleshooting. Generally speaking, only a few things can go wrong with a CD-ROM drive: Its connections become loose, in which case the drive seems to have power, but inserting a disc has no effect; the drive has no power, which generally means that the drive is dead; or, the drive intermittently reads data, which means that the lens needs cleaning.

✔ Don't use a CD drive cleaning kit on a CD-R/RW or DVD-R drive. Those drives have self-cleaning laser heads, and using a cleaning disc on them can damage the drive.

✔ Speaking of which, a CD-R/RW drive that cannot write may have a hardware problem and need replacing. But first, try burning another disc. CD-R discs do go bad. When they do, toss them out and try again with another disc.

✔ Yes, CD-ROM drives do die. Remember that anything with moving parts is more likely to die than something fully electronic.

✔ If the CD-ROM drive ever goes AWOL, consider running the Add New Hardware Wizard (from the Control Panel's Add New Hardware icon) to reinstall it.

✔ If you can't eject a disc, use the "beauty mark" hole on the front of the drive. Stick a straightened paper clip into the hole. Push gently. This action ejects the disc — even when the computer is off or the drive totally lacks power.

Turning autoplay on or off

Windows comes configured to automatically play any CD you stick into the CD-ROM drive. This means that music discs should play automatically and that the autoplay programs on most data CDs run a Setup or Install program when the disc is inserted.

You can turn the AutoPlay feature on or off, or you can control how the disc is to be treated when Windows recognizes what types of files it contains. Here's how to do that:

1. **Open the My Computer icon on the desktop.**

2. **Right-click your CD-ROM drive's icon.**

3. **Choose Properties from the pop-up menu.**

   The CD-ROM drive's Properties dialog box appears.

4. **Click the AutoPlay tab.**

   You're presented with a slate of options, as shown in Figure 15-1. Here's what to do:

   - If you want nothing to happen, choose the item labeled Select an Action to Perform. Then, from the list, choose the item labeled Take No Action. That way, the computer does nothing whenever you stick in a CD.

   - If you want Windows to do different things depending on the disc's contents, choose the contents from the drop-down list. For example, to automatically play a music CD, choose Music CD from the list. Then, select from the list in the dialog box the program or media player to use.

Figure 15-1: Controlling AutoPlay for your PC's CD-ROM drive.

5. **Click the OK button after you have made your choices.**

6. **Close the My Computer window.**

If you have a second CD-ROM or DVD drive, you need to repeat these steps for that drive as well. Remember that a DVD drive can also read CD discs.

CD-R and CD-RW drive stuff

CD-R and CD-RW drives present other problems in addition to that of the normal CD-ROM drive. That's because, as their name implies, these drives can actually write discs, either the CD-R recordable discs or the CD-RW read-write discs — or both!

The biggest problem folks have with their CD-R drives is that they cannot get the drive to record. I cover specific steps to accomplish that task in my book *PCs For Dummies* (Wiley Publishing, Inc.). But, you must ensure that the drive is configured for recording. Here's how to check:

1. **Open the My Computer icon on the desktop.**

2. **Right-click your CD-ROM drive's icon.**

3. **Choose Properties from the pop-up menu.**

   This step displays a Properties dialog box for that CD-ROM drive.

4. **Click the Recording tab.**

   The Recording tab has lots of information on it, as shown in Figure 15-2. But, the key is the item labeled Enable CD Recording on This Drive.

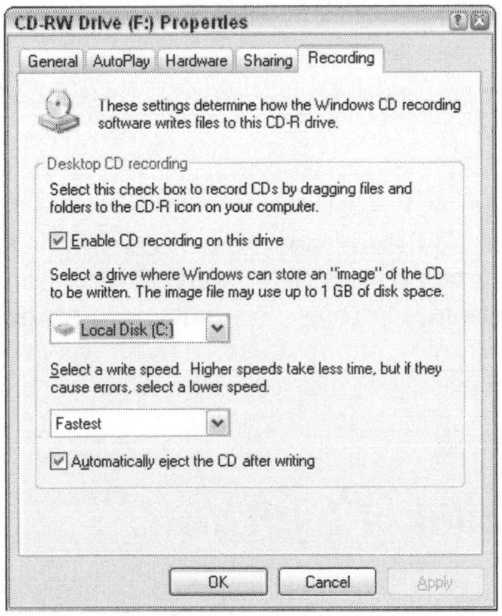

Figure 15-2: Here's where you activate CD-R recording.

5. **Ensure that there's a check mark by the item labeled Enable CD Recording on This Drive.**

6. **Click OK.**

7. **You can close the My Computer window as well.**

Obviously, if there's no Recording tab in Step 4 in these steps, the drive is *not* a CD-R/RW drive. Don't argue with me about it! Contact your dealer!

Here are some thoughts:

- I don't recommend using CD-RW discs any more. First, they're more expensive than CD-R discs. Second, they don't always reliably erase, and the number of times they can be reused is limited. Third, using them seems to be more time-consuming. Therefore, I recommend that you simply buy and use CD-R discs instead.

- My advice is to "burn" data to a CD-R disc in big chunks, and the larger the chunk, the better. Using a CD-R drive like a regular disk drive may result in less usable storage space on the drive; the extra overhead required to keep track of all the small recording sessions adds up.

- Though it appears that you can delete files on a CD-R disc, the space used by the files isn't recovered. No, Windows merely "masks" the deleted file. Don't be surprised when you delete 50 megabytes of stuff from a CD-R or CD-RW and don't see an extra 50 megabytes of storage appear on the drive.

- CD-R discs fail, just like other types of discs. If the CD-R disc cannot be written to, throw it out.

- The CD-R drive may appear to be dead, but most likely the disc is full. Try replacing the disc and see whether it still works.

Floppy Disk Woes

Pity the poor floppy disk. My friend Reza, from the United Kingdom, believes them to be doomed. Alas, they may be underused and ignored on many PCs, but they're still standard equipment. Quite a few smaller programs and utilities still come on floppy disks. They're cheap; easy to mail; easy to transport. But, they can cause woe and distress just like any other disk in the system.

"The floppy disk doesn't format!"

All floppy disks need to be formatted before you can use them. Even those preformatted disks should be formatted by your own floppy drive. If they can't be formatted, *toss them out!*

Floppy disks are cheap enough that you shouldn't waste any of your time trying to get one to format.

Why don't some of them format? The answer is alignment. Floppy drives aren't manufactured with the same rigid precision as other disk drives in your PC. Because of that, the alignment from drive to drive varies. A disk formatted in one drive (at the factory, for example) may not work in your own PC's drive. Likewise, you may find that your floppy disks can't be read on other drives because of bad alignment.

Floppy disks are unreliable

Please don't use floppies as your primary form of disk storage. The hard drive is where you're supposed to put all your vital stuff. Floppy disks are for transport or backup use, for that second copy.

The reason you shouldn't rely on floppy disks is that they just aren't as reliable as other disks. The floppy drive read/write head literally rubs the disk media every time you use the disk. Eventually, the head rubs the magnetic material off the disk and renders the disk useless.

Chapter 16

Correcting Graphics Disgrace

• •

In This Chapter

▶ Understanding graphics resolution

▶ Using the dots per inch (DPI) measurement

▶ Knowing about image size verses resolution

▶ Changing the monitor's resolution

▶ Viewing large images

▶ Setting graphics resolutions for e-mail

▶ Setting image resolutions in a digital camera

▶ Changing an image's size or resolution

▶ Understanding graphics file formats

▶ Using JPG compression

▶ Converting between graphics file formats

• •

O, shame! The powerful computer is slowly consuming the gentle, patient art of photography. While the camera companies continue to strive toward making things easier, computer users' graphical efforts are often met with disgrace and shame. Grandma bemoans, "It took me 40 minutes to download that baby's picture, and all I can see on the screen is one big eye!" Then, to make matters worse, she adds, "I thought you were supposed to be some sort of computer genius!"

The problems surrounding graphics images, scanning, and digital photography aren't centered as much on computer problems as they are on misunderstanding. Graphics is a big arena. There are plenty of places where things can go wrong and problems can crop up. This chapter helps smooth down those rough edges and offers soothing words of advice for grappling with graphics.

Unraveling Resolution

Most of the basic graphics questions and problems orbit the mysterious planet of resolution. Before you can understand why an image appears too large on the monitor or prints too tiny on paper, you need to understand resolution.

This section helps break down the concept of resolution, as well as other graphical terminology, into easy-to-digest, byte-size chunks.

What are pixels?

All graphic images — whether on the screen, in a file, or printed — are composed of tiny dots. On the computer screen, these dots are called *pixels,* which is a contraction of *pic*ture *el*ements. A typical pixel is shown in Figure 16-1.

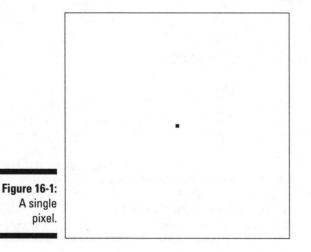

Figure 16-1:
A single
pixel.

Most of the talk about computer graphics deals with pixels: An image is formatted with so-many pixels across (horizontally) and so-many down (vertically). The monitor's resolution is set in pixels (refer to Chapters 6 and 13).

The printer, on the other hand, doesn't use pixels. Instead, the printer uses *dots,* which are merely a printed representation of the pixels on the screen. Every printer is capable of printing so-many dots per linear inch.

Dots and pixels are really the same thing: an individual piece of an electronic photograph. The difference is only in the name; the same pixel on the monitor becomes a dot on the printer.

The mysterious depths of color

Each pixel on the screen is assigned a specific color or tone. Back in the old days of monochrome monitors, there were no colors: The pixel was on or off, which translated into black or white. (A typical black pixel appears in Figure 16-1.) With color monitors, the pixel's color value is more diverse: It ranges from a basic 16 colors on up to millions of colors.

Obviously, having a high color depth is good; more colors render images more realistically than a limited range of colors can. Images with fewer colors look flat and phony — like a cartoon.

Though a higher color depth is better, there's a premium to pay: Having more colors requires more video memory to store the pixels' information; plus, more microprocessor speed is required in order to manipulate that vast amount of information; plus, more hard drive space is required in order to store the image. That's why the system resource requirements are so great for graphics and photo-editing applications.

The number of dots per inch

An image's resolution comes into play when you set the number of pixels, or dots, per inch for an image. You see, this value varies. Unlike other measure-ments in computers — characters per kilobyte, speed in GHz, crashes per hour — the number of pixels that can be crammed into an inch isn't a con-stant thing.

The higher the resolution, the more pixels or dots per inch.

The lower the resolution, the fewer pixels or dots per inch.

Figures 16-2, 16-3, and 16-4 illustrate the same image taken at different resolu-tions, or numbers of dots per inch.

In Figure 16-2, the resolution is low enough that you can see the pixels. (The stair-stepping phenomenon is called *aliasing.*) In Figure 16-3, the resolution is double that of Figure 16-2, and Figure 16-4 is doubled again.

- ✔ The more dots per inch, the higher the resolution and the more realistic the image appears.

- ✔ Higher-resolution images take up a tremendous amount of disk space. Those pixels cost RAM!

- ✔ If you're editing an image by using photo-editing software, such as Adobe Photoshop Elements, you *want* a very high resolution. The more pixels that are available, the easier it is to work with the image.

Figure 16-2:
A very low-
resolution
image.

Figure 16-3:
The same
image as
shown in
Figure
16-2, at
double that
resolution.

Figure 16-4:
The same image again, at four times the resolution of the image shown in Figure 16-2.

- ✔ The fewer dots per inch, the lower the image's resolution and the less realistic it appears.

- ✔ Lower-resolution images have the advantage of taking up less disk space.

- ✔ More color depth can be used to compensate for lower resolution, which is how television sets work. But, more color depth also makes the file size larger without necessarily increasing any detail in the image.

"Why does the image look so large on my monitor?"

When you use the term *resolution* to refer to a computer monitor, the values discussed are the number of pixels horizontally and vertically. For example, the monitor's resolution is 800 x 600 pixels or 1024 by 768 pixels. But, those numbers mean nothing. The true resolution is the number of dots per inch. The typical PC monitor has a resolution of about 96 dots per inch (dpi).

Suppose that you have a graphics image that uses 300 dots per inch as its resolution. That image appears *three times larger* on the PC's monitor when it's displayed at a 1-to-1 ratio, dots per pixel, as shown in Figure 16-5.

Image at 300 DPI resolution

Image appears "big" on monitor

Monitor set at 96 DPI

Figure 16-5:
A high-resolution image shows up *big* on the screen.

If the image's size is less than the monitor's "resolution" — 1024 by 768 pixels, for example — you can still see the whole thing on the screen. But, most images with a 300 dpi resolution have much larger dimensions than 1024 x 768 pixels. Therefore, the whole thing cannot show up on the monitor at once.

Changing the monitor's resolution

Your monitor's resolution isn't stuck at 96 dpi. It can be adjusted up or down, depending on the monitor and graphics adapter's abilities. Follow these steps to see whether you can change your monitor's resolution:

1. **Open the Control Panel's Display icon.**

   This step summons the Display Properties dialog box. You can also beckon this dialog box by right-clicking the desktop and choosing Properties from the pop-up menu deal.

2. **Choose the Settings tab.**

3. **Click the Advanced button.**

   A dialog box detailing your video hardware, both monitor and graphics adapter, pops into view.

4. **Locate the Display area on the General tab.**

You can see the DPI Setting drop-down list, as shown in Figure 16-6. In the figure, it's shown as Normal Size (96 DPI).

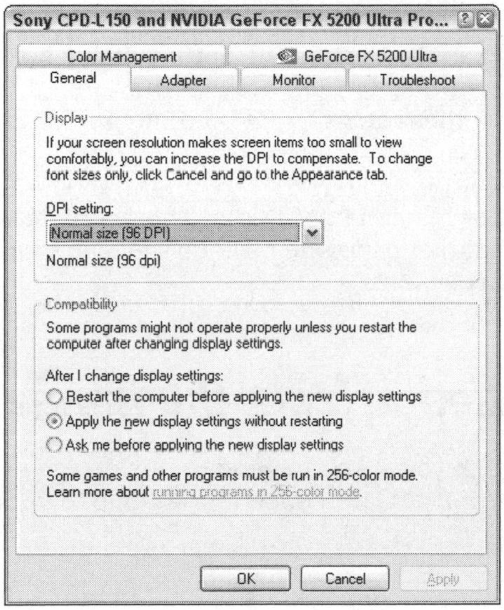

Figure 16-6:
Lord it over your computer's video hardware here.

5. **Choose Custom Setting from the drop-down list labeled DPI Setting.**

The Custom DPI Setting dialog box can be used to adjust the monitor's resolution, as shown in Figure 16-7. The more pixels per inch, the smaller the images appear on the monitor. The fewer pixels per inch, the larger images appear.

6. **Select a new resolution in the Custom DPI Setting dialog box, or just leave well enough alone.**

You can also use the mouse to drag the ruler in the Custom DPI Setting dialog box to the left or right.

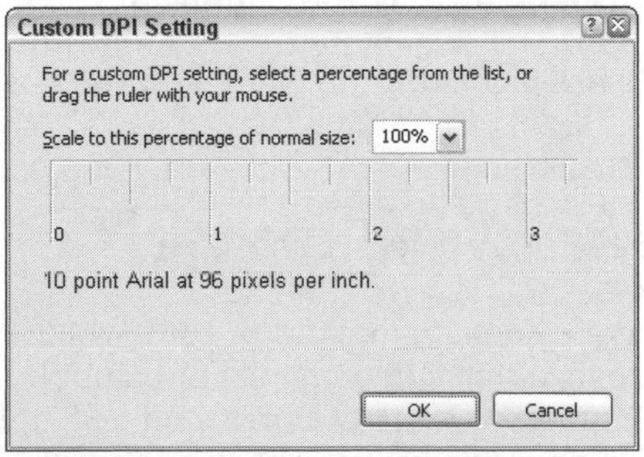

Figure 16-7:
Change your monitor's resolution here.

7. Click the various OK or Cancel buttons to back out of the open dialog boxes. Close the Control Panel window, if necessary.

Note that the monitor's resolution isn't *exactly* 1 inch per one inch. For example, if you get to Step 5 in this set of steps, put a ruler up to the monitor to see whether those tick marks in the Custom DPI Setting dialog box (refer to Figure 16-7) are *really* one inch wide. I would bet that they aren't! This is why some graphics mavens follow these steps to set their monitor's resolution to exactly one inch per inch.

The Macintosh uses a monitor resolution of 72 dpi. This is one reason that graphics designers prefer that platform: One pixel on the Mac's monitor is equal in size to one typesetter's point.

How the resolution affects the image size

The image resolution and its physical size depend on the device used to either capture or display the image. This concept is strange to understand, so pay heed!

Suppose that an image has physical dimensions of four inches by five inches. If that image is captured at 100 dpi, its resolution is 100 dpi. But, the image's dimensions are 400 pixels by 500 pixels.

Once again, suppose that the same image (4 x 5 inches) is captured at 300 dpi. Its dimensions are now 1200 x 1500 pixels. That image would be too large to display on a monitor that shows 1024 x 768 pixels. But, consider what happens when you print the image on a printer with a resolution of 600 dpi: The image is printed twice as small: 2 inches by 2.5 inches.

✔ The image's real size depends on the resolution of the device used to render the image.

✔ The best way to set the resolution is to know in advance where the image will end up. For e-mail, a resolution of 100 dpi, or roughly what the computer's monitor displays, is fine. For printing, try to match the printer's resolution. For photo editing, higher resolutions are best to ensure that enough pixels are present to properly edit the image.

"How can I see the whole image?"

Most graphics applications have a Zoom command or tool, which can be used to reduce or enlarge the image that's displayed. For example, an image taken at 300 dpi appears three times larger than normal on a 96 dpi monitor. If you use the Zoom tool to zoom out and reduce the image's visual size, you can see the entire thing on your monitor.

Likewise, when an image is too small, you can use the Zoom tool to enlarge it. However, the computer cannot create pixels where none exists. So, zooming in on a low-resolution image results in the kind of pixel-laden image you see in Figure 16-2.

Setting Resolution

One of the decisions you must make when you create a graphics image is the resolution. What is the proper number of dpi for that image? The real key here is to know where the image will end up. After all, there's no point in oversizing an image's resolution when you don't really need to.

"At what resolution should an image be for e-mail?"

Images captured for the Web or for e-mail need have no higher a resolution than the computer's monitor. Because PCs are set at 96 dpi, 96 dpi is a fine resolution, though most professionals choose 100 dpi simply because it's a round number.

At 100 DPI, you need to gauge the scale of the image. That's because most graphics programs do the math for you and though you set the resolution at a certain DPI value, the program displays the results in pixels horizontal and vertical. What I do is this:

> Set the image's longest edge to a value between 300 and 400 pixels.

This action ensures that the image fixes on the screen, no matter what the monitor's resolution. If the image doesn't look good at that size, set a higher size. But, be aware that sizes larger than 600 or 800 pixels may not appear on some folks' monitors.

✔ Most digital cameras, and indeed some scanners, have a *Web* or *E-mail* setting, which is a rather low resolution, but one specifically designed for viewing the image on a monitor.

✔ If you need the image for purposes other than the Web or e-mail, create a copy of the original image and reduce the copy to a size and resolution best suited for the Web.

✔ Not every computer monitor is the same! In addition to size and resolution matters, not every monitor has the same color balance. What the image looks like on your monitor will be different on other monitors.

"At what resolution should an image be for photo editing or enlarging?"

For photo editing you want lots and lots of those juicy pixels available, so the higher the resolution, the better.

For snapping digital pictures, set the camera to its highest available resolution, which is typically the *camera raw* format. At that resolution, the images are huge in size (several megabytes), but that abundant and glorious information makes all the difference when you're photo editing or reproducing or enlarging the images.

"How can I change my image's resolution?"

Technically, you cannot change an image's resolution. Pixels are stuck like stars in the firmament. New ones cannot be plucked from the ether, just as a magician doesn't really pull coins out of the air. So, if you snap an image at 100 dpi, you cannot magically convert it to 800 dpi for output on a high-quality digital printer.

Or, can you?

Photo-editing programs have commands for increasing resolution. But, they cheat. They *approximate* pixel values. Some programs do this quite well; Photoshop is the master, by using complex algorithms and software trickery to approximate and interpolate pixels where none existed before. Keep in mind that the result is never as good as when the image was captured at the proper resolution in the first place.

"How can I resize an image?"

Changing an image's size is done in photo-editing or any type of graphics application. The key is to find the resizing command. For example, in Photoshop the command is Image⇨Image Size. That command allows you to resize an image based on its horizontal and vertical pixel measurements. (It may also let you set the image's resolution.)

When you're changing an image's size, be sure to *constrain* the image. That is, when you resize the number of horizontal pixels, ensure that the vertical pixels are resized in a similar way so that the image doesn't appear stretched or skewed.

Figure 16-8 shows the Image Size dialog box from Photoshop Elements. See the linked chains to the right of the Width and Height areas? That means the values are linked, or constrained, so that when one is resized, the other dimension follows accordingly. The Constrain Proportions option (at the bottom of the dialog box) is what ensures that things remain together.

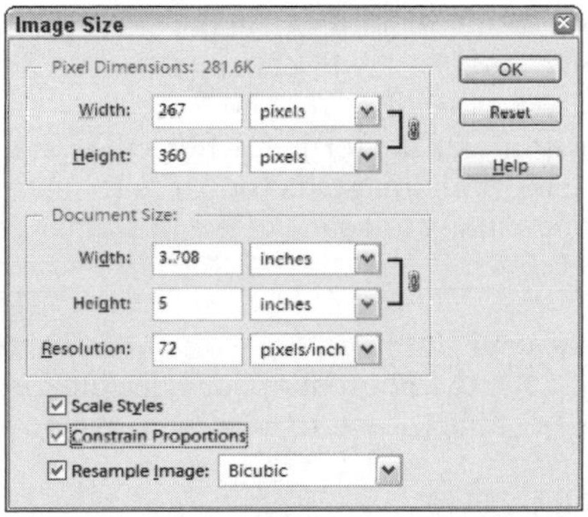

Figure 16-8:
Resizing an
image is
done here.

Glorious Graphics File Formats

Beyond the confusion of image resolution, there exists the multiple mania of graphics file formats. You may think that one format would be enough, but there are literally *hundreds* of computer graphics file formats. These document the different computer platforms as well as the gradual improvement of graphics technology over the years. The good news is that only a few of the graphics file formats are popular now, which narrows the choice and waters down the confusion.

Graphics file format reference

Out of gazillions of graphics file formats, there are only six common ones you need to confuse yourself over.

TIFF: This is the most compatible, common graphics file format, though it's best suited for documents or sharing images between different applications. TIFF images are too large to use for sending e-mail photos. But, for long-term storage or archiving images, I highly recommend using TIFF.

JPG: This is the most common graphics file format. JPG, or JPEG, renders real-life images, like photographs, very well. Unlike TIFF, JPG files can be compressed so that they don't take up huge amounts of disk space. The smaller file size also makes JPG images the ideal format for the Internet.

GIF: This is an older file format, though it's still popular on the Internet. GIF images aren't as good as JPG, however, because of a limited number of available colors. Therefore, you see graphic designs or art rendered in the GIF format, but not photographs.

PNG: This is the graphics format of the future. Called PNG, it's perhaps the most versatile graphics file format developed. It's slowly gaining adoption on the Web; however, I wouldn't recommend it for e-mail because not every e-mail program can properly recognize and display PNG images.

BMP: This is the old Windows graphics file format, where BMP stands for bitmapped image. The file size for BMP images is too large to make them practical for use in e-mail, though many folks make the mistake of e-mailing BMP images all the time.

Native: This is whatever format your photo-editing software uses to save its images. In Photoshop Elements, it's the Photoshop, or PSD, file format. Generally speaking, this is the best file format to save images you edit.

- ✓ For the Internet, use the JPG file format.

- ✓ JPG is pronounced "jay-peg." Note that the files can also end with the JPEG extension.

- ✓ GIF is pronounced "gif" with a hard G, as in "give." Some folks say "jiff" instead.

- ✓ BMP images are still used by Windows. In fact, the Paint program that comes with Windows uses BMP as its *native* format.

The JPG compression stuff

JPG graphics files achieve their small size thanks to built-in compression. When the image is saved to disk, a dialog box appears, such as the one shown in Figure 16-9, from Photoshop Elements. The dialog box prompts you to set the compression, either 1, or Low, for lots of compression or 10, or High, for no or little compression.

The low compression values yield smaller file sizes, which is good. But the image tends to get very fuzzy and ill-defined at tight compression values.

The higher values ironically indicate little compression. That means that the file size is larger, but the image quality is better.

I have never been in a situation where I have had to use compression values less than 5. I don't like the way the images look at those settings, so I save images at 6 or higher. For images where I want lots of detail I use 8, 9, or 10 values. For other images, values of 6 or 7 are just fine.

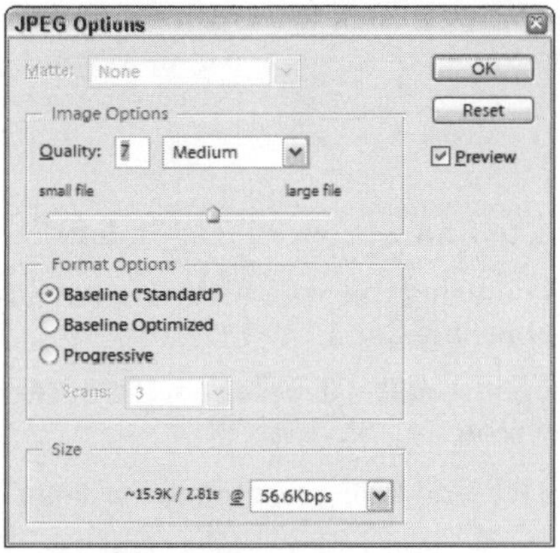

Figure 16-9:
Setting a
JPG image's
compres-
sion.

JPG graphics use what's called a *lossy* compression routine. That is, every time a JPG image is saved to disk, some of the image's information is lost. The more you open and resave JPG images to disk, the worse the image looks over time. If you just open and view an image, this isn't a problem. If you plan on editing or reusing an image, save it in the TIFF file format instead.

"What's the best graphics file format for e-mail?"

JPG.

"How can I convert my image from the [whatever] format into JPG?"

Some wonderful graphics conversion programs are available, but in Windows the only way to convert graphics images is to use the Paint program. It's clumsy, but it works:

1. **Start the Paint program in Windows.**

   The program can be found on the Start button's menu: Choose All Programs⇨Accessories⇨Paint.

2. **Choose File⇨Open.**

3. **Use the Open dialog box to locate the file you want to convert.**

   From the drop-down list labeled Files of Type, choose the All Pictures Files option. That directs Paint to display any picture file it can open.

4. **When you find the file to convert, click the Open button to open its image inside the Paint program.**

   There it is.

5. **Chose File⇨Save As.**

6. **Use the Save As dialog box to find a proper location for the file.**

   I offer specific instructions on using the Save As dialog box in my book *PCs For Dummies* (Wiley Publishing, Inc.).

7. **Choose the graphics file type from the drop-down list at the bottom of the Save As dialog box, by selecting Save As Type.**

   There, you find JPEG, GIF, TIFF, and PNG as options. For e-mail, you want to choose JPEG.

8. **Click the Save button to save the file.**

Now, you can use your e-mail program to send the picture in the best graphics file format. Don't forget where you saved it!

✔ The Paint program may also be called MS Paint or Windows Paint.

✔ The Paint program can open BMP (Native), JPG, GIF, TIFF, PNG, and ICO graphics file types. (ICO files are icon graphics images.)

✔ A great alternative graphics program is IrfanView, which is free, from www.irfanview.com.

✔ These steps can also be used to convert between any of the five popular graphics file formats: TIFF, JPG, GIF, PNG, and BMP. Just choose the proper format in Step 7.

Chapter 17

Internet Connection Mayhem

· ·

In This Chapter

▶ Dealing with disconnection disaster

▶ Connection frustrations in Outlook Express

▶ Losing the connection (let me count the ways. . . .)

▶ Taking care of call waiting

▶ Adjusting the automatic disconnect/idle time values

▶ Making the Internet go faster (or not)

· ·

I survived! For my research into this chapter, I read the technical description of how the typical PC connects to the Internet. The reading was tough — even dangerous. No pictures. And, it wasn't a *Dummies* book, either. I read lots of jargon about layers and protocols and bits hither, thither, and yon. The process is all so complex that it makes you wonder how it ever happens at all, but you know that it does. In a way, I could compare it to the differences between reading about sexual reproduction in biology class versus a backseat experience in a GTO at a drive-in movie, but I think that my publisher would strenuously object.

Fortunately, you don't ever have to learn the ins and outs of what goes on behind the scenes when you make an Internet connection happen. With any luck, it just does. When it doesn't, you can turn to this chapter for some solutions or soothing words of advice.

Just a Sampling of the Zillions of Things That Can Go Wrong with Connecting to the Internet with a Dial-Up Modem

It's supposed to work like this: You start an Internet program, and your computer automatically connects to the Internet and dishes up whatever data it is you're requesting: a Web page, e-mail, file — whatever.

This section, presented in a somewhat logical order, describes the things that can go wrong or may go wrong, or they're just general questions about connection calamities and losses.

Please note that these issues deal with dial-up Internet connections only.

"Windows doesn't remember my password!"

You go to connect to the Internet and, sure enough, you have to reenter your connection password. Again and again. And the Save option is dimmed, meaning that you cannot save the password. What's up?

The problem is that your account doesn't have a password in Windows XP. When you log in properly and provide the Login dialog box with a name and password, Windows activates the *password chain,* which is simply a location where Windows remembers all your various passwords.

The solution? Log in properly; give your account a password in Windows XP. Here's how:

1. **Open the Control Panel's User Accounts icon.**

2. **Click your account in the User Accounts window.**

   Your account name and its pretty little icon appear in the window.

3. **Click the link labeled Create a Password.**

4. **Fill in the blanks on the next screen to assign yourself a password and password hint.**

   Enter the password twice, as the window beckons you to. Also enter a password hint, which should not be the same thing as the password, but a *hint* to remind you of the password.

   For example, a good password has a combination of letters and numbers and is generally more than six characters long. So, if you once lived at 123 Ash Street, a password could be 123ash. The hint would be "My address when I was 15." Good password, good hint.

5. **Click the Create Password button when you're done.**

6. **Close various windows and such.**

By having a password-protected account in Windows, you can direct all the other places where passwords are entered to remember the passwords. That way, for example, you never have to keep typing the Internet or e-mail pass-word. Everything is locked up under that main, Windows XP account password.

✔ The username and password used to log in to Windows is different from the username and password you use on the Internet.

✔ Also refer to Chapter 9 for information on creating the password reset floppy disk.

Automatic-connection dilemmas

People automatically complain about two things in connecting to the Internet: They want it to happen, or they want it not to happen.

For example, if you enjoy automatic connection, when you start an Internet application, such as Internet Explorer, the connection box just pops up, and the modem dials in to the Internet. That's automatic connection in action.

On the other hand, some people prefer to have the Connect dialog box pop up and then have to click the Dial button to manually connect to the Internet.

Either way is possible, controlled from the Internet Options dialog box, as shown in Figure 17-1. Here's how to dig that up:

Figure 17-1:
The
Internet
Options/
Connections
dialog box.

1. **Open the Control Panel's Internet Options icon.**

   You can also get to this dialog box by choosing Tools⇨Internet Options inside the Internet Explorer Web browser program.

2. **Click the Connections tab.**

3. **Choose the option labeled Never Dial a Connection.**

4. **Click OK.**

   You can close the Control Panel window too, if needed.

The Never Dial a Connection option isn't stupid; it doesn't mean to *never* dial a connection. In fact, it should be relabeled Never *Automatically* Dial a Connection. That way, you have to manually connect to the Internet, which is why you would choose such a setting. Control!

Here's a description of each of the connection choices listed in the Internet Properties/Connections dialog box:

> **Never Dial a Connection:** Windows doesn't automatically connect to the Internet. You must manually dial in by using the Connect dialog box. You do this by opening the Internet Connection icon in the Network Connections window. Or, the Connect dialog box may appear whenever any program attempts to connect to the Internet.
>
> **Dial Whenever a Network Connection Is Not Present:** This option is the one that most people with traditional modems should select. It tells Windows to connect to the Internet whenever you open an Internet program.
>
> **Always Dial My Default Connection:** This option is puzzling because it sounds like the one you should check, but you should check the preceding option instead.

Most people get into trouble in the Internet Properties/Connections dialog box when they choose Always Dial My Default Connection rather than Dial Whenever a Network Connection *Is Not* Present.

You can still connect to the Internet if you choose the Never Dial a Connection option. You must summon the Connect To dialog box, like this:

1. **Open the Network Connections window.**

   If you're lucky, there's a Network Connections item on the Start button's menu. Otherwise, you open the Control Panel and then open the Network Connections icon.

   The Network Connections window is shown in Figure 17-2. The dial-up modem connections are listed in the Dial-Up area.

Figure 17-2:
The
Network
Connections
window.

 2. **Open your ISP's connection icon in the Dial-Up area of the Network Connections window.**

This step displays the Connect dialog box, as shown in Figure 17-3.

Figure 17-3:
The
Connect
window,
where the
dial-up
Internet
connection
is made.

3. **Click the Dial button to make the connection.**

After some annoying screaming from the modem over the PC's speaker, you're connected to your ISP and the Internet.

Note that some national online services, such as AOL, may require you to connect to the Internet by using their own icons and their own methods. If so, follow those instructions and not what's written here.

What if you're always connected?

High-speed, or *broadband,* Internet connections are always on. If you have DSL, cable, satellite, wireless, or even a T1 type of connection, your computer is always connected to the Internet. In that case, you don't ever see the connection dialog box because the connection is made instantly whenever you turn on your computer. That's the advantage to having a high-speed Internet connection.

If you would rather not connect to the Internet with a high-speed connection, choose File➪ Work Offline from the menu of whichever Internet application you're using. What this command does is to temporarily suspend the connection for that application; the command makes the program pretend that it's not talking to the Internet. You see Working Offline displayed on the application's title bar.

To reconnect the application, choose File➪ Work Offline again, and the connection is reestablished. Or, you may see a dialog box asking you to reconnect. It's a mere formality; with a high-speed connection, you're always connected.

(The only way to truly disconnect a high-speed connection is to turn off the DSL or cable modem. Or, if the connection is through some type of Ethernet cable, disconnect the Ethernet cable. That temporarily suspends Internet access both to and from your PC. You rarely have any reason to do this, however.)

✔ If you have a DSL, cable, or other broadband Internet connection, you should choose Never dial a connection from the Internet Properties/ Connections dialog box. That's right: You don't need to "dial" anything; you're always connected.

✔ The default connection is your preferred connection if you have more than one. You can always select another connection, from either the list in the Internet Options dialog box (refer to Figure 17-1) or from the Network Connections window (refer to Figure 17-2).

The PC dials in to the Internet at seemingly random times

In many instances, your computer attempts for some reason to dial into the Internet. It seems random because you may not be doing anything directly related to the Internet at the time. Or, it may happen when you start the computer. Is the computer possessed? Call the digital exorcist!

Obviously, *something* in your computer is trying to connect. What it could be is anyone's guess. The way I deal with the problem is to turn off the automatic-connection feature, as described in the preceding section. That way, when I see the Connect dialog box, I click the Cancel button and the computer stops dialing into the Internet.

✔ Some startup programs may connect to the Internet because they confuse your Local-Area Network (LAN) address with the Internet. So, rather than try to connect directly with some other computer that's local to you, the computer dials the Internet and looks for that computer. It's dumb, but it happens.

✔ The same type of situation may happen if you print to a networked printer; your computer may attempt to dial up the Internet to try to find the printer.

✔ Also consider contacting the printer manufacturer or software developer to see whether anyone there has any information on the product dialing into the Internet. Refer to Chapter 5 for tech-support information.

✔ Consult with your network administrator if you suspect that your computer is dialing the Internet to find a local computer. Consider changing the local IPs to the 10.0.0.*x* range of addresses. Again, the network person knows how to do this.

Connection mysteries in Outlook Express

Two mysteries must be unraveled regarding Outlook Express (OE) and your Internet connection: The first is when OE fails to automatically connect (which may or may not be wanted), and the second is when OE immediately disconnects after picking up your mail, which is mostly unwanted.

Whatever the case, you need to wander off to the Options dialog box in OE: Choose Tools⇨Options. This command displays the Options dialog box. Ensure that the General tab is selected, as shown in Figure 17-4.

Figure 17-4: Setting the OE connection options, Part I.

The main thing you need to notice is the drop-down list near the middle of the dialog box. It's titled If My Computer Is Not Connected at This Time, and three options are on the list:

- ✔ Do not connect.
- ✔ Connect only when not working offline.
- ✔ Connect even when working offline.

The first item is obvious: If you start OE and don't want to dial into the Internet, choose that option. OE should (and I'm sorry, but this is a "should" situation) not dial into the Internet. Sometimes, it does — specifically, if you also have checked the option labeled Send and Receive Messages at Startup. Better uncheck that item too if you really don't want to connect.

Another way to avoid connecting — even if you have a broadband connection — is to choose File➪Work Offline. This command tells OE to pretend that it's not connected to the Internet, even if it is. When you choose that option, the second two items in the drop-down list come into play, and OE connects or not depending on which option you have chosen.

Confused? If so, and if you really don't want OE to connect, remove the check mark by Send and Receive Messages at Startup and choose Do Not Connect from the drop-down list.

- ✔ Be careful to note the commands on the drop-down list. One says If My Computer Is Not Connected at This Time. That means that if the computer *is* connected, the instructions on that list are ignored — unless you choose File➪Work Offline, in which case OE pretends that it's not connected anyway.
- ✔ And Pooh said "Oh, bother!"
- ✔ If you detest that the Windows Messenger program always starts up when you run OE, uncheck the item Automatically Log On to Windows Messenger.

Disconnection mysteries in Outlook Express

One frustrating option in Outlook Express (OE) is found on the Connection tab of the Options dialog box, as shown in Figure 17-5. It's the Hang Up after Sending and Receiving option.

If you choose that option, OE itself kills your dial-up Internet connection, no matter what else is going on.

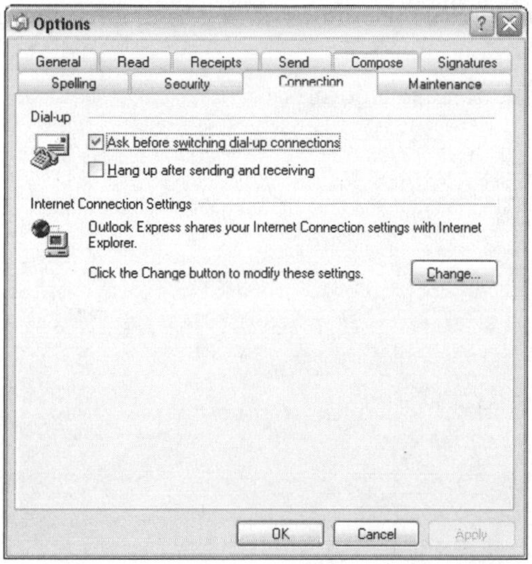

Figure 17-5:
The
Connection
tab in the
OE Options
dialog box.

I have had readers who are happily surfing on the Web discover that they have been disconnected simply because OE has automatically picked up some new e-mail *and then disconnected.* It can be a frustrating thing, especially if you don't know where to look for turning it off. Now you know.

Missing modem guys!

Whenever a dial-up connection is active in Windows, what I call "the little modem guys" appear in the system tray/notification area, as shown in the margin. These guys not only let you know that you're connected to the Internet, but they also provide instant access to the Connect dialog box, which can be really handy.

The first thing to assume is that the modem guys have just been shoved off to the side, which is normal behavior. Click the Show More chevron to see whether the fellows are merely hiding.

The second reason is that you may not have the option to show the modem guys turned on. Check it by following these steps:

1. **Open the Network Connections window.**

   You can do this by opening the Network Connections icon in the Control Panel.

2. **Right-click your Dial-Up Networking icon.**

3. **Choose Properties from the pop-up menu.**

4. **In the dial-up connection's Properties dialog box, click the General tab, if necessary.**

What you see should look like Figure 17-6.

Figure 17-6:
Controlling
the little
modem
guys'
visibility is
done here.

5. **Click to put a check mark by the option labeled Show Icon in Notification Area When Connected.**

6. **Click OK to close the Properties dialog box.**

You can optionally close the Network Connections and Control Panel windows.

You may also want to refer to the section in Chapter 6 about annoying programs in the system tray/notification area for more information on things that wither in the system tray/notification area.

Hanging up the modem without restarting the computer

Somewhere, someone along the line told computer users that in order to hang up their Internet connections, they had to restart Windows. This is dumb, dumb, dumb. Computers are much smarter than that. Such nonsense is like telling someone to turn her car off when she pulls up to a stop sign. It's just not necessary.

To hang up the modem, you must click the Disconnect button in the Status dialog box, similar to what's shown in Figure 17-7. That hangs up the modem and disconnects you from the Internet — no restart required.

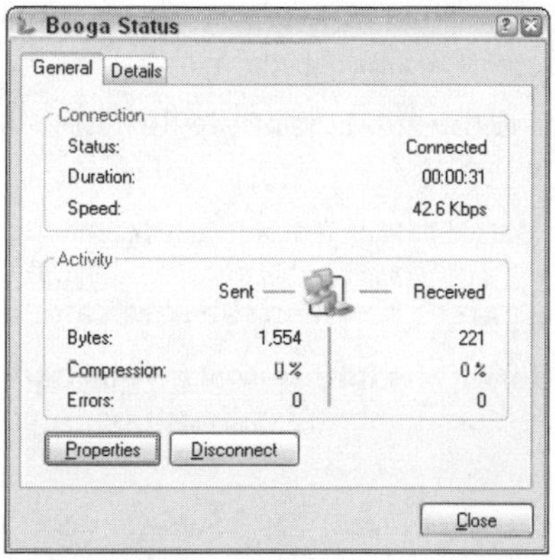

Figure 17-7:
Hang up
the modem
here.

Now, the real question is "How do you get to the Status dialog box?"

The first way is to find the little modem guys in the system tray/notification area. Double-click them to see the Status dialog box. Or you can just right-click them and choose Disconnect from the pop-up menu.

The second way is to open the Network Connections window (instructions are in the preceding section) and then right-click your dial-up connection icon and choose the Disconnect command from the pop-up menu. That method also works just swell, though using the little modem guys is most likely faster for you.

Losing the Connection

Internet connections drop for a gazillion reasons — anything from squirrels on the line (I kid you not) to someone else in the house picking up the phone extension. The phone connection is a delicate thing, and just about anything short of wishful thinking can bring it down.

- ✔ Do you suspect your phone lines to be to blame? If so, you can have your phone company test the wires all the way up to your house for reliability. The wires inside your house, however, must be tested by an electrician. See whether your ISP can recommend an electrician familiar with digital communications.

- ✔ By the way, the phone company can do nothing to improve slow service. It only guarantees a certain speed over its phone wires — nothing faster. (You have to see what the speed is for your area, which depends on the age of the equipment and, well, how lazy your particular phone company is.)

✔ Sometimes the connection works better at night. Radio interference from the sun can wreak havoc with communications.

✔ For you people living in Oregon, the sun is that big, bright thing in the sky that most of us see during the day.

✔ At two times during the year, satellite modems get interference from the sun: during the fall and vernal equinoxes. It typically happens about noon or so, when the satellite passes between the earth and the sun.

✔ Call waiting can sure knock you off the Internet. See your phone book or features manual for information on disabling call waiting in your area. See the following section.

✔ The connection can drop because of inactivity. (See the section "Adjusting the Connection Time-Outs," later in this chapter.)

✔ Sometimes, your ISP may drop the connection, especially during a busy time of day. AOL doesn't admit to it, but that doesn't mean that it never happens.

✔ The modem may drop the connection because of the heat. In this type of situation, you can connect for only about 20 to 30 minutes before getting disconnected. Ensure that your PC's fan is working and that your computer is in a well-ventilated place.

Disabling the Annoying Call Waiting

Windows can be taught to automatically switch off the call waiting feature so that you don't get accidentally disconnected by it when you're on the Internet. You do that by heeding these steps:

1. **Open the Phone and Modem Options icon in the Control Panel.**

   The Phone and Modem Options dialog box comes forth.

2. **Click the Dialing Rules tab.**

3. **If locations are entered, select the current location and click the Edit button. Otherwise, click the New button to create a new location.**

   The location feature is best used on PC laptops, where the computer's location can change from place to place. On a desktop system, you need only enter the computer's permanent location.

   After creating the location, click the Edit button to proceed to the next step.

4. **Put a check mark by the item labeled To Disable Call Waiting, Dial.**

   It's near the bottom of the dialog box, as shown in Figure 17-8.

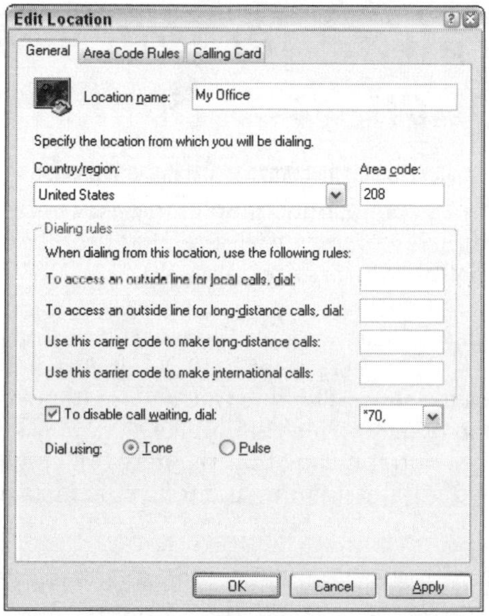

Figure 17-8:
Disable
call wait-
ing here.

5. **From the drop-down list, select the proper dialing sequence for your area to disable call waiting.**

   This information can be found near the front of your area's phone book.

6. **Click OK to close the Edit Location dialog box.**

7. **Click OK to close the Phone and Modem options dialog box.**

   You can optionally close the Control Panel window as well.

After you make these adjustments, Windows automatically disables call waiting for each call the modem makes.

✔ For more information on using a PC laptop, get my book *Laptops For Dummies* (Wiley Publishing, Inc.).

✔ If you would rather keep call waiting on, but have the computer not disconnect and instead notify you, you can check out the following Web pages for specialized software:

```
www.buzzme.com
www.callwave.com
www.catchacall.com
```

✔ The AOL service also has a feature, called AOL Call Alert, that notifies you of a pending call while you're dialed into AOL.

Humble Words of Advice for When Your Broadband Connection Goes Bonkers

Broadband modems — those of the cable, DSL, and satellite varieties — are really more like remote network connections than modems. Therefore, any problems they have are most likely to be network-related problems other than the typical problems that plague dial-up users.

The first thing to check when you suspect a problem with your broadband modem is the modem's lights. You see a power light, a network light, and maybe a few other lights just for show. The one that's most important is the connection light, which may be the one that blinks as data is sent and received. When that light goes out, it means that the network connection is down. Phone your DSL provider to let it know, and follow its instructions on what to do next.

When all the lights are on and no connection can be found, it could be that your broadband provider is having trouble. In other words, *its* computers that are kaput! In that case, all you can do is wait. Be sure to phone up the provider after a few minutes of no Internet action to confirm that it's having problems.

The final thing you can do when everyone else says "Nope — nothin' wrong here!" is to disconnect your broadband modem. Wait a while (about a minute). Then, reconnect the thing. In many cases, that fixes the problem.

- Broadband modems are fairly robust and reliable. If your broadband connection has been up and running for a few weeks, chances are that it will perform flawlessly for a long time.

- When the broadband modem is inside the computer, such as on some satellite modems, you have to turn the computer off, wait, and then turn it on again to restart the modem.

- Yes, it's okay to leave the broadband modem on all the time. In fact, many ISPs and broadband providers want you to keep the modem on.

- Broadband modems go down during power outages. Consider plugging the broadband modem into a UPS, or uninterruptible power supply. That way, the modem stays on during brief power outages. (Sometimes, it takes a while for the broadband connection to reestablish after a power outage, but not if you're using a UPS.)

Adjusting the Connection Time-Outs

To ensure that you don't waste precious Internet connect-time, Windows has built in a connection time-out system to disconnect your dial-up modem after a period of inactivity. You can adjust this value up or down, or even turn it off, which is nice. What's not nice is that there are *two* places to look in Windows XP for the time-out information. Better take these one at a time.

First comes the modem time-out settings:

1. **Open the Control Panel's Phone and Modem Options icon.**

2. **Click the Modems tab in the Phone and Modem Options dialog box.**

3. **Choose your modem from the list.**

   It's probably selected already, especially when you have only one modem in the computer.

4. **Click the Properties button at the bottom of the dialog box.**

   Another Properties dialog box opens, one specific to your brand of modem.

5. **Click the Advanced tab.**

6. **Click the Change Default Preferences button.**

   Finally, you hit pay dirt in the modem's Default Preferences dialog box, as shown in Figure 17-9.

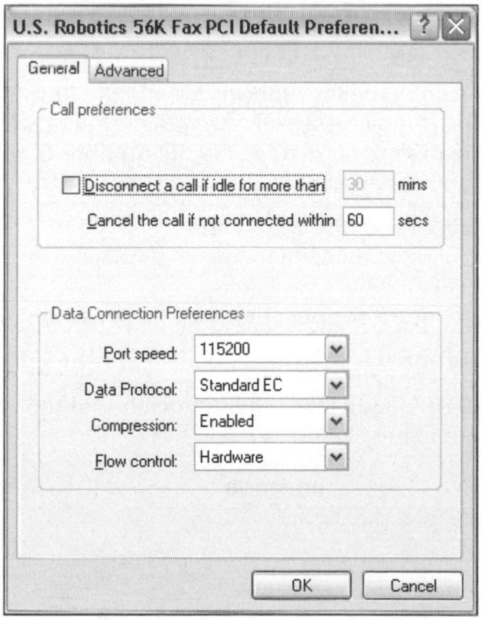

Figure 17-9:
The modem time-out setting is buried way down here.

To set an automatic disconnect, put a check mark by Disconnect a Call If Idle for More Than [blank] Mins. Then, enter the amount of minutes to wait for a disconnect.

 7. **Make the settings your heart desires.**

 8. **Click OK to close the Default Preferences dialog box.**

 9. **Click OK to close the modem's Properties dialog box.**

10. **Click OK to close the Phone and Modem Options dialog box.**

Okay! Okay! Okay!

That's just the first location, and they hid it most effectively, don't you think? The second location deals with your ISP's connection information, which you can get to from the Internet Options icon, also located in the Control Panel:

11. **Open the Internet Options icon in the Control Panel.**

12. **Click the Connections tab in the Internet Properties dialog box.**

13. **If necessary, choose your ISP from the list.**

If you have only one ISP, it's already selected for you.

14. **Click the Settings button.**

A dialog box for your ISP's Settings appears. Believe it or not, you can check in *two* places for time-out values.

15. **Click the Properties button.**

You're not there yet!

16. **Click the Options tab in your ISP's Properties dialog box.**

There it is! Located in the Redialing Options area is the first idle-time-before-hanging-up item. It may be specific to redialing, but why take chances? Set the idle time-out value to a specific number of minutes or to Never to not hang up automatically.

17. **Make your adjustments to the idle time value.**

18. **Click OK.**

Now comes the second, more serious, time-out value setting for your ISP.

19. **Click the Advanced button.**

Ah, the Advanced Dial-Up dialog box is just chock-full of time-out and idle values, as shown in Figure 17-10.

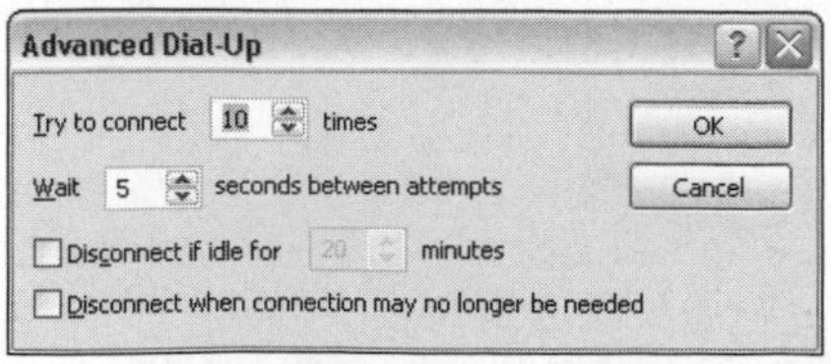

Figure 17-10:
Even more
time-out
options!

Advanced Dial-Up	? X
Try to connect 10 ⬍ times	OK
Wait 5 ⬍ seconds between attempts	Cancel
☐ Disconnect if idle for 20 ⬍ minutes	
☐ Disconnect when connection may no longer be needed	

To disable the idle disconnect, uncheck the Disconnect If Idle for [blank] Minutes option, as shown in Figure 17-10. Or, check that item and enter the number of minutes of inactivity after which the computer should disconnect.

In this dialog box, you also find the handy Disconnect When Connection May No Longer Be Needed item. That's the item that tells Windows to automatically display the Disconnect dialog box when you close your last Internet application's window — a handy item to turn on.

20. Make the necessary settings and adjustments.

21. Click OK to close the Advanced Dial-Up dialog box.

22. Click OK to close your ISP's Settings dialog box.

23. Click OK to close the Internet Properties dialog box.

24. Close the Control Panel window while you're at it.

Be sure to bring in the trash cans before the neighbor's dogs get into them!

Obviously, if you have a broadband connection, you don't need to worry about time-out values; you're connected all the time anyway. Nya! Nya! Nya!

Improving Your Internet Connection Speed

You can do little to improve your Internet connection speed. I know that many products out there claim to improve download times and connect speeds and many Web pages, advertisements, and magazine articles give you lists of things to tweak and adjust. But the time savings that are made, if any, are minute.

The ugly fact is that connection speed is a hardware thing. Unless you get faster connection hardware, the speed is roughly the same all the time. Honestly, this isn't even a troubleshooting issue.

✔ Even a fast Internet connection can meet with a slow Internet from time to time. When major parts of the Internet go down or servers are turned off for backups or upgrades, the overall speed of the Internet drops. Again, you can do little about it.

✔ Some "tips" have you delete temporary Internet files, check your proxies, reset the modem, reboot the computer, and do a host of other chants and genuflections. Do they help? I'm not sure. But if such actions make you feel better, by all means continue.

✔ If your Internet connection gets slower over time, you can try to disconnect, reset the modem, and start over again.

✔ To reset an internal modem, simply restart Windows. You reset an external modem by turning it off and on again. Be sure to wait before turning the modem on again; you want to avoid a fast off-on flip of the switch, which may not have any effect on the hardware.

✔ Download accelerators are available, which, although they don't change your connection speed, do make downloads take less time because of how the information is managed.

✔ Cable modems do slow down the more people are on the circuit. So, if you're on the Internet and then all the neighbor kids come home from school, that would explain a drop in connection speed.

Chapter 18

Web Weirdness with Internet Explorer

*I*nternet Explorer gets lots of the blame for things that aren't really its fault. You see, a *Web browser* is merely a window through which you can view information on the World Wide Web. If a Web page screws up — which happens often — you really have to blame the Web page itself and not Internet Explorer for merely passing on the bad news.

Yeah, verily, even though you can pass blame off on the Web, Internet Explorer does have enough quirks and oddities that warrant its own chapter in this troubleshooting book.

✔ Throughout this chapter, I use the abbreviation *IE* to refer to Internet Explorer.

✔ Though the information here is about IE (Internet Explorer — just checking to see whether you're reading all the bullet points), much of it applies to other Web browsers as well.

Maintaining and Configuring Internet Explorer

Internet Explorer is a relatively easy program to use and configure. It has only a few areas where it tends to frustrate people. I have listed the more popular frustrations and solutions in this section.

Changing the home page

The *home page* can be anything you want to see when you first start Internet Explorer. Here's how to set the home page to something special or to nothing at all:

1. **Start IE.**

   That's Internet Explorer, in case you were silly and skipped reading this chapter's introduction.

2. **Visit the Web page you want as your home page.**

   For example, visit Yahoo! or my own Web page, www.wambooli.com/. Displaying that Web page now makes choosing it as your home page much easier.

3. **Choose Tools⇨Internet Options.**

   You set the home page in the Internet Options dialog box, in the top part of the General tab, as shown in Figure 18-1.

   You have three choices:

   - **Use Current:** Choose the current page as the home page. You notice that the current page's address appears in the box.

   - **Use Default:** This choice would be the Microsoft preference, which is probably the MSN home page.

   - **Use Blank:** This option tells IE to start with a blank page — an item popular with many folks.

4. **Select whichever option you want.**

   For example, to switch to the page you were viewing, click the Use Current button.

5. **Click OK.**

   Now, that page is the first thing you see when you start IE.

These steps should reset your home page, but the change may not be for good, as the following subsections demonstrate.

Figure 18-1:
Selecting a
home page.

"I cannot change the home page!"

Sometimes, changing the home page may not be possible. These times include any of the following circumstances:

- Your computer has been infected by a virus that disables your home page selection. The solution is to run antivirus software to remove the problem and regain control.

- Your computer has been infected with spyware or software that has changed your home page. The official term is *hijacked* your home page. The solution here is to run anti-spyware software, as covered in Chapter 24.

- You have installed software that changes the home page for you, either on purpose or against your wishes. The page may be a feature of a "Web enhancement" program. The solution here is to remove that program.

- IE has been customized to prevent you from changing or using a home page. It happens at large companies or other large institutions where the system administrator restricts your computer's features for security purposes — or just to be mean.

"Why does it tell me that there's a new version of Internet Explorer?"

From time to time, Microsoft releases newer versions of its software and feels compelled to let the world know. When this happens, you don't see your regular home page when IE starts. Instead, you're redirected to an update page. That's normal; annoying, but normal.

- ✔ After choosing to update the software, your Web page *should* return to normal. Sometimes, it doesn't, in which case you can reread (or just read) the section "Changing the home page," earlier in this chapter, about changing the page back.

- ✔ It's up to you whether you want to upgrade to the newer version of any program. I generally don't do it unless the newer version offers me some feature that I think I need or fixes a problem I'm having.

- ✔ Other Web browser software also pulls this same home-page-direction stunt, so don't go off blaming Microsoft for being evil or anything.

Adjusting the temporary file size

IE stores megabytes and megabytes of temporary files on disk. Officially, this area is known as the *cache* (say "cash"). By storing images, sounds, text, and other information on your computer's hard drive, you make those Web pages you visit frequently load faster. After all, it takes less time to load an image from the temporary file cache than it would to squeeze that same image through the wires connecting you to the Internet.

The problem? The temporary file size can get huge! The bigger it is, the longer it takes IE to search through it, so cutting down on the size may truly improve your Web browsing performance.

Here's how to view or adjust the temporary file size for IE:

1. **Choose Tools⇨Internet Options.**

   The Internet Options dialog box appears. The center part of the General tab deals exclusively with temporary Internet files.

2. **Click the Settings button.**

   Various settings litter the Settings dialog box, as you would expect and as shown in Figure 18-2. The key setting to adjust here is the amount of disk space used for storing temporary files. That adjustment is made by using the slider in the center of the dialog box or by manually entering a new size in the MB (megabytes) box.

3. **Adjust the size as needed.**

   Normally, the file size is set to about 1.5 percent of your hard drive's total capacity. You can adjust this setting to 1 percent, for example, and see how that number affects things; just move the slider left or enter a new value in the MB box.

Figure 18-2:
Temporary
Internet file
control.

Another item to change is the first one. I would select Every Visit to the Page to keep IE from wandering off to look for new copies of stored stuff.

If you select Never from the list, which effectively disables the cache, you must use the Refresh command (or press the F5 key) to load a new version of a Web page. It's definitely an option *not* worth selecting.

4. **Click OK.**

Some folks say to delete the temporary files as another way to speed up Web performance. I'm not certain whether that method works, though it does increase disk space.

If you want to delete the files, simply click the Delete Files button in the Internet Options dialog box.

Common Puzzles and Solutions

Here are a few of my favorite and most common Web browsing puzzles and their solutions. Consider this the short list; the full list would consume many more pages — perhaps an entire book in itself!

"The text is too small to read!"

I don't know why some Web page designers seem hell-bent to make us old folks squint at the computer monitor. Unless it's the text that says "Copyright," way down at the bottom of the Web page, then — dernit! — I want to read it!

Fortunately, IE has a solution for any Web page where you may find the text too teeny to interpret: Choose View⇨Text Size⇨Larger.

If that doesn't work, try View⇨Text Size⇨Largest.

What that command does is to temporarily boost the size of the text you see on the screen. (Graphical images aren't affected, so if the text is really a graphic, the size doesn't change.) Then, you can read at your leisure.

Note that this command is a page-only thing and that IE doesn't remember the next time around which pages you magnified.

Pop-up porn puzzles

Nothing is more shocking or irritating than a pop-up parade of porn windows. Or, they can be any advertisements, but most often it's shocking pornography — not just once, but as many as 64 different windows all hogging up the screen. Closing the windows is like pounding down a lump in the carpet.

I have known many people who just shut down Windows whenever the porn pop-up parade begins. The newest version of IE, however, includes some anti-pop-up blocking tools. To ensure that the pop-up blocker is on, choose Tools⇨Pop-up Blocker⇨Turn On Pop-up Blocker. That should fix the problem.

You can make adjustments to the Pop-up Blocker by choosing Tools⇨Pop-up Blocker⇨Pop-up Blocker Settings. That command displays a dialog box, as shown in Figure 18-3. Use the Filter Level drop-down list (at the bottom of the dialog box) to set how aggressively you want IE to block those dang pop-up windows.

Not every pop-up window is bad, however. Some Web sites use pop-up windows to display extra information. In that case, you may want to type the Web page's address in the text box labeled Address of Web Site to Allow. Then, use the Add button to put that Web site on the list of OK pop-up sites.

- ✔ Other Web browsers also offer anti-pop-up features.

- ✔ Pop-up windows that appear when you try to close a Web page window or attempt to visit another Web page are referred to as *mouse traps*. The IE pop-up blocker should quash those. If not, use the Back button in IE to back out of the suspect Web page and then close the window.

- ✔ Beyond porn pop-ups, another way to fight porn is to get antiporn software for IE. I recommend either NetNanny or Cybersitter:

```
www.netnanny.com/
www.cybersitter.com/
```

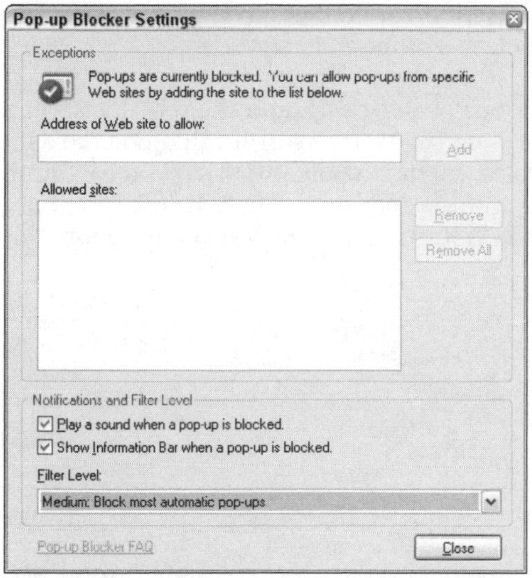

Figure 18-3:
Knock
down pop-
ups here.

Where did the download go?

Saved a file to disk, didja? And now, you can't find the file. It happens. Mostly, it happens because folks are so eager to save to disk that they forget *where* they saved to disk. But it's an easy solution: Use the Search or Find command in Windows to locate any file that was recently created. Refer to Chapter 9 for more information.

✔ When you download a file, be sure to choose the option that *saves* the file to disk. Don't choose the option that *runs* or *opens* the file.

✔ Sometimes, it's necessary to right-click the file's link and choose the Save Link to Disk option.

✔ Some types of files cannot be downloaded to disk. Certain MP3, Real Audio, Flash, and other media file formats can be played only over the Internet. Any attempt to download them results in a tiny file, which is merely an Internet shortcut back to the original file's location on the Internet.

JavaScript errors, or "Error on page"

JavaScript is a programming language used to automate certain things on a Web page. One of its features is that it can open new windows, which is how you get those annoying pop-up window advertisements (or "infestations"). JavaScript does good things too, such as display rollover buttons and change graphical images on a Web page — stuff you normally wouldn't care about until you get a JavaScript error message.

The telltale sign of a Javascript error is the text "Error on Page," which appears in the lower-left corner of the IE window.

 Normally, you wouldn't notice such a thing, and there really isn't anything you can do about it; the error is on the Web page, and that could exist anywhere on the Internet on the planet earth. If you're curious, you can double-click the warning icon to see more information, as shown in Figure 18-4, but that's really of use to no one except the Web page designer or programmer.

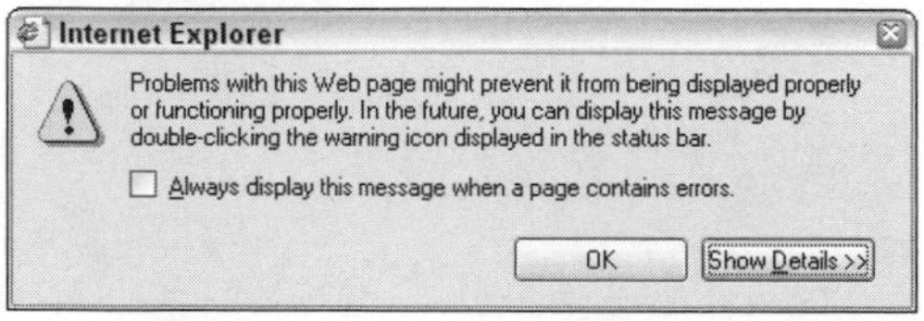

Figure 18-4:
Yawn.

> **Internet Explorer**
>
> Problems with this Web page might prevent it from being displayed properly or functioning properly. In the future, you can display this message by double-clicking the warning icon displayed in the status bar.
>
> ☐ Always display this message when a page contains errors.
>
> [OK] [Show Details >>]

If you find that these errors appear in the form of pop-up windows that you must address, you can stifle them. Try these steps:

1. **Choose Tools⇨Internet Options to display the Internet Options dialog box.**

2. **Click the Advanced tab.**

3. **Put a check mark by the item Disable Script Debugging.**

   If there are two such options, put the check mark by both of them.

4. **Click OK.**

   You never see the error messages again.

These steps don't disable JavaScript! They merely turn off the error message display so that it's just one less thing to be annoyed by.

> ✔ JavaScript isn't the same thing as Java. No, *Java* is a programming language that creates programs you can run on the Internet, such as Yahoo! Games or MSN Games.

> ✔ Don't bother reporting the JavaScript error to the Webmaster. I mean, well, you can *try*. But it has been my experience that such reports go unnoticed.

Disabling ActiveX

ActiveX is an IE add-on that allows you to run programs over the Internet. In many cases, the programs are helpful and innocent. But, the ActiveX programs can also do damage, such as run nasty software on your computer or infect your PC with a virus or install other unwanted junk. I feel that it's best to disable Active X. Here's how:

1. **In IE., choose Tools⇨Options to display the Internet Options dialog box.**

2. **Click the Security tab.**

3. **Ensure that the Internet icon is selected.**

4. **Click the Custom Level button.**

The Security Settings dialog box is displayed, as shown in Figure 18-5.

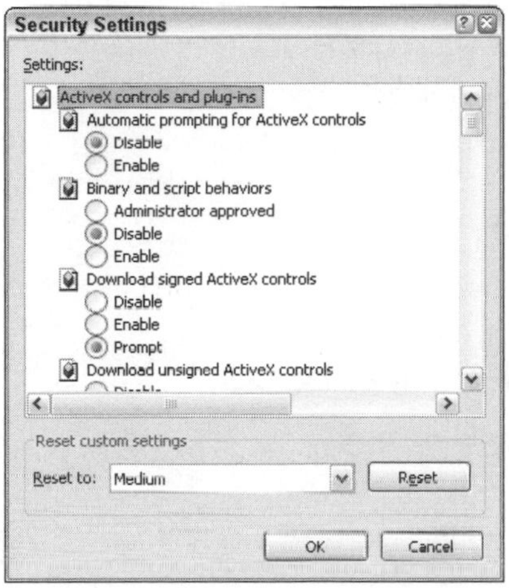

Figure 18-5:
Disable
those
annoying
ActiveX
controls
here.

5. **Set the options for any ActiveX control or plug-in to Disable.**

There are seven items. Choose Disable for all of them.

6. **Click the OK button to confirm your settings and dismiss the Security Settings dialog box.**

7. **Click OK to close the Internet Options dialog box.**

After making these changes, use IE for a while and visit a few Web pages. As you do, you may receive a warning about the page not being displayed correctly or not functioning properly because you disabled the ActiveX controls. In many cases, that's good news; because you don't know what the ActiveX control could do, saying "No" is a good idea. But, for Web sites you trust, you may want to override the settings.

For example, if you use the Google Gmail program, you need to have ActiveX controls working in order to read your mail. To tell IE that ActiveX controls are okay on that page, follow these steps:

1. **Choose Tools⇨Options in IE to display the Internet Options dialog box.**

2. **Click the Security tab.**

3. **Click the Trusted Sites icon.**

4. **Click the Sites button.**

   The Trusted sites dialog box appears, as shown in Figure 18-6. This is where you can specify those sites where it's okay for Active X controls to run.

5. **Type the name of the Web site in which you want ActiveX controls to be run.**

   You can use the asterisk character (*) as a wildcard to permit subdomains to be accessed on various Web sites. For example, in Figure 18-6, you see *.microsoft.com, which allows all Microsoft sites (`support.microsoft.com` and `updates.microsoft.com`, for example) to be accessed with no restrictions.

6. **Click the Add button.**

   This step puts that site on the list.

   If you cannot add the site, ensure that the check box at the bottom of the dialog box isn't checked.

7. **Click OK to close the Trusted Sites dialog box.**

8. **Close the Internet Options dialog box.**

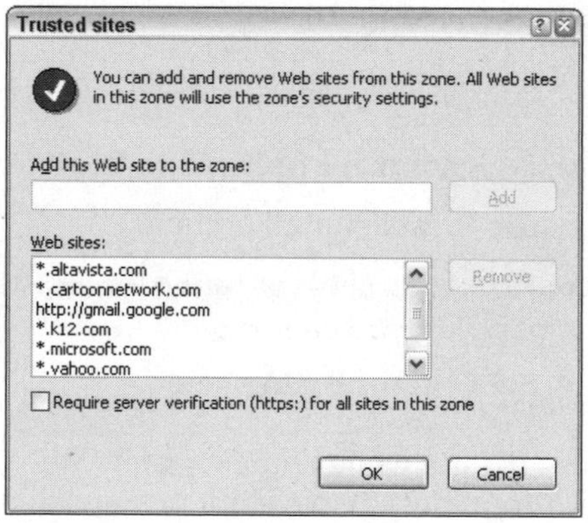

Figure 18-6:
Put your
trusted
sites here.

Trusted sites

You can add and remove Web sites from this zone. All Web sites in this zone will use the zone's security settings.

Add this Web site to the zone:

[   ]   Add

Web sites:

*.altavista.com
*.cartoonnetwork.com
http://gmail.google.com
*.k12.com
*.microsoft.com
*.yahoo.com

Remove

☐ Require server verification (https:) for all sites in this zone

OK   Cancel

Now, you can visit those sites you trust and have them run ActiveX controls, yet ActiveX controls on unknown sites are cut off — a good thing.

- ✔ If you find yourself locked out of more Web sites because of ActiveX restrictions, consider changing the options for ActiveX controls from Disable to Prompt.

- ✔ The check box at the bottom of the Trusted Sites dialog box, labeled Require Server Verification (https:) for All Sites in This Zone, is used to ensure that only secure Web sites appear on the list. This isn't really necessary for sites you know and trust, such as Microsoft or Google. Also see the nearby sidebar, "About that HTTPS thing."

About that HTTPS thing

That HTTP thing you see at the start of some Web page addresses is the abbreviation for the protocol used to receive the Web page. My Lord, that is technical! Let me try again: HTTP is what tells the Internet how to send a Web page to your computer. Better? Anyway.

HTTP stands for HyperText Transfer Protocol, and a protocol is a set of rules and such for sending information to and fro over the Internet. The extra S you see in HTTPS stands for *secure.* Such Web pages send and receive information

in an encrypted manner that is more secure than normal HTTP over the Internet.

For example, if you do online banking or pay for something online, you note an S at the end of the HTTP in the Web site's name. You may also notice a padlock icon appearing on the bottom status bar in Internet Explorer (or any Web browser). That also assures you that the information you're sending is safe and that the Web site you're accessing can be trusted.

Printing Web pages

What seems like one of the easiest things to do can confound Internet users like nothing else: that is, print a Web page. For some reason, this simple activity can drive people nuts. It's not the actual printing or even finding the Print command. It's the *results* that drive people batty.

Most Web pages don't have a fixed width, so their margins are whatever the window size could be. Those Web pages print nicely. But, fixed-width Web pages, or Web pages that are wider than a sheet of paper can handle, don't print as smoothly. Here are some things you can try:

- ✔ Choose File➪Page Setup. In the page Setup dialog box, locate the Orientation area (in lower-left corner) and choose Landscape mode. That may just get all the information on a page. (Choose File➪Print Preview to confirm.)

- ✔ Save the Web page to disk. Choose File➪Save As and ensure that Web Page, Complete is chosen from the Save As Type drop-down list. Then, after getting the page on disk, open it in Microsoft Excel. You can then print the whole thing across several pages, which Excel does nicely. (Word works too, but not as well as Excel.)

- ✔ When you're only after the text, use the mouse to carefully drag over and select the text you want. (This procedure takes patience and practice.) Then, open your word processor and paste in the text. You may have to do a little editing and tuning, but that way, you have more control over the text and can print it as slick as any other document.

Content Advisor Woes

Internet Explorer has a feature called the Content Advisor. Its role is to control what you see on the Internet, by helping to restrict access to sites that have what you may consider to be offensive content — like that Vegetarian Recipes site.

I don't recommend activating the Content Advisor. Instead, I suggest using third-party programs, such as NetNanny and Cybersitter, which I cover in "Pop-up porn puzzles," earlier in this chapter. Just leave the Content Advisor alone!

The main problem with the Content Advisor is that it's password-protected. So, if you make some settings and go overboard with them — but you forget your password — tough luck! So, rather than risk using Content Advisor and getting stuck, I feel that it's better just to avoid the issue in the first place and *never* enable the Content Advisor.

Removing the Content Advisor password (when you have forgotten it)

It's possible to eradicate the Content Advisor Password, if you set it (against my advice) and then forget it later. Here are the tricky steps:

1. Choose Run from the Start menu.

2. Type **REGEDIT** into the box and click the OK button. This step runs the Registry Editor.

3. Open the HKEY_LOCAL_MACHINE folder.

4. Open the following folders, one after the other: Software, Microsoft, Windows, CurrentVersion, Policies, Ratings.

5. Click to select an item, named Key, on the right side of the window.

6. Press the Delete key on your keyboard to remove the Key item.

7. Click the Yes button to confirm the deletion.

8. Close the Registry Editor window.

9. Restart Windows.

10. After Windows restarts, run Internet Explorer.

11. Choose Tools⇨Internet Options.

12. Click the Content tab.

At this point, you can get back into the Content Advisor and make whatever adjustments you need. To truly disable it, click the General tab and remove the check mark by the item labeled Supervisor Can Type a Password to Allow Users to View Restricted Content. Click OK to close the Content Advisor. Then, you can go back and click the Disable button in the Internet Options/Content dialog box. Good riddance to the password!

If you can remember the password, you can disable the Content Advisor:

1. **Choose Tools⇨Internet Options from the IE menu.**

2. **In the Internet Options dialog box, click the Content tab.**

3. **Click the Disable button.**

4. **Type your password (which you remember).**

5. **Click OK.**

   A dialog box appears, to tell you what you just did.

6. **Click OK to get rid of the dialog box that tells you what you just did.**

I don't go into the details of Content Advisor, mostly because I seldom get any troubleshooting questions on the subject. If you do set up restrictions, however, you may occasionally see a message that tells you something like "Sorry! Content Advisor doesn't allow you to see this site." Oh, well.

Dealing with Cookies

So it comes down to this! Cookies, huh? What do you think that this chapter should end with — dessert? You are gravely mistaken! Cookies are nothing you eat. On the Internet, they're simply a bad name for a controversial Web browsing feature.

What's a cookie?

A *cookie* is merely information a Web page saves to disk — and it isn't even that much information; it's more like random notes. The information is stored on your computer in a special Cookies folder.

When you go to visit the same Web page again, it can open the cookie it saved. That way, for example, Eddie Bauer remembers your pants size and that you enjoy seersucker. Or, Amazon.com says "Hello, Dan Gookin! Welcome back! Boy, have we got some books for you!" I find that handy.

Some people, however, find the whole cookie thing annoying. They would prefer *not* to have a Web page save anything. And that's fine because you can delete cookies, disable them, turn them off, and stomp them into cookie dust! This information is all covered in this main section.

✔ Web pages can open only the cookies they saved. Cookies saved from other Web pages cannot be opened. (Even if they could, the content is usually so specific that no critical information would be compromised.)

✔ All cookies expire. Some are automatically deleted when you close IE. Some are deleted in several hours or in a day or so. Some last for up to six months. But they all have expiration dates, and they are, with few exceptions, automatically deleted on those dates.

The official way of deleting cookies

If you're in for the cookies, you can delete them, swiping them from your hard drive like some frenzied couch potato urgently starting a crash diet:

1. **Choose Tools⇨Internet Options from the IE menu.**

   The Internet Options dialog box appears, with the General tab selected (refer to Figure 18-1).

2. **Click the Delete Cookies button.**

   An annoying confirmation dialog box shows up.

3. **Click OK in the annoying confirmation dialog box.**

   Lo, all your cookies have been smote.

An unofficial (yet effective) way to delete cookies

Though I admonish my readers *never* to delete any file they didn't create themselves, sometimes you can delete a file you didn't intentionally create. One of those instances happens to be with Internet cookies, which you kinda created, but not directly.

Yes, you can zap any or all of your cookies to kingdom come. First job: Find the cookies.

In Windows XP, each user has his own set of cookies for each user's account. You need to find your own account's cookie jar, which can be done this way:

1. **Open the My Computer icon on the desktop.**

2. **Open the Drive C icon.**

3. **Open the Documents and Settings folder.**

4. **Open your account's folder.**

   On my computer, the folder is named Dan Gookin, which, coincidentally, happens to be my name.

5. **Open the Cookies folder.**

Second job: Delete the cookies. There's nothing simpler:

6. **Select one or all of the cookie icons in the folder.**

7. **Press the Delete key on your keyboard.**

They're gone.

A-ha! A trick: I prefer to delete ancient cookies myself. So, with Details view on the screen (choose View⇨Details), I click the Date Modified column header to sort the cookies by date. Then, I drag the mouse to delete any old, ancient cookie on the list — anything older than three months.

Close the Cookies window when you're done eating.

- ✔ The keyboard shortcut for selecting all the files in a window? Ctrl+A.

- ✔ Yes, cookies are simple text files. Most are only a handful of bytes long.

- ✔ The cookie is given your computer's or your account's name, followed by an at sign (@) and then the Web page domain name. Note that some Web pages save several cookies.

- ✔ You can delete an INDEX.DAT file along with the cookies. Don't worry about this file; IE rebuilds the DAT file when it needs to.

Preventing cookies in the first place

Why bother with cookies and deleting them? If they really bug you, turn them off at the source. Heed these steps:

1. **Open the Control Panel's Internet Options icon.**

2. **Click the Privacy tab.**

   Yes, cookies are a matter of privacy, not really security.

3. **Click the Advanced button.**

   The Advanced Privacy Settings dialog box appears (see Figure 18-7), but it should really be called the Cookie dialog box.

4. **Click to put a check mark by Override Automatic Cookie Handling.**

   You must do this step to enable the other options in the dialog box.

5. **Choose Block for the Third-Party Cookies option.**

   That pretty much shuts down cookies from advertisers on any Web pages you visit. If you don't mind cookies, this is an excellent option to choose.

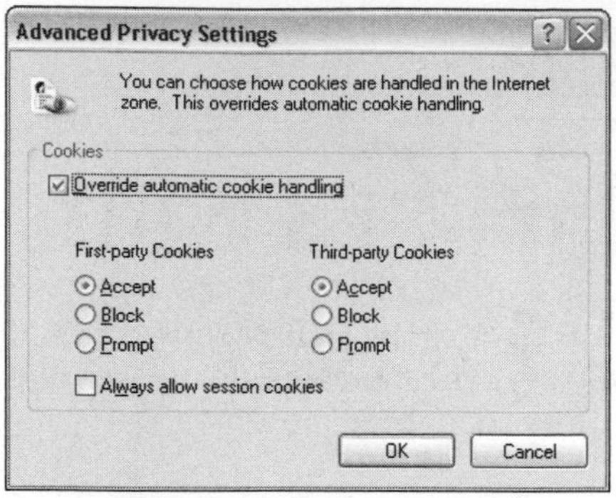

Advanced Privacy Settings

You can choose how cookies are handled in the Internet zone. This overrides automatic cookie handling.

Cookies
☑ Override automatic cookie handling

First-party Cookies	Third-party Cookies
⊙ Accept	⊙ Accept
○ Block	○ Block
○ Prompt	○ Prompt

☐ Always allow session cookies

[OK] [Cancel]

Figure 18-7:
Death to all
cookies!

6. **Choose Block for the First-Party Cookies option.**

   This option is necessary only if you really, *really* hate cookies. Otherwise, I leave this option set to Accept.

7. **Click OK to close the Advanced Privacy Settings dialog box.**

8. **Close the Internet Properties dialog box.**

No more cookies!

✔ Cookies that are "stored on your computer" are any cookies that a Web page wants to save. They don't, however, include per-session cookies.

✔ *Per-session* cookies are deleted when you close the IE window.

✔ *First-party* cookies are cookies owned by the Web page you're viewing.

✔ *Third-party* cookies are cookies saved by the advertisements on the Web page you're viewing.

✔ Avoid choosing the Prompt option in the Advanced Privacy Settings dialog box (refer to Figure 18-7). Many, many Web sites use cookies. Being prompted for all of them can certainly drive you nuts!

Chapter 19

E-Mail Calamities with Outlook Express

● ●

In This Chapter

▶ Resolving the missing spell-check issue

▶ Finding the lost Contacts panel

▶ Dealing with duplicate messages

▶ Making messages more readable

▶ Working in the Drafts folder

▶ Undeleting a message

▶ Figuring out file attachments

▶ Fighting spam

▶ Unblocking blocked senders

● ●

Some people just live for e-mail. Therefore, you could understand that not getting e-mail or having trouble with an e-mail program (chiefly, Outlook Express) can be the cause of much teeth gnashing and anguish. Nay, even hair-pulling can accompany the many frustrations that mix with the joys of Internet e-mail.

This chapter concentrates on e-mail as the Windows Outlook Express program delivers it (or not, as the case may be). I am aware that lots of people have frustrations with Hotmail and questions about Yahoo! Mail or perhaps problems with other e-mail programs in general. But, Outlook Express is the one program that ships with Windows, so, to keep this chapter short, poignant, and beautiful, I concentrate only on its own troubles.

> ✔ The abbreviation *OE* is used in this chapter to refer to Outlook Express.
>
> ✔ There's a difference between OE and the Outlook program that ships with Microsoft Office. The programs do similar things, but they're different programs. This book covers only OE.

General Outlook Express Nonsense

E-mail is such a simple thing, yet your e-mail program is perhaps the most complex application you will ever use. I could pack an entire book full of OE tips and tricks, and not a single one of them would be considered advanced or obtuse. That's just the nature of the e-mail beast.

It was a tough task, but I was able to pinpoint a few key nonsensical issues with OE and stuff these and their solutions into this section.

"The links don't work!"

Most e-mail programs have the ability to properly interpret Web page addresses as active links in e-mail. So, when someone types `http://www.wambooli.com/` into an e-mail message, the e-mail program properly changes that text into a link you can click. Clicking the link opens that Web page in your Web browser program. Or, it's supposed to.

Sometimes, however, the links don't work. There could be a number of reasons why, so mull over the following solutions.

Ensure that HTML options are on. This is perhaps the most common reason that the links don't work: You have disabled them! Check out these steps:

1. Inside OE, choose Tools⇨Options.

2. Click the Read tab in the Options dialog box.

3. Remove the check mark by the item labeled Read All Messages in Plain Text.

4. Click OK to close the Options dialog box.

That should fix it. If not, keep working through the next set of steps:

Change the Internet connection type. You need to ensure that Windows is properly configured to dial in to the Internet so that the links in your e-mail can work. This advice is for dial-up Internet users only! Check to confirm that things are properly set, by following these steps:

1. Open the Control Panel.

2. Open the Internet Options icon.

3. Click the Connections tab.

4. **Ensure that the option Always Dial My Default Connection is selected.**

5. **Click the OK button.**

   Optionally, close the Control Panel's window.

Now, give the link a try in OE and see whether it works. If not, you have still more things to try:

Fix OE. This trick is a bit technical, but folks tell me that it works. Obey these steps carefully:

1. **Close OE in case you have it open.**

2. **Choose Run from the Start button's menu.**

   Or, you can press Win+R on the keyboard. Either way, the Run dialog box appears, as shown in Figure 19-1.

Run
Type the name of a program, folder, document, or Internet resource, and Windows will open it for you.
Open: REGSVR32 URLMON.DLL
OK   Cancel   Browse...

3. **In the text box, type** REGSVR32, **and then a space, and then** URLMON.DLL.

   Don't follow URLMON.DLL with a period! Make sure that it looks like what you see in Figure 19-1. Carefully review your typing!

4. **Click the OK button.**

   If all goes well, you may hear a tone and then you see a RegSvr32 dialog box that says "DllREgisterServer in URLMON.DLL succeeded."

   If you get any other error message, you most likely mistyped the command in Step 3. Start over again in Step 2.

5. **Click the OK button to dismiss the RegSvr32 dialog box.**

6. **Open the Control Panel.**

 7. **Open the Internet Options icon.**

8. **Click the Programs tab.**

9. **Click the button labeled Reset Web Settings.**

10. **Click the Yes button in the Reset Web Settings dialog box.**

    Note that this step resets your Web home page as well as other settings you may have made for cookies and Internet security.

11. **Click OK when you're told that your Web settings have been reset.**

12. **Click OK to close the Internet Properties dialog box.**

    Or, before you close the dialog box, you can review the settings on the General, Security, Privacy, and Content tabs to reset things the way you like.

These past few steps fix nonworking links in an e-mail message in Outlook Express. Consider following some of the advice I offer in Chapters 17 and 18 to readjust your Internet settings.

Note that some pop-up blocker utilities may also prevent OE from opening links in e-mail messages. Try disabling your pop-up blocker software and see whether that helps. (See Chapter 24 for more information on pop-up blocker software.)

"Spell check doesn't work!"

Rotten spelling and e-mail often go hand in hand. And I'm not referring to silly spellings, like CU L8R ("see you later"), but rather to common things like *recieve*, *acceptible*, or *preceed*. To fix these mistakes in OE, you use the Spell Check button when you're finished composing e-mail. But, why is that button dimmed and the command unavailable?

The answer is that spell checking is provided not by Outlook Express itself, but by another program, either Microsoft Word or the Microsoft Works program. (You can add Microsoft Office to the list because Office includes the Word word processor.) If you don't have any of those programs, spell checking in OE doesn't work.

✔ The solution for OE is to get Word or Works or Office. Then, spell checking works.

✔ Note that there's a difference between Word and Works. One is the word processor that comes with Microsoft Office — a high-end program. The other, Works, is for beginners and home use — or so they say.

✔ Other e-mail programs, such as my favorite Eudora, come with built-in spell checking, and no other programs are required. Check out the free version of Eudora at

```
www.eudora.com/
```

"The Contacts panel is missing!"

Outlook Express divides its screen into several panels, as shown in Figure 19-2. These panels are customizable and utterly controllable by you, though most folks prefer to keep things set up as shown in the figure.

The problem? The Contacts list (in the lower-left corner) as well as the Folders list (just above Contacts) have X Close buttons on them. So, it's possible to accidentally close those panels and then freak out at their absence.

To get the missing panels back, choose View⇨Layout. This command displays the Window Layout Properties dialog box, as shown in Figure 19-3. You can restore any or all or even more of the OE window by choosing the proper items from the dialog box.

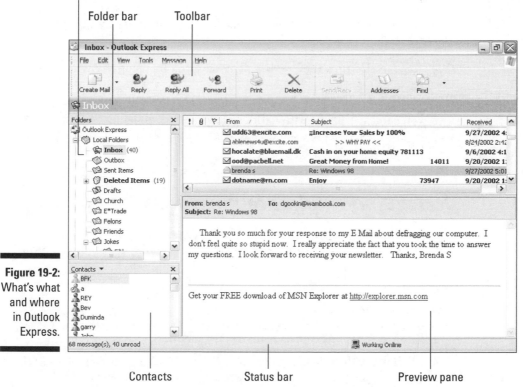

Figure 19-2: What's what and where in Outlook Express.

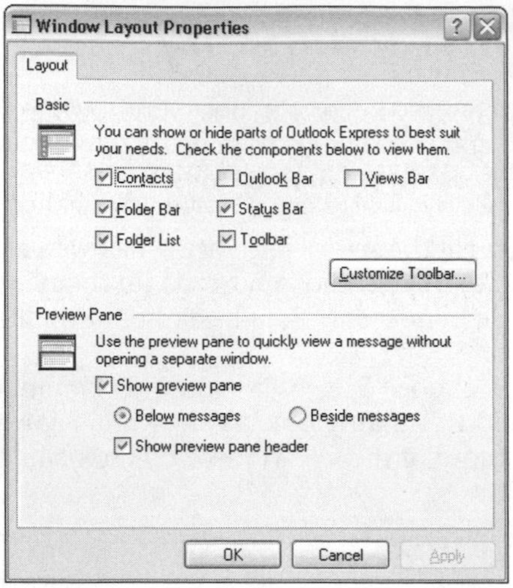

Figure 19-3:
The secret
location
where stuff
is restored.

For example, to restore the Contacts list, put a check mark by Contacts and then click OK.

 ✔ You can also turn the Preview pane on or off by using the Window Layout Properties dialog box.

 ✔ Because OE appears behind the Window Layout Properties dialog box, you can experiment with various views and arrangements. Just click to add or remove a check mark and click the Apply button to see how the OE window is affected.

Receiving duplicate messages

If your ISP is sending you two copies of every message, you should check with them first to find reasons that it may be happening. It could be a problem on their end.

If the problem isn't with the ISP, you can check another place (isn't that always true?):

1. **Choose Tools⇨Accounts from the OE menu.**

2. **Click the Mail tab.**

3. **Select your mail account from the list.**

   Or, it may be the only account on the list.

4. **Click the Properties button.**

   Your e-mail account's Properties dialog box appears.

5. **Click the Advanced tab.**

   In the bottom of the dialog box is a Delivery option, as shown in Figure 19-4. If the option Leave a Copy of Messages on Server is checked, that explains your duplicate pick-up.

6. **Uncheck the box by Leave a Copy of Messages on Server.**

   That fixes it.

Figure 19-4:
Checking for
that nasty
Leave Mail
on Server
option.

Displaying the BCC field

The problem? OE doesn't normally display the BCC field when you go to create a new message. BCC, the Blind Carbon Copy field, is used to send e-mail to people secretly; e-mail addresses put in the BCC field don't appear when the final message is received. The stealth nature of this feature makes the BCC field ideal for sending to a batch of people and not having each of them see the whole list of e-mail addresses — very tidy.

The solution: Choose View➪All Headers from the New Message window. That command displays the BCC header, and away you go.

For more information on the BCC header, refer to my book *PCs For Dummies* (Wiley Publishing, Inc.).

Fragmenting large messages

Another obscure option that OE has is to split large messages into separate chunks. I assume that this feature has some pressing, possibly historical, purpose. But, most of the time, what happens is that your recipient complains that rather than get that MPEG movie of you at Niagara Falls, he gets 50 smaller junk files from you that make no sense.

Here's how to prevent OE from splitting up a long message:

1. **Choose Tools⇨Accounts.**

2. **Click the Mail tab.**

3. **If your e-mail account isn't selected, click it on the list.**

4. **Click the Properties button.**

5. **Click the Advanced tab.**

    Yes, it's the same dialog box shown earlier, in Figure 19-4. This time, note the Sending area. Is that item checked?

6. **Uncheck the Break Apart Messages Larger than [blank] KB item.**

    This step tells OE *not* to split apart large messages.

People complain that you send them unreadable messages

Outlook Express sends e-mail using the Web page formatting language, HTML. That way, you can add pictures, formatted text, and other fun things to your e-mail, to make it more exciting than plain text.

The problem is that not everyone uses OE. Some people use e-mail programs that cannot properly interpret the HTML-formatted e-mail that OE sends. For those cases, you need to send those folks plain, or *unformatted,* e-mail.

To switch over to plain text in a New Message window, choose Format⇨Plain Text. You may see a warning dialog box, but it's just telling you what you need to know; click OK.

To send out all your e-mail as plain text, follow these steps:

1. **Choose Tools⇨Options in the OE main window.**

    The Options dialog box appears.

2. **Click the Send tab.**

3. **Choose Plain text from the Mail Sending Format area.**

4. **Click OK.**

I consider the sending of plain text to be a courtesy to other, non-Windows users on the Internet. People forget that fancy formatting and colored text may look good on your computer, but may appear too small or even invisible on someone else's screen.

- ✔ When you choose plain-text formatting, the formatting toolbar in the New Message window disappears.

- ✔ To get an idea of how your message may look in an e-mail program that doesn't support HTML messages, click the Source tab in the New Message window. Yuck.

Folder Folderol

Folders are a great way to organize your e-mail — and I'm talking about folders beyond just the basic Inbox, Outbox, Sent Items, and Deleted Items folders. As you can see from Figure 19-2, I have many folders that I play with for stashing and hoarding my e-mail. You should too — but this isn't the place to lecture you about folders. Instead, let me just get to the two key OE folder issues I often get quizzed about.

The mystery of the Drafts folder

The Drafts folder should really be called the I'm-not-quite-ready-to-send folder. But it's too late to change that now! Instead, the Drafts folder merely poses a puzzle to those who often find their e-mail in there.

How does a message get into the Drafts folder? The Drafts folder is the Outlook Express dead-letter office. It holds e-mail you don't want to send. Rather than click the Send button for a message, you instead closed the messages window. OE asked whether you wanted to save the message, and you said Yes. So, OE stuck the message in the Drafts folder, where it's lingering until you're ready to try to send it again.

How does one get a message out of the Drafts folder? Open the message, edit it if you will, and click the Send button. That sends the message off.

- ✔ Newer versions of OE *tell* you that the message is being saved in the Drafts folder. Most of the Drafts folder questions I get via e-mail are from users of older versions of OE, where it didn't explain how the messages got into the Drafts folder.

✔ You can also drag a message out of the Drafts folder and into any other folder. Or, if you find that dragging doesn't work, select the message and choose Edit➪Move to Folder from the menu. Then, choose the destination folder from the Move dialog box.

Copying an e-mail folder to a "real" folder

E-mail folders aren't the same thing as real folders in Windows. They're *fake* folders. In fact, an e-mail folder is nothing more than a very large text file hidden somewhere on your PC's hard drive. It only looks like a folder in Outlook Express.

This folder puzzle brings up an interesting issue: How would someone save all the messages in a folder to a real folder out there on the hard drive? The answer is: with much time and patience.

Although you can save any individual message to disk (choose File➪Save As), you cannot save groups of them to disk at a time. You're stuck with going through the folder and individually saving each message in a "real" folder on the hard drive.

✔ An e-mail folder in OE is basically a long text file. OE itself splits up the text file so that it appears that there are separate messages — but what you're really looking at is simply a very long text file.

✔ The location of the mail folder or text file is kept secret in Windows; Microsoft really doesn't want you messing with the files.

✔ They're not *exactly* text files. But, they contain enough text that you can open them in Notepad or WordPad and be able to read some of the mail.

✔ If you want to search for the file's location, use the Search or Find command, as described in Chapter 9, and look for a file named INBOX.DBX. That's the official name of your e-mail Inbox folder and file.

Any way to undelete a message?

When you delete a message in OE, the message is put into the Deleted Items folder and not really deleted. To undelete the message, open the Deleted Items folder and right-click the message you want to undelete. Then, choose Move to Folder from the pop-up menu. That command allows you to recover the so-called deleted message to a specific folder.

Unfortunately, if you empty the Deleted Items folder, the e-mail is gone for good and cannot be recovered. Alas.

- ✔ No, not even Norton Utilities or any other unerase program can recover e-mail deleted from the Deleted Items folder.

- ✔ To empty the Deleted Items folder, choose Edit⇨Empty 'Deleted Items' folder. (This command is available only if messages are in the Deleted Items folder.)

- ✔ You can also have OE automatically dump out the Deleted Items folder every time you quit OE: Choose Tools⇨Options and in the Options dialog box, click the Maintenance tab. Put a check mark by Empty Messages from the 'Deleted Items' Folder on Exit. Click OK.

Attachment Adversity

Along with e-mail comes . . . attachments! What a remarkable invention. Attachments make boring old e-mail all the more exciting. You can see pictures of the grandkids. Get a silly tune from Uncle Charlie. Or, have Aunt Ruth forward you *another* e-mail virus. It's a thrill-a-minute with e-mail attachments!

This section gives you some attachment highlights for troubleshooting. If you want more detailed information on attachments in general, you should see my book *PCs For Dummies* (Wiley Publishing, Inc.), which goes into all sorts of painless e-mail attachment detail.

You just cannot open this attachment!

Try as you can, the attachment doesn't open. Either you have no option to open it or, when you open it, Windows presents you with an Open With What? dialog box, and no apparently obvious or useful choice is available. What to do? What to do?

My advice: Give up. I'm serious. If your computer cannot open the attachment, Windows simply lacks the necessary software. Other than rush out and buy that software (and remember that you don't exactly know which software it is), there's nothing you can do.

In this situation, I respond to the message by telling the sender that I cannot open the attachment and asking whether they can resend it in a more common format. For pictures, JPEG or JPG is the most common format. For documents, HTML, RTF, and PDF are common.

- ✔ Those PSS files are PowerPoint Slide Show files, which people often e-mail to others without considering that not all of us have the PowerPoint program. (You can, however, pick up a free PowerPoint viewer from www.microsoft.com; follow the links for Microsoft Office downloads.)

- ✔ PSD files are Photoshop images. Have the sender resend the image in JPG format.

- ✔ WPD and WPS files are WordPerfect files: *Attention, WordPerfect users:* Save your documents as either plain-text (TXT) or RTF files. Thank you.

- ✔ MPG, MOV, and AVI are movie files. They represent three different movie file formats. Your computer is guaranteed to play at least two of them, and the third format is the one that everyone always e-mails to you.

But my Macintosh friend swears that it's a real JPG image!

The Macintosh, as well as other computers, uses a different method to identify files on disk. In Windows, the last few characters of a file's name (following a period) indicate which type of file you have. So, MONALISA.JPG is a JPG file — a graphics image. But, MONALISA.TXT is a TXT file, which is a text file.

A *file extension* — the .jpg part of a file that lets a Windows computer know that you have a JPG image — isn't required on a Macintosh. So, if some Mac dweeb sends you a file named MONALISA, your PC will have a tough time figuring out what type of file it is.

If the Mac dweeb swears that it's a JPG file, rename the file to MONALISA.JPG (or whatever the file's first name is, followed by JPG).

You just can't go around randomly naming files. If someone sends you a file named SOMETHING, ask what type of file it is. That way, you can properly rename the file so that Windows recognizes it.

- ✔ Text files end in TXT.

- ✔ Graphics files can end in GIF, BMP, TIFF, JPG, and a host of other *file-name extensions*. You must check with whoever sent you the file to see which type it is.

Beware of AOL .ART files

AOL uses a proprietary graphics format named ART. These files appear as graphical images when AOL users e-mail them to each other or view them on their own computers. But, ART files are utterly incompatible with computers that don't have AOL installed. (You *must* use AOL to view an ART file.)

If you're an AOL user and want to send graphics, ensure that the image isn't an ART file. Likewise, if you receive an ART image from an AOL user, understand that you cannot view it.

The solution lies on the AOL user's side. In the Web Graphics section of the Preferences, choose Setting B, Never Compress Graphics. That action fixes the ART problem and makes your images more compatible with other software and other people on the Internet.

"The attachment never got there!"

For a number of reasons, a file attachment may not make it to its recipient:

✔ An attachment may be too large and get rejected (based on its size) by either your own ISP or the recipient's ISP.

✔ If the recipient is using AOL, AOL doesn't accept certain types of file attachments.

✔ Antivirus or firewall software can prevent an attachment from arriving.

✔ The recipient may be using an e-mail program that doesn't allow or understand attachments.

✔ The recipient may not notice or may ignore the attachment.

In most cases, you can try sending the attachment again. If that fails, you have to use a floppy disk, Zip disc, or CD-R and mail it through regular postal mail.

Printing an e-mail attachment

OE has no method to print an e-mail attachment. Sure, you can print e-mail, but if you just want to print the attachment, you have to save the attachment to disk, open a program to view the attachment, and print from within that program.

"I forward a message, and the image is replaced by a little red X!"

Two types of images can appear in an e-mail message: attached and embedded. When you see the red X, you're dealing with an embedded image. In that case, you cannot forward the image, and it cannot be saved to disk. That's just the nature of an embedded image.

The solution here is to reply to the message and have the original sender attach the image and not embed it. Here's the difference:

To attach an image, choose Insert⇨File Attachment. That way, anyone can receive the image and save it to her hard drive, just as though it were her own file.

To embed an image, choose Insert⇨Picture. That command sticks the image into the message body, like a picture of a Web page. The recipient can see the message, but he may not be able to save it to disk or forward it.

Vain Efforts to Filter Spam

Congratulations if you're one of the few who has figured out how to use the message rules or Blocked Senders list in OE to help cut down on that filthy, unwanted e-mail known popularly as *spam*.

I would love to get into the whole message-rules creation stuff, but that's not the point of this book. Instead, here's a major section about various problems that come up when you get resolutely bold in your spam-fighting efforts.

Reviewing your message rules

Alas, I don't have the space to get into creating message rules here, though I can help guide you with fixing them:

1. **Choose Tools⇨Message Rules⇨Mail.**

   This step displays the Message Rules/Mail Rules window, as shown in Figure 19-5.

2. **Review each rule: Click a rule to select it.**

   Read through the rule description. Fortunately, the descriptions are English-like, so they make sense. Watch out for rules that delete mail. Ensure that the proper mail is getting deleted and that the rule cannot be misinterpreted.

   If you're concerned about deleting mail, change the various mail-deleting rules so that the mail goes instead to a specific folder, where you can review it later.

3. **Select and review the next rule.**

   And so on, until you have reviewed them all.

4. **Close the Message Rules window.**

   Click OK.

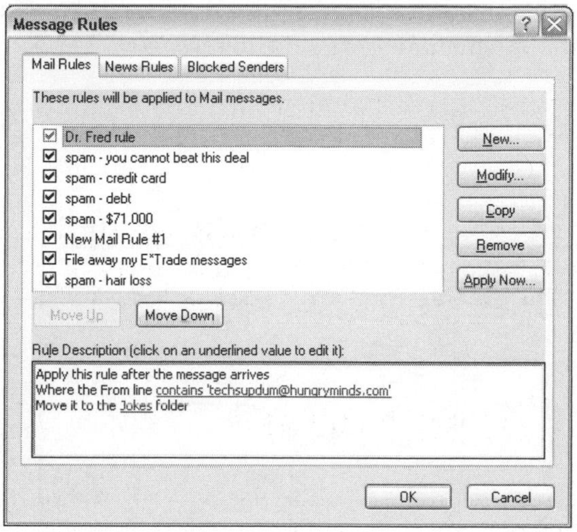

Figure 19-5:
Review-
ing the
message
rules.

Be careful with rules! I once made an overly aggressive rule that deleted *all* my incoming mail. Oops! Before you assume that it's a light mail day, double-check your rules!

Unblocking accidentally blocked senders

Rather than create rules, many people simply choose Message➪Block Sender, which instantly deletes any new mail from a specific person. It's a handy trick to use because most of your unwanted e-mail does come from the same idiots most of the time.

Occasionally, you may add someone unintentionally to the Blocked Senders list. If so, you can easily remove that person and unblock his e-mail:

1. **Choose Tools➪Message Rules➪Blocked Senders List.**

   You see a dialog box listing all blocked senders.

2. **Scroll though the list for the person you accidentally added.**

3. **Highlight the name you want to unblock.**

4. **Click the Remove button.**

   This step puts the person back to unblocked status — and restores peace in the family if she just happens to be a relative.

"Here's a little tip on disassembly that you won't find in the manual."

Chapter 20

General Windows Disruption (Or, "Is This PC Possessed?")

* * *

In This Chapter

▶ Dealing with weird things on the screen

▶ Windows run amok!

▶ Taskbar done gone crazy!

▶ Properly opening a file

▶ Fighting programs that don't uninstall

▶ The "reinstalling Windows" question

▶ The "reformatting the hard drive" question

* * *

Any time you have a visual operating system, such as Windows, you see weird stuff on the screen. Perhaps it's not weird, but more like unexpected or unwelcome. It's like the computer is possessed at times. You may be in the driver's seat, but something else is definitely steering!

I don't need to lead everyone down the fearful path of superstition and panic. Although everyone definitely goes through PC rituals (I like pressing and holding the Enter key when I save a file), most of the weird or common disruptions can be blamed on logical, explainable things. Granted, there are probably lots of them, but I tried to limit this chapter's coverage to the most common, interesting, and, well, plain weird.

"That Looks Stupid"

Sure, it looks stupid! And, calling something stupid is quite offensive. But, you know what? Stupid is easy to recognize. I know stupid when I see it. This section covers some of the most stupid-looking things in all of Windows.

Screwy colors

Perhaps you intended that bright red-and-pink theme for Windows? Certainly, the colors are striking. No? Not to you? Then, to your 4-year-old, perhaps? The dark purple and black-on-black theme makes such a statement. Obviously, the kid has talent!

Colors can grow screwy in two ways. The first is the most definite way, which is when you go nuts inside the Advanced Appearance dialog box, as shown in Figure 20-1. Windows really doesn't care about your taste, so you can choose some really odd combinations there — and live to regret it later.

Figure 20-1: Don't go nuts in this-here dialog box.

How to undo the nonsense? If you can *see* the screen just fine, follow these steps as written. If you're having trouble seeing things, start the computer in Safe mode to make your corrections (refer to Chapter 24 for more information on Safe mode):

1. **Right-click the desktop.**

2. **Choose Properties from the pop-up menu.**

3. **Click the Themes tab.**

4. **Choose Windows XP from the Theme drop-down list.**

5. **Click OK.**

   That should fix it.

Well, it may not fix the screen, but it restores Windows to its standard screen setup. At least you can get work done.

✔ If you have your own set of custom colors defined, I recommend saving that set to disk as its own theme: On the Display Properties/Themes tab, click the Save As button. Give your settings a name and click OK. That way, you can restore your favorite colors and screen settings whenever you like.

✔ For handling problems with the screen's resolution, refer to Chapter 6.

Fuzzy icon trouble

It's not that the icons get fuzzy, but rather that your desktop icons — and the Start button — seem to flash or rapidly change color — like the transporter effect from *Star Trek*. That's the sign of a bad or corrupted video driver. Refer to Chapter 6 for information on upgrading or restoring your video driver.

Jiggling icons

The infamous jiggly icon weird thing happens like this: You go to point the mouse at an icon, and the icon moves away from the mouse. You try again, and the same thing happens. It's like the icons are afraid of the mouse. Annoying? Or, could it be amusing?

You see, this jiggly icon thing is someone's idea of a joke. I consider it to be a *virus*, not a prank. The virus exists as an e-mail attachment that's probably hanging on some message in the Outlook Express Inbox.

The quick solution: Go through your Inbox and remove every message. Just empty the Deleted Items folder: Choose Edit⇔Empty 'Deleted Items' Folder. That fixes it in a drastic way.

If you want to be less drastic, just go through your Inbox and look for any e-mail with an attachment. Graphics attachments are okay, but anything else is suspect as the cause of the virus. Delete 'em.

Of course, buying and using antivirus software would prevent this and other viruses from happening in the first place.

Getting more stuff on the screen

You can't make the screen bigger. I wish you could! But no such thing as a screen-stretcher exists; a 17-inch monitor can display only so much information. If you want more stuff on the screen, the solution is to increase the screen's resolution.

Chapter 6 contains information on setting the screen's resolution. Look there for more information.

Resetting the screen's resolution to something higher makes things look smaller on the screen. You can do two things:

First, in your applications, you can take advantage of the Zoom command, usually found on the View menu. The Zoom command magnifies the contents of the window so that everything is easier to read.

Second, you can make Windows own icons appear larger:

1. **Right-click the desktop.**
2. **Choose Properties from the pop-up menu.**

   This step conjures up the Display Properties dialog box.

3. **Click the Appearance tab.**
4. **Click the Effects button.**
5. **Put a check mark by the Use Large Icons item.**
6. **Close the various dialog boxes.**

   When the last one is closed, you see the new, larger icons on the screen.

You can also use a command to change the icon size on the Start button's menus, though these are already set to Large in most configurations. To check the icon size on the Start button menu, follow these steps:

1. **Right-click the Start button.**
2. **Choose Properties from the pop-up menu.**
3. **Click the Customize button.**

   You see two Customize buttons. Click the top one, next to the Start menu item.

   The Customize Start Menu dialog box appears. The icon size item is right there on top on the General tab.

4. **Choose Large Icons (if it's not chosen already).**

5. **Click OK and then OK again.**

The window has slid off the screen

Moving a window on the screen is so easy that few beginning Windows books even bother to explain it in any detail: You use the mouse to *drag* the window around. Simple. But it's not so simple when you can't pinch the top part of the window by using the mouse. In fact, I have known some folks who get so desperate to get the window back that they just end up reinstalling Windows. Bad move!

The trick to getting any window to move when it's off the screen is the same trick you use to move a window when the mouse is broken: Use the keyboard!

These steps assume that a window you want to move is on the screen. Click that window to make it "on top" and selected and then follow these steps:

1. **Press Alt+spacebar.**

   This command activates the window's Control menu.

2. **Press M, for *m*ove.**

   Now, you can use the keyboard's arrow keys to move the window.

3. **Press the left, right, up, or down arrow to move the window in that direction.**

4. **When you're done moving the window, press the Enter key.**

The window is too large for the screen

Resizing a large window is next to impossible when you can't grab its edges with the mouse. The solution here is to use the keyboard to help resize the window:

1. **Ensure that the window isn't maximized.**

   You cannot resize a maximized window; click the Restore button (the middle button in the window's upper-right corner) to unmaximize the window.

2. **Press Alt+spacebar.**

   This keyboard command drops down the window's Control menu.

3. **Press S, for *size*.**

   You can now move each of the window's four sides in or out. You do that by first choosing a side and moving the side in or out.

4. **Press the left, right, up, or down arrow to move that side of the window.**

   For example, press the left-arrow key to choose the left side of the window.

5. **Use the left–right or up–down arrow keys to move the window's edge.**

   For example, if you chose the left side of the window, press the left or right arrow keys to move that side of the window.

6. **Press Enter when you're done resizing that edge.**

7. **Repeat Steps 2 through 6 to resize another edge of the window.**

   For example, to resize the bottom edge of the window, press Alt+ spacebar, S, and then the down-arrow key to select the bottom edge. Then, use the up- or down-arrow keys to move that edge in or out.

These steps may seem confusing, but if you work through them and mess with the window's size, they make sense. Just be thankful that such an alternative window-resizing technique exists.

The window is too tiny

Windows remembers the size and position of any window you open on the screen. When you return to a program or open a folder again, Windows sticks the window back in the spot in which it originally existed and at the same size as when you last used the window.

The problem is that sometimes Windows restores a window that you have resized to be very tiny. Most people just maximize the window at this point, but the problem is that Windows doesn't remember maximized windows. No, instead, the window is opened again at its tiny size.

The solution is to resize the window *without* maximizing it: Use the mouse to drag out the window's edges (top, bottom, right, left) to the size and position you prefer on the screen. With the window larger — but not maximized — you can close it. Then, when that window is reopened, it opens to the larger size.

The taskbar has moved

On my long sheet of Windows regrets is the ability to move the taskbar. I'm certain that someone at Microsoft thought it would be handy to have a taskbar on the left, right, or top of the computer screen. In practice, in my experience? I have *never* seen a taskbar anywhere except the bottom of the screen. Even so, the ability to move the taskbar exists, and many people do accidentally move it — and then desperately want it back on the bottom.

You can move the taskbar just as you can move any window on the screen: Drag it with the mouse. The key, however, is to *close all open windows* so that you can easily grab the taskbar with the mouse.

To move the taskbar back to the bottom of the screen, follow these steps:

1. **Point the mouse at the taskbar (on a spot that has no buttons).**

2. **Press the mouse button.**

3. **Drag the mouse pointer to the bottom of the screen.**

If these steps don't work, you can try using the keyboard and mouse together:

1. **Click the taskbar once.**

   Click a blank spot that has no buttons.

2. **Press Alt+spacebar.**

   This step pops up a menu, as shown in Figure 20-2. If not, start over again with Step 1.

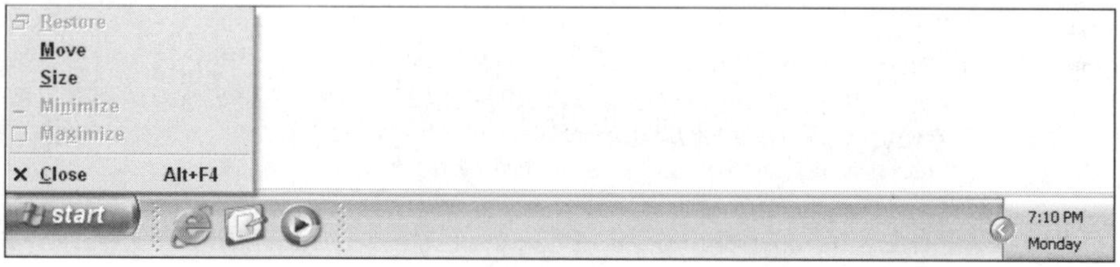

Figure 20-2:
Properly
accessing
the taskbar's
control
menu.

3. **Press M, for *m*ove.**

4. **Press and hold the down-arrow key until the mouse pointer is close to the bottom of the screen.**

   If this step doesn't move the taskbar, press the left-arrow key and hold it down. If that doesn't work, press the right-arrow key and hold it down.

5. **Click the mouse when you're done.**

The object is to use the keyboard to move the mouse pointer to where you want the taskbar. Use all four arrow keys — left, right, up, and down — to move the taskbar.

 ✔ Yes, you can accidentally move the taskbar. It happens all the time.

 ✔ Also, mean people move or hide the taskbar. They call it a practical joke, though there's nothing practical about it, nor is it funny.

 ✔ If the moving taskbar frustrates you, lock it down. See the section "Locking the taskbar," later in this chapter.

The taskbar has disappeared

The taskbar cannot disappear, but it can hide. It can also grow so thin as to seem invisible, although it's still there.

First, make sure that you're not using a program in full-screen mode, which would hide the taskbar. Most full-screen programs keep one button or menu item available to allow you to de-full-screen the program. Or, you can try pressing the F10 key to summon the menu bar and try to restore the screen. In Internet Explorer, press the F11 key to unzoom from full-screen mode.

Second, see whether the taskbar is simply too skinny to see. Check each edge of the screen for a thin, gray strip. If you find it, you have found the taskbar: Point the mouse at the strip, and it changes into an up-down pointing arrow (or a left-right pointing arrow if the taskbar is on the side of the screen). Press the mouse button and *drag* the mouse toward the center of the screen. As you drag, the taskbar grows fatter. Release the mouse button when the taskbar is the proper size.

Third, the taskbar may be automatically hidden, which is an option. To check, point the mouse to where the taskbar normally lives and wait. The taskbar should pop right up. (If not, try pointing at the other three edges of the screen to see whether some joker moved *and hid* the taskbar.)

If the taskbar pops up, you can switch off its autohide feature:

1. **Right-click the Start button.**

2. **Choose Properties from the pop-up menu.**

 The Taskbar and Start Menu Properties dialog box appears.

3. **Click the Taskbar tab.**

 You see a dialog box specifically customized to deal with taskbar ways and woes, as shown in Figure 20-3.

4. **Remove the check mark by the item labeled Auto-Hide the Taskbar.**

5. **While you're at it, click to select the item labeled Keep the Taskbar on Top of Other Windows.**

6. **Click OK.**

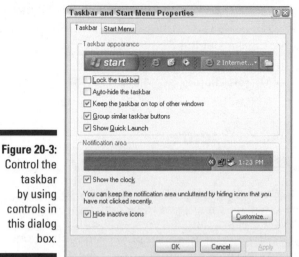

Figure 20-3:
Control the
taskbar
by using
controls in
this dialog
box.

Locking the taskbar

There's a solution for all this taskbar madness! After many releases, finally in Windows XP you can blissfully *lock down* the taskbar:

1. **Right-click the Start button and choose Properties from the pop-up menu.**

2. **Click the Taskbar tab.**

3. **Ensure that there's a check mark by the item labeled Lock the Taskbar.**

4. **Click OK.**

You get two subtle visual clues that the taskbar has been locked. The first is that the extra "lip" atop the taskbar disappears. The second is that the dimple dots that separate toolbars on the taskbar go away; yes, the various toolbars on the taskbar cannot be resized after the taskbar is locked.

"The menu, button, or some other element in the program, is missing!"

Without listing the 50,000 variations for every program and application, generally speaking you can fix missing visual elements by checking either the View or Window menu.

The View menu can contain commands that control which toolbars and buttons are visible.

The Windows menu controls which of the windows or palettes are visible.

Before giving up, consider checking the View or Windows menu for the missing things you yearn for.

You Open the File and You Get Crap

It's supposed to work like this: You choose File⇨Open and pluck out a file, and there it sits on the screen, all happy and eager to be edited or otherwise messed with. But, what *really* happens is this: You choose File⇨Open or you double-click some icon to open it, and you get . . . crap! Not the content, but visually: junky text. It's definitely not what you saved. What happened?

First, it's not *your* fault. (You may remember that from Chapter 1.)

Second, you may be using the wrong format to open the file, which is a common screw-up in most Open dialog boxes.

Suppose that you try to open a file in Word just to recover text. If so, choose the option Recover Text from Any File (*.*) from the Files of Type drop-down list in Word's Open dialog box, as shown in Figure 20-4. So, you open the file and mess around and you're happenin'.

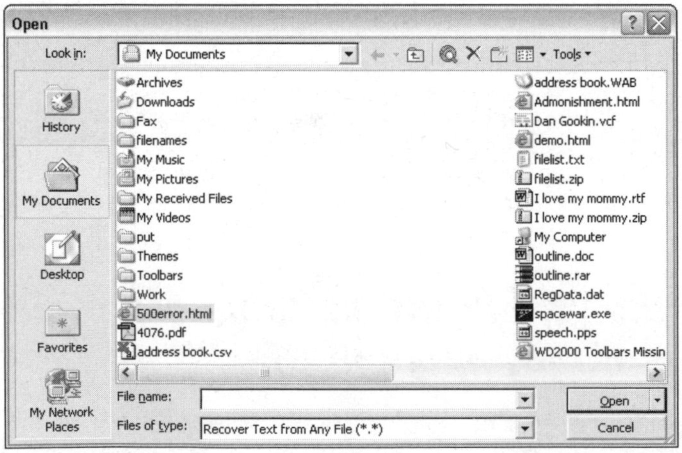

Figure 20-4:
Beware the Files of Type drop-down list!

Then, you go to open the document you have been working on and . . . you get crap! Okay, maybe it's not pure ugliness, but you may notice that your formatting is gone or that perhaps random characters have infiltrated the text. Or, in a graphics program, the colors may be all screwed up.

Relax! What happened is that you misused the Open dialog box and opened a file of one type as another. For example, if you open a Word document but choose Recover Text from Any File (*.*) from the Files of Type drop-down list in Word's Open dialog box, you see plain text on the screen — not a formatted Word document.

The solution is to close the document. Don't save any changes! Then, reopen the document by first selecting the proper document type from the Files of Type drop-down list in the Open dialog box.

✔ This error is quite common, particularly with Microsoft Word.

✔ Sometimes, files do get corrupted. If the file still opens as garbage, it probably is garbage. That happens, usually because of some type of disk error. Run ScanDisk on your hard drive to check for errors; see Chapter 23.

Uninstalling Uninstalled Programs

You never delete a program from Windows. No, you're supposed to *uninstall* it instead. You use the Add/Remove Programs icon on the Control Panel, choose the installed program, and then schedule it for proper termination and removal. That's the *proper* way to remove the software.

Secretly, what the Add/Remove Programs window does is to run the installed program's Uninstall routines. That's a special program — often, the same program that installed the software — which goes about removing bits and pieces of the program, redoing settings, and doing other necessary things in a complex operating system like Windows. All those tasks are necessary, which is why simply deleting a program is considered a no-no.

Another way to uninstall

Many programs put their uninstall utility on the Start thing's Programs menu, right there with other commands. For example, the Zone Alarm firewall software, from Zone Labs, puts its Uninstall command right there on the Start menu along with other commands, as shown in Figure 20-5. Choosing the Uninstall command removes the program. Of course, not every program's developer is as smart as Zone Labs.

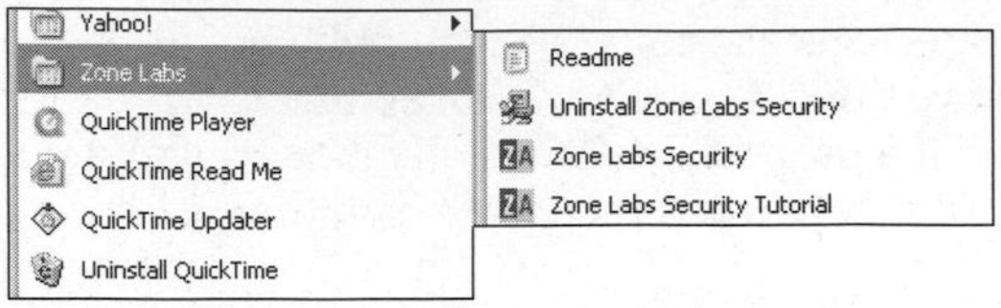

Figure 20-5:
The uninstall
program is
on the Start
thing's
Programs
menu.

Yahoo!	▶
Zone Labs	▶
QuickTime Player	
QuickTime Read Me	
QuickTime Updater	
Uninstall QuickTime	

| Readme |
| Uninstall Zone Labs Security |
| Zone Labs Security |
| Zone Labs Security Tutorial |

✔ Using firewall software is covered in Chapter 24.

✔ Visit Zone Labs at `www.zonelabs.com`.

Use CleanSweep, my boy!

When you're having serious uninstall issues, my best suggestion is to buy the Norton CleanSweep program. CleanSweep does a much, *much* better job of analyzing a program's installation so that uninstalling the same program with CleanSweep yields fewer problems. Plus, CleanSweep archives uninstalled programs so that you can reinstall bits and pieces of it later, if that proves necessary. I highly recommend this product, though you should be aware that it works best on applications installed *after* CleanSweep is installed.

For more information on CleanSweep, see `www.symantec.com/`.

Giving up and deleting the damn programs

This suggestion is rather sneaky: You may notice that after you attempt to uninstall a program the "real" way, remnants of the program still litter your hard drive. In this case, my advice is simple: Delete the remnants. Specifically, delete any files left in the application's main folder.

Suppose that you do away with a program named Last Continent to be Discovered Online (LCDO). You have resigned from the service. You have uninstalled the program. Yet, you notice that you still have an LCDO folder with plenty of files installed. In that case, feel free to delete that folder and its contents.

This action may have adverse side effects, so be prepared to undelete the folder if necessary. Or, better, just rename the folder and see whether it affects anything. Rename the LCDO folder to LCDO.KILL, for example. If this trick doesn't seem to bother the rest of Windows, feel free to delete the folder and its contents.

- ✔ I recommend that you don't delete any program that you didn't create yourself. However, if a program doesn't fully uninstall and you need the disk space, you can delete remnants of the program from its old folder.

- ✔ Don't delete any program remnants saved in the Windows folder or any of the subfolders beneath the Windows folder.

- ✔ Sometimes, the remnants are left around in the hope that you may reinstall the program later. For example, I uninstalled a game, but noticed that it kept personal data — saved missions and high scores — in the folder.

- ✔ You can freely delete remnants such as shortcut icons: Right-click any shortcut icon and choose Delete from the pop-up menu to rid yourself of that icon. You can do that on the desktop as well as on the Start menu.

- ✔ Feel free to delete any .zip or .exe files you downloaded. After installing that software, you can delete the original download — if you like. (I tend to keep those files.)

- ✔ Sometimes, new computers come with folders full of yet-to-be-installed programs. For example, the Online or similar folders may contain icons for various online systems. Delete 'em all!

- ✔ Also consider checking with the System Configuration utility (MSCONFIG) and its Startup tab to see whether bits and pieces of the program are still being started there. (LCDO is notorious for this.) See Chapter 24 for more information on the System Configuration Utility.

The uninstalled program remains on the stupid Add/Remove Programs list

Here's a pain in the arse: You do everything properly and go about uninstalling a program the way Lord Gates intended, yet the stupid program name still appears on the list of installed programs in the Add or Remove Programs dialog box. How maddening! How rude! How wrong!

The solution is surgical:

1. **Carefully note the name of the program as listed in the Add/Remove Programs dialog box.**

2. **Close the Add/Remove Programs dialog box.**

3. **Choose Run from the Start menu.**

4. **Type** REGEDIT **into the box.**

5. **Click OK.**

   This step runs the Registry Editor.

6. **Open the following folders:**

   HKEY_LOCAL_MACHINE

   Software

   Microsoft

   Windows

   CurrentVersion

   Uninstall

   This location is where Windows keeps the installed program list for the Add/Remove Programs dialog box.

7. **Look for your program's folder inside the Uninstall folder.**

   The folder is named with the program name or perhaps the developer's name. If you can't find the folder, give up! The program most likely has some other tricky way of removing itself and has already outguessed you here.

8. **Select your program's entry.**

9. **Press the Delete key on the keyboard.**

10. **Click the Yes button when you're asked to confirm.**

    The item is now gone from the list.

The Big, Scary Question of Reinstalling Windows

At some point, reinstalling Windows became acceptable. And, I'll be honest: Reinstalling Windows works. It absolutely restores your computer to the way it was when you first got it or when Windows was last upgraded. It's a guaranteed fix, but it's a cheat.

It's a cheat because you usually have a simpler, easier way to fix the problem than to resort to reinstalling Windows. For example, consider going to the doctor for an irregular heartbeat, and she recommends a heart transplant. Or, go to a mechanic because your engine knocks, and he recommends replacing the entire engine. Reinstalling Windows is the same overblown, waste-of-time solution.

Fundamentally, an operating system should never need to be reinstalled. Just quiz a Unix wizard on how many times he has to reinstall Unix, and you get this puzzled, insane look. Even in the days of DOS, reinstalling DOS was never considered a solution. But, with 12-minute time limits on tech-support phone calls (refer to Chapter 5), suddenly reinstalling Windows isn't only a potential solution, most often it's *the* solution.

Poppycock!

- ✒ Reinstalling Windows is a solution only when the system has become so corrupted that no other solution exists. For example, if your computer is attacked by a virus or somehow major portions of Windows are destroyed or deleted, reinstalling Windows is an option.

- ✒ Reinstalling Windows is also necessary to recover from a botched operating system upgrade.

- ✒ Yes, often, reinstalling Windows does fix the problem. But it has also been my experience that it has caused more problems than it has solved. I feel that tech-support people who recommend it should be held personally and legally responsible for the consequences of such a drastic recommendation.

- ✒ No, reinstalling Windows isn't the same thing as rebuilding the kernel in Unix. The kernel is one file, similar to Windows own KERNEL32.DLL file. In fact, you can reinstall single files in Windows, which is one way to avoid reinstalling *every* file. You do this by using the System File Checker (SFC) utility, which is covered in Chapter 24.

"Are there any benefits to reinstalling Windows?"

I have been to various Web sites that tout the virtues of reinstalling Windows. It's almost a religious experience for them, like getting a high colonic. The sites remind me of reading those ancient alchemy, or "medical," documents that heartily recommend drinking mercury to cure a fever.

Argument 1: Reinstalling Windows removes much of the junk that doesn't get uninstalled when you remove programs. So (blah, blah, blah), you end up with a cleaner system.

Rebuttal 1: Well, yeah, you end up with a cleaner system *until* you reinstall all your applications, which reintroduces all the junk right back into the system. Cleaner system? No. Wasted time? Definitely!

Argument 2: Reinstalling Windows results in a faster system.

Rebuttal 2: No argument there. But, the reason that it's faster is that reinstalling has the marvelous effect of defragmenting the entire hard drive, especially nonmovable clusters. So, like, *duh!* The system is faster — for a time. Fragmentation eventually does creep back in.

Rebuttal 2 ½: Also, don't forget the time wasted reinstalling Windows. Count your computer system down for at least half a day.

Argument 3: Reinstalling Windows fixes a number of problems.

Rebuttal 3: You can fix problems without reinstalling Windows.

I could go on. And, I would love to, but I have run out of arguments in favor of reinstalling Windows. If you hear of any, please e-mail them to me for this book's next edition: dgookin@wambooli.com. Thanks!

What about reformatting the hard drive?

Reformatting the hard drive is another evil activity that's foisted on the computing public as a necessary thing. It's not. In fact, you should never, *ever,* have to reformat your computer's hard drive. It's something they do at the factory. It's something a computer technician does. It's no longer anything a computer user has to do.

As with reinstalling Windows, in only one circumstance do I suggest reformatting a hard drive: when a virus has attacked the computer so thoroughly that the only solution to rid it of the virus is to reformat the hard drive. And, that's a pretty rare thing; an ugly thing; a thing that I hope never happens to you.

Chapter 21

Windows Can Be Your Friend

● ●

In This Chapter

▶ Checking the event logs

▶ Stopping your running programs

▶ Halting your antivirus and firewall software

▶ Checking processes and services

▶ Troubleshooting System Restore

● ●

*A*fter several trial versions of Windows, Microsoft finally hit its stride with Windows XP. It's not a bad version of Windows, nor is it a bad operating system, as far as operating systems go. The proof of this is that many of the old jokes about Windows just don't get laughs any more. Few people really remember the pain associated with a "General Protection Fault." Fewer still have even seen that infamous Blue Screen of Death. It's all trivia now.

As part of its new robustness, Windows is laden with a slew of interesting places to visit and things to try that can help you review your PC's state, diagnose errors, or help resolve certain problems. This chapter covers those things and gives you more resources to review while you attempt to diagnose exactly what the heck is wrong with your PC.

Windows Event Logs

Whenever a little kid gets a booboo, he rushes off to find his mother or any handy parental-unit-type person. The booboo is displayed. In return, verification and sympathy are given. Perhaps a bandage is prepared, and finally a kiss is applied to make everything better. The child then goes off and continues performing the same activity that caused the booboo in the first place. Such is life.

In your computer, electronics imitates life. When a booboo happens, Windows XP makes a note of it. Sometimes, the note is helpful; sometimes, it's not. But all of the time the note confirms that the booboo has happened, and validation is an important part of that process.

In the computer, the booboo is referred to as an *event*. The thing that keeps track of events is the *event log*. Here's how to view the thing in Windows:

1. **Open the Control Panel.**

2. **Open the Administrative Tools icon.**

   You may also be able to get to Administrative Tools from the main Start thing menu, if Windows is configured that way.

3. **In the Administrative Tools window, open the Event Viewer icon.**

   This step opens the Event Viewer window, which is shown in Figure 21-1. The left side of the window lists three event logs that Windows keeps track of: Application, Security, and System. The right side lists the individual events, as shown in the figure.

	Event Viewer						
File Action View Help							
Event Viewer (Local)	System 1,839 event(s)						
Application	Type	Date	Time	Source	Category	Event	User
Security	Warning	11/22/2004	10:35:20 ...	W32Time	None	36	N/A
System	Information	11/21/2004	8:56:53 PM	Service Control Manager	None	7035	SYSTEM
	Information	11/21/2004	8:56:53 PM	Service Control Manager	None	7036	N/A
	Information	11/21/2004	8:56:43 PM	Service Control Manager	None	7036	N/A
	Information	11/21/2004	8:56:37 PM	Service Control Manager	None	7036	N/A
	Information	11/21/2004	8:56:37 PM	Service Control Manager	None	7035	SYSTEM
	Information	11/21/2004	8:56:31 PM	Service Control Manager	None	7036	N/A
	Information	11/21/2004	8:56:30 PM	Service Control Manager	None	7035	SYSTEM
	Information	11/21/2004	8:56:28 PM	Service Control Manager	None	7036	N/A
	Information	11/21/2004	8:56:28 PM	Service Control Manager	None	7035	SYSTEM
	Information	11/21/2004	8:56:27 PM	Service Control Manager	None	7036	N/A
	Warning	11/21/2004	8:56:11 PM	RemoteAccess	None	20192	N/A
	Information	11/21/2004	8:56:11 PM	Service Control Manager	None	7036	N/A
	Information	11/21/2004	8:56:10 PM	Service Control Manager	None	7036	N/A
	Information	11/21/2004	8:56:10 PM	Service Control Manager	None	7035	SYSTEM

Figure 21-1: The Event Viewer tells the tale.

Here are some of the types of events that can be listed in the Event Viewer:

- **Error:** Could indicate a major problem. Basically, an Error event means that something went wrong.

- **Warning:** For events not as serious as error events, but things you should potentially be aware of.

• **Information:** Indicates that a successful or normal operation has begun, been completed, or perhaps anything else that happens and is noted in the event log.

4. **To view the details of an event, double-click the mouse to open that event.**

   For example, in Figure 21-2, you see the details of a failed disk operation. The date and time are given, along with the other information. The Description area details the message and often shows you a link you can click for more information on the Web. Finally, a data *dump* is listed at the bottom of the dialog box, which is information only a techy would love.

   Many details in the dialog box also appear in the Event Viewer window's columns.

5. **Close the various windows when you're done looking around.**

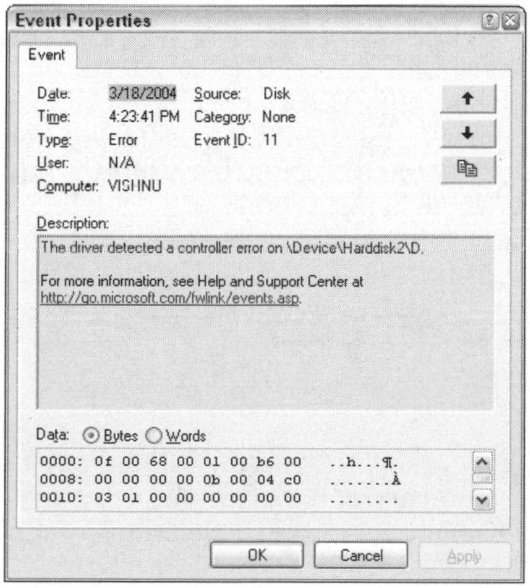

Figure 21-2:
Details of a
specific
event.

The Event Viewer is good in two instances. First, when you suspect that there's a problem, you can quickly open the Event Viewer to ensure that you're not crazy. For example, when I recently experienced CD-ROM drive problems, a quick check of the Event Viewer confirmed that the computer was having trouble.

Second, the Event Viewer can alert you to certain problems you may not know about. For example, I noticed just now that I was getting W32Time Warning errors (Figure 21-1). That explains why my computer's clock is wrong. After reading the event log, it explained that the time server I'm using is no longer available. A quick trip to the Date and Time icon in the Control Panel fixes that up just fine!

- ✔ The Event Viewer is also part of the Computer Management console in Windows XP.

- ✔ You can quickly start the Event Viewer by using the Run command. Type **EVENTVWR.MSC** into the box and click the OK button.

- ✔ The technical information at the bottom of each event detail is really of use only to the programmer or to someone who has access to the program's code. Tech-support people don't need to see it. I don't want to see it. You may remember what I say in Chapter 5: Give the tech-support people only what they ask for. That keeps them happy.

Shutting Down All Running Programs

One of the most common yet frustrating tasks a computer user faces is giving the order to "shut down all running programs" when installing new software. Believe it or not, such a thing isn't an ordeal. But, it's a serious question that folks raise, and one that's answered in this section.

How to shut down all your running programs

Most programs you install like to install themselves with no other software running on the computer. So, they say, right there in the setup instructions, "Please quit all other programs now, before you install the Mondo Number Whacker 3000." Of course, they don't tell you *how* to shut down other programs or even why.

The *why* I'm guessing at: Most new programs need to restart Windows to fully install. Because the computer is restarting, it's a good idea to save your documents. By quitting other programs, you're ensuring that your documents are saved.

The second why-reason is that some installation programs monitor what the computer is doing so that the software can be successfully uninstalled at a later date. Having a second program running, and writing stuff to disk, during that operation may screw things up. It's just best to shut down your other running programs. Here's how:

1. **Press Alt+Tab.**

   This command switches your focus to the next running program or open window.

2. **If pressing Alt+Tab does nothing — you just return to the same Install or Setup program window, for example — you're done. Otherwise:**

3. **Close the program or window.**

4. **Start over with Step 1.**

By using Alt+Tab, you can successfully switch to each running program and shut it down, one after the other. When Alt+Tab doesn't appear to work any more, you're done shutting things down and can continue with the installation.

Don't bother trying to shut down any *processes*. No, the advice is to shut down other running *programs*. Windows has lots of processes going, and I don't recommend that you kill them all off just to install a new program. (Processes are killed in the Task Manager's Processes tab.)

Disabling your antivirus, firewall, and so on

After you shut down any running programs, the next annoying thing you're requested to do for a new software installation is to shut down or disable your antivirus software. You may also be asked to disable the Internet firewall. Yeah, in other words, *strip naked and bare your computer's soul to the cruel universe!*

Well . . . it's not that terrible.

Most antivirus and firewall programs leave their marks as icons in the system tray/notification area. Shutting them down or disabling them is as easy as finding their tiny icons and right-clicking them. From the pop-up menu that appears, choose a Suspend, Disable, or even Shutdown command, to temporarily do away with that icon's papa program.

For example, in Figure 21-3, the tiny icon representing the Norton AntiVirus program appears. After you right-click the icon, a menu pops up. Choosing the Disable command from that menu temporarily suspends the antivirus program, which allows you to install a new program.

Similar steps can be taken for your firewall. For example, to shut down the Zone Alarm firewall, right-click its icon and choose the Shutdown command from the pop-up menu.

Figure 21-3:
Disabling
Norton
AntiVirus.

> **Open Norton AntiVirus**
> Disable Auto-Protect
> Configure Norton AntiVirus

Immediately after installing the new software, be sure to restart Windows.
That way, you ensure that your antivirus, firewall, and any disabled software
are restarted as well.

Processes and Services Here, There, and Everywhere

The Processes tab in the Windows Task Manager window displays all the programs and individual processes going on in your computer. It's a like a peek
into the computer's brain; you see *everything,* even supersecret programs
that the operating system runs behind the scenes, as shown in Figure 21-4.

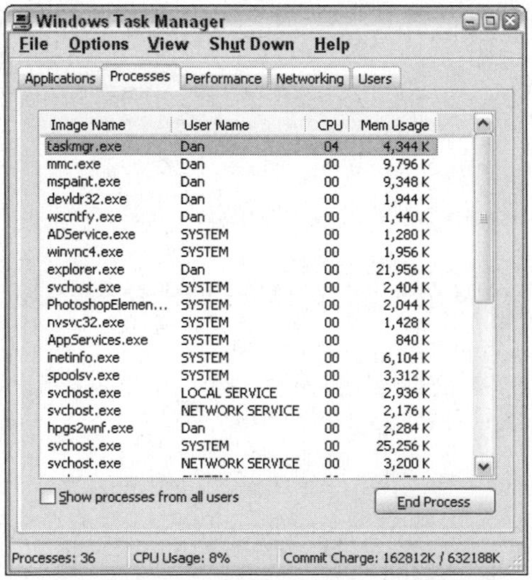

Figure 21-4:
Processes
running, and
shown in
the Task
Manager.

To see the Task Manager window, press Ctrl+Alt+Delete on the keyboard. You
can also use the Run command from the Start menu (or press Win+R) and type
TASKMGR into the box. Then, click the Processes tab to see which processes
are running on your computer.

Some processes are linked to the programs that are running, which are displayed in the Applications window. Otherwise, the processes are started by programs that run when the computer starts, some processes are represented as icons in the system tray/notification area, and some processes are part of Windows and carry out specialized tasks.

You can end a process by selecting it in the Processes window and clicking the End Processes button. But, I suppose, that's a *bad thing* to do. Indeed, there's a better way to disable and even prevent some specific processes from running.

Close the Windows Task Manager window, if it's open.

The processes, or *services,* that Windows runs are controlled from the Services console, which can be accessed from the Administrative Tools window. Here's how:

1. **Open the Control Panel.**

2. **Open the Administrative Tools icon.**

   Your version of Windows may also be configured to show Administrative Tools as a menu item on the Start button's menu.

3. **In the Administrative Tools window, open the Services icon.**

   This step opens the Services console window, which is shown in Figure 21-5. The left side of the window is pretty much useless; all the action happens on the right, which lists all the services available to Windows or those installed by various applications. Various columns display information about the services, but you can get specific information by clicking a resource, as shown in the figure.

4. **Double-click the Messenger service to open it.**

   Locate the Messenger service on the list, and then double-click it to display the dialog box that controls that service, similar to what's shown in Figure 21-6.

   In the Messenger Properties dialog box (refer to Figure 21-6), there are buttons available to start, stop, pause, or resume the service's activity. For stopping a service, clicking the Stop button here is preferred over ending the service's process in the Task Manager window.

   Note that you can also prevent a service from even starting by choosing Disabled from the Startup Type drop-down list (in the middle of the dialog box's General tab).

5. **Click OK to close the Properties dialog box, and close the Services window and any other open windows.**

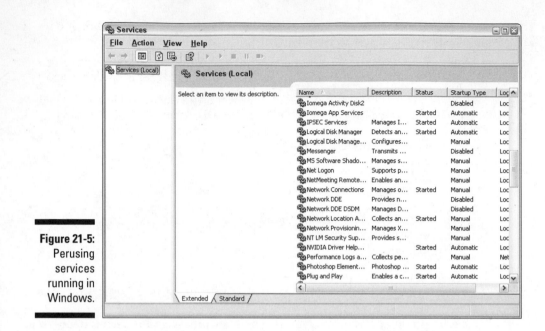

Figure 21-5:
Perusing
services
running in
Windows.

You may be directed to disable or stop a service as part of some trouble-shooting activity. Or, some Web pages recommend disabling certain services merely as a way to optimize your PC's performance. I cannot vouch for any Web sites, but when you find them, you then know where to go to carry out their recommended tasks.

Figure 21-6:
Specifics
on the
Messenger
service.

✔ Don't go around disabling or stopping services unless you're directed to do so by a reliable source.

✔ The Services thingy is also part of the Computer Management console in Windows XP, just like the Event Viewer (covered earlier in this chapter).

✔ You can quickly start the Event Viewer by using the Run command. Type **SERVICES.MSC** into the box and click the OK button.

Checking System Restore

The System Restore tool should always be on and running. If it's not, you need to check a few things or even fix the program. This section offers some suggestions and help.

Confirming the status of System Restore

The System Restore control center is found in the System Properties dialog box. Here's how to get there from wherever you are:

1. **Open the Control Panel.**

2. **Open the System icon.**

3. **Click the System Restore tab.**

   The System Restore tab displays summary information about System Restore. Most importantly, there you find a check box labeled Turn Off System Restore on All Drives.

4. **Ensure that there's *not* a check mark in the box labeled Turn Off System Restore on All Drives.**

   Unless you're running an alternative System Restore-like utility, keep Windows System Restore on!

5. **Close the dialog box and various windows when you're done with them.**

The following subsections delve deeper in the System Restore tab of the System Properties dialog box.

✔ When you turn System Restore off, Windows automatically deletes all the Restore Points for that drive. Don't expect them to magically reappear if you decide to reenable System Restore later!

✔ One alternative program to System Restore is the Go Back utility, sold by Symantec (the Peter Norton people).

Peering deeply at the System Restore service

The System Restore program automatically creates restore points as you use Windows. That's because System Restore is run as a service, going on all the time in Windows XP. To find the service, refer to the section, "Processes and Services Here, There, and Everywhere," earlier in this chapter. You're looking for a service called System Restore Service. (This is a look-only exercise.)

If there are any problems with the System Restore Service, they appear in the Event log. Refer to the section, "Checking the Event Logs," earlier in this chapter. In the Event Viewer window, choose the System event category. Then on the right side of the window, click the Source column heading to sort the list by the source. Any System Restore errors or events appear under the source System Restore Services.

Setting the amount of disk space used by System Restore

Face it: System Restore is just a quick-and-dirty utility that helps people become lazy. If you seriously backed up your computer's hard drive, you wouldn't need System Restore. But, it exists, so you may as well take advantage of it.

On the downside, System Restore is a great consumer of hard drive space. When disk space is low, or when you back up anyway, you may consider reducing the copious amount of storage space System Restore consumes. Here's how:

1. **Open the System Properties dialog box and the System Restore tab therein.**

   Refer to the preceding section.

2. **If more than one hard drive is listed in the window, click to select it.**

3. **Click the Settings button.**

   You see a dialog box illustrating how System Restore consumes space on the hard drive, as shown in Figure 21-7.

4. **Adjust the slider to the left to decrease the amount of disk space used by System Restore.**

   Or, if you find yourself using System Restore often, increase the disk space it uses by moving the slider to the right. The more room, the more Restore Points the utility can remember.

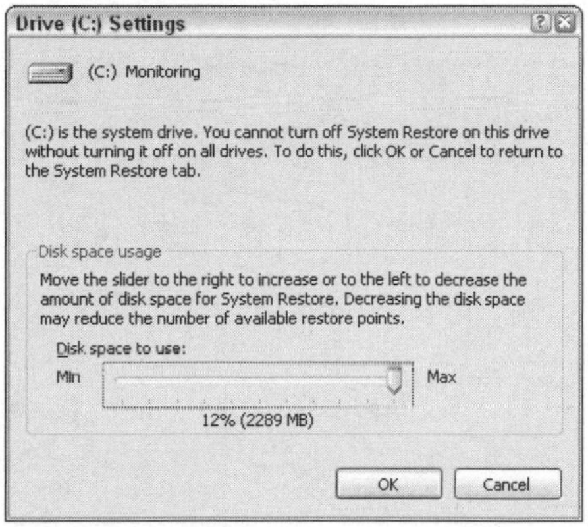

Drive (C:) Settings

(C:) Monitoring

(C:) is the system drive. You cannot turn off System Restore on this drive without turning it off on all drives. To do this, click OK or Cancel to return to the System Restore tab.

Figure 21-7:
Set the
amount of
disk storage
consumed
by System
Restore.

Disk space usage

Move the slider to the right to increase or to the left to decrease the amount of disk space for System Restore. Decreasing the disk space may reduce the number of available restore points.

Disk space to use:

Min ▢ Max

12% (2289 MB)

OK   Cancel

5. **Click OK.**

6. **Repeat Steps 2 through 5 for any additional hard drives monitored by System Restore.**

7. **Close up everything when you're done.**

Note that on hard drives other than Drive C, an extra option appears in the Settings dialog box. You can click to put a check in the box labeled Turn Off System Restore on This Drive, which disables System Restore monitoring for that drive only.

✔ System Restore points take up a lot of disk space!

✔ You can help free up the disk space used by Restore Points by using the Disk Cleanup program. See Chapter 23.

✔ System Restore tries to keep Restore Points for at least 90 days, after which they're automatically removed.

✔ After a restore point has been removed, it cannot be recovered!

Chapter 22

Shutdown Constipation

• •

• •

*I*t is the height of good manners to know when it's time to leave. Alas, Windows has no manners, so it's up to you to shut 'er down when you're done. But, even though you go through those proper procedures, something in the box *refuses* to shut down. Good-bye already!

So, you sit and wait and wait and wait. "Shutting down Windows," it says. Yeah, right. And the check is in the mail, and the government is here to help you, and so on. What's to believe? With any luck, you can find the cure for your PC's shutdown constipation in the text that follows.

What to Do When Your Computer Doesn't Shut Down

Give the computer about two or three minutes before you're certain that it's stuck. Then, just turn the sucker off. I know — that's "bad," but what else can you do?

Well, yeah: You can get the situation fixed. Windows is supposed to shut down and, in many cases, turn off the computer all by itself. When it doesn't work that way, you need to fix things.

✔ If the power button doesn't turn the computer off, press and hold that button for about three seconds. That usually works.

✔ If the power button still doesn't turn the computer off, unplug it. Or, if your computer is connected to a UPS (uninterruptible power supply), turn off the UPS.

"Why doesn't it shut down?"

Windows refuses to shut down for the very same reason that some guests refuse to leave a party: rude behavior. Inside the computer, usually some stubborn program has been given the signal to shut down, but — like the guest who doesn't leave despite your walking around in your pajamas and bathrobe — it refuses to leave.

Get a hint, will ya?

The solution is finding that stubborn program and either forcing it to quit before you shut down or just not running the program in the first place. As luck would have it, the list of programs that could possibly not get the hint to quit is quite long.

✔ Some older versions of antivirus software were usually to blame for not letting the computer shut down all the way. The programs would monitor the shutdown to ensure that no viruses were installed, but then they would "forget" to quit themselves.

✔ In fact, if you're looking for anything to blame, older software is generally your number-one suspect. Though Windows is supposed to shut down all open programs before it quits, you probably should manually close older programs before you give Windows the command to shut down.

Common things that stop up shutdown

Of course, it's not always Windows fault. Any of the following situations can also lead to shutdown constipation:

✔ Older, out-of-date, or conflicting device drivers may hang a computer on shutdown.

✔ Software you have recently uninstalled, but that still has sad little pieces of itself remaining around to gum up the works, may be the culprit.

✔ Any devices flagged as nonfunctioning by the Device Manager can also be causing the problem. See the appendix in this book for information on the Device Manager.

✔ A bad hard drive may be the problem.

✔ A virus or worm may be the problem.

✔ If your computer plays a sound file when it shuts down and the sound file is corrupted or damaged, that could also cause the system to hang; Windows just sits there and waits for the sound file to "fix itself."

If the shutdown problem is new, consider what you have installed, removed, or updated recently. Odds are that the new software, the removed software, or changes in hardware may be causing the conflict that's preventing the system from shutting down.

Try this first! (System Restore)

The first thing to do: Try a System Restore. Odds are that restoring the system to a point where it shuts down properly fixes the problem.

To fix a problem with a corrupt shutdown sound

If the problem happens because Windows is playing a sound at shutdown and that sound is screwing things up, follow these steps to fix it:

1. **Open the Control Panel.**

2. **Open the Sounds and Audio Devices icon and click the Sounds tab.**

3. **Scroll through the list of events until you find the Exit Windows item.**

   If no sound is listed there — and no icon is by the Exit Windows event name — you're okay. Skip to Step 6.

4. **Click the Play button.**

   This step tests the sound to see whether it's working, though it's no guarantee that the sound isn't the thing that's hanging the computer on shutdown.

5. **Choose (None) from the drop-down list of sounds.**

   By choosing no sound, you effectively disable the sound playing at shutdown.

6. **Click OK.**

If the computer continues to hang when it's shut down, you know that the problem lies elsewhere. Continue reading in the next subsection.

Restart Windows quickly

Sometimes, the problem may be with some program you're running — one of those *memory leak* situations discussed in Chapter 11. If you're having that type of trouble, follow these steps:

1. **Start Windows as you normally would.**
2. **Wait for all the startup activity to settle down.**
3. **Shut down Windows.**

If Windows shuts down normally without any hang-ups, you're assured that it's probably some other program you're running and not Windows itself to blame. The job then becomes one of elimination to see which program is hanging the system.

Of course, this technique doesn't disable the many other startup programs that are not a part of Windows. Keep reading for more information on those.

Try shutting down in Safe mode

One trick you can try is to start the computer in Safe mode. After you're there, try shutting down. If the computer shuts down successfully, you can be sure that the problem is not with Windows and most likely not with your computer hardware. No, the problem is either a device driver or a third-party program that's not shutting down properly.

See Chapter 24 more information on Safe mode.

Check logs and error messages

Refer to the Event Viewer to see whether any errors or troublesome events have been logged just before shutdown. Also read the screen to see whether any programs display an error message just before the problem occurred.

After checking the messages, simply try to disable the program or service that is displaying the message. If you can kill the thing off, try shutting down. When shutdown is successful, you have found the bad program or service.

- ✔ Windows is quite good about writing error messages to the event logs, even right before it shuts down.
- ✔ Refer to Chapter 21 for information on the Event Viewer as well as instructions on how to stop a process in Windows XP.

> ✔ Also see Chapter 24 for information on disabling programs by using the System Configuration Utility.
>
> ✔ Defective programs should be reinstalled, or check with the developer for information on updates or new versions.

Disabling Some Things to See Whether They're at Fault

Three main areas cause woes in Windows:

✔ The graphics adapter

✔ The power-management hardware

✔ The networking hardware

Fixing any of these is easy; you just reinstall the software or update the software driver with a newer version. You can obtain the newer version from the manufacturer's Web page at no cost. The problem, of course, is to properly identify which of those suckers could be at fault.

Disabling the graphics adapter

To see whether the video driver is causing the problem, you need to disable the video hardware in your computer. Obey these steps:

1. **Open the System icon in the Control Panel.**

2. **Click the Hardware tab.**

3. **Click the Device Manager button.**

    This step opens the Device Manager window.

4. **Open the item labeled Display Adapters.**

    You see a list of graphics adapters installed in your computer. These are the hardware devices that control graphics.

5. **Double-click to open your computer's graphics adapter.**

    The graphics adapter's Properties dialog box appears, as shown in Figure 22-1.

6. **From the Device Usage drop-down list (at the bottom of the dialog box in Figure 22-1), choose the option labeled Do Not Use This Device (Disable).**

NVIDIA GeForce FX 5200 Ultra Properties

General | Driver | Resources

NVIDIA GeForce FX 5200 Ultra

Driver Provider: NVIDIA
Driver Date: 5/2/2003
Driver Version: 4.4.0.3
Digital Signer: Microsoft Windows Hardware Compatibility Publ

Driver Details...	To view details about the driver files.
Update Driver...	To update the driver for this device.
Roll Back Driver	If the device fails after updating the driver, roll back to the previously installed driver.
Uninstall	To uninstall the driver (Advanced).

OK   Cancel

Figure 22-1:
Disabling
the video
software.

You may also want to just skip over this step and click the Troubleshoot button to see whether the troubleshooter can find any problems. My experience shows that disabling the video hardware works faster.

7. **Click OK to close the Properties dialog box.**

   A warning dialog box appears and begs you to restart your computer now.

8. **Click the Yes button to restart Windows.**

   You're asked whether you want to restart Windows. You do.

9. **Click the Yes button to restart Windows.**

   Or, if you're not prompted, just restart Windows as you normally would. Granted, it may not be restarting — which is the core of the problem here. If so, just unplug the computer or do whatever is necessary to restart the sucker.

   When Windows comes back on the screen, it may or may not look any different. Regardless, the video driver has been disabled, and now you can seriously test to see whether it's causing your problem.

10. **After Windows comes back up, shut it down again.**

    You're testing to see whether shutdown works with the video driver disabled.

If the system shuts down just fine, you need to update or upgrade your video driver. Refer to Chapter 6, the section about updating your graphics device driver, for more information.

If the system still refuses to shut down, the problem is *not* the video system. You need to repeat the preceding steps, but in Step 6, click the Enable button to restore your graphics hardware. (You may not need to restart Windows.)

Disabling power management

 Turn off that power-management stuff and see whether that's the cause of your shutdown woe. Open the Control Panel's Power Options icon. Set everything to Never. Shut down Windows (as best you can). Then, restart and try shutting down again. Often, the power-management feature may be stopping you up.

- ✓ Also, access your PC's Startup program and see about disabling power management there.

- ✓ Another term for the PC's power-management system is ACPI. That stands for Advanced Configuration and Power Interface.

- ✓ Check with the Device Manager to see whether you have a problem with power management. See the preceding section, Steps 1 through 4, to display the Device Manager. The power-management hardware is listed under System Devices.

Disabling the network

The final punk in the nasty trio of problem bullies is your computer's networking hardware. The main situation here is usually that the dang thing wasn't properly installed in the first place. It's probably not sharing an IRQ or is trampling on some other device's DMA or something else technical-sounding.

The first way to check your networking hardware or software is to see whether any diagnostic programs are available. Check the Programs menu (off the Start thing panel) to see whether your PC dealer or manufacturer has a menu item for the networking hardware. If so, check there for a diagnostic tool or utility. That tells you right away whether there's a problem — though it probably doesn't tell you how to fix it. (Generally, the hardware needs to be reconfigured and reinstalled.)

The next thing to do is to run a networking troubleshooter. Open the Device Manager as covered earlier in this chapter. Then, open the Network Adapters item to see your network hardware listed. Double-clicking your network hardware displays a Properties dialog box, similar to what's shown in Figure 22-2.

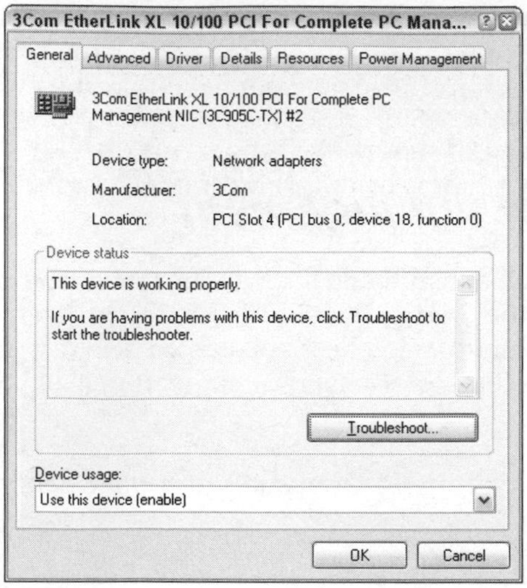

Figure 22-2:
The networking hardware's Properties dialog box.

Click the Troubleshoot button to begin the troubleshooter.

Finally, you can try disabling the networking hardware. This action works just like disabling the video hardware, as covered in the section, "Disabling the graphics adapter," earlier in this chapter. The difference is that you're opening the Network Adapters item in Step 4.

Be very careful when disabling and reenabling your networking hardware. Setting up a computer for networking isn't the easiest or most pleasurable thing to do. If any of this causes pangs in your chest, definitely consider paying someone else to do it!

The Annoying Shutdown/Instant Restart Problem

A sadly common problem in Windows XP is its frustrating ability to restart right in the middle of a shutdown. The good news is that such a thing can be fixed. The bad news is that the shutdown/restart problem is a symptom and not the cause. The true cause is hardware trouble, but first follow these steps to fix the shutdown/restart problem:

1. **Open the Control Panel's System icon.**

   You can open this icon from the Control Panel's window, and also by right-clicking the My Computer icon on the desktop and choosing Properties from the pop-up menu.

2. **Click the Advanced tab in the System Properties dialog box.**

3. **In the Startup and Recovery area, click the Settings button.**

   Mind which button you click! Three buttons are on the Advanced tab, all annoyingly named Settings. Clicking the proper one displays the Startup and Recovery dialog box, as illustrated in Figure 22-3.

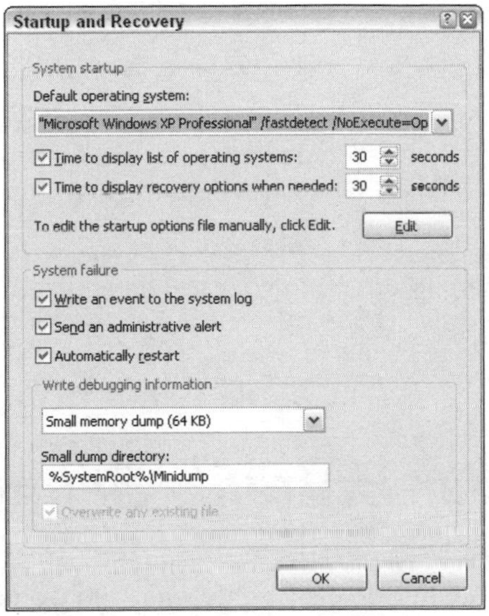

Figure 22-3:
Windows deals with startup and shutdown problems here

4. **Remove the check mark by the item labeled Automatically Restart.**

   This step effectively removes the restarting symptom.

5. **Click OK.**

6. **Close any other dialog boxes and windows that you opened.**

The symptom has been addressed, but the problem has not been cured. The next time you start Windows, immediately check the Event Viewer and review the System messages to see what exactly is going wrong at shutdown. That helps you nail down the problem, or at least arms you with enough information for tech support.

✔ Refer to Chapter 21 for information on using the Event Viewer.

✔ Also refer to Chapter 8 for information on the boot menu. That helps you to stop the restart problem when Windows first starts.

Help Me, Microsoft!

Microsoft takes careful notes on all the problems that happen with Windows, by keeping a large database, or *Knowledge Base,* of all the trouble and the solutions offered. That's good. Even better is that Microsoft makes all this information available to anyone with Internet access. The Microsoft Knowledge Base Web site can be accessed at

```
support.microsoft.com/
```

This Web site can be especially useful for diagnosing shutdown problems. After all, you're probably not the only person in the world who has had this type of issue. (Nope, no one is picking on you!)

Use the Search text box on the main Knowledge Base Web page. Type the word **shutdown**, plus any other words key to your problem. (If you cannot think of any extra words, **shutdown** is fine by itself.) Click the Search button and see what the Knowledge Base comes up with.

Controlling the Power Button's Behavior

In the old days — and I'm talking pre-1990 here — computers all came with an On-Off button or switch. That button did exactly what you would expect: On was on. Off was off. Today, with all the emphasis on power management and energy efficiency and *la-di-da,* the computer's On-Off button has become the *power button.*

On all computers, the power button most definitely turns the computer on. Good.

On a small number of computer models, the power button definitely turns the sucker off. But, on most other computers, the power button can have any of a number of functions. That's why it's the power button and not the on-off switch.

Forcing the power button to turn the computer off

Yeah, it may seem like the power button isn't turning the computer off, but that's because you don't know the secret:

Press and hold the power button for about eight seconds.

Even when the computer seems locked up beyond all hope, the hardware is down in Hades playing rummy with a washing machine and 8-track tape deck, and the software has taken your credit card number and set off dancing and singing to the mall, the power button *always* turns the computer off if pressed and held for eight seconds. Magic.

Changing the power button's function

When the computer is behaving nicely, you can program the power button on many PCs to obey your whim. The options that are available depend on your computer's power-management hardware. To see what's available, as well as to change the power button's function, comply with these steps:

1. **Open the Control Panel.**

2. **Open the Power Options icon.**

3. **Click the Advanced tab.**

   If the function of your PC's power button can be changed, you see a Power Buttons area in the dialog box, as shown in Figure 22-4. If you don't see the area, your computer lacks this feature.

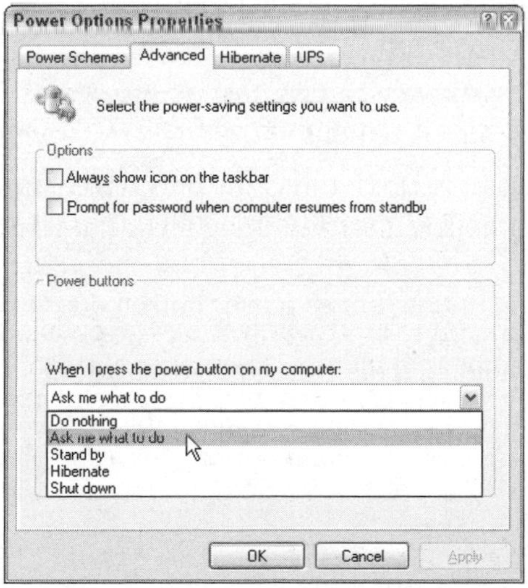

Figure 22-4: Change the power button's function here.

[Figure: Power Options Properties dialog box]

Power Options Properties

Power Schemes | Advanced | Hibernate | UPS

Select the power-saving settings you want to use.

Options
- [ ] Always show icon on the taskbar
- [ ] Prompt for password when computer resumes from standby

Power buttons

When I press the power button on my computer:

Ask me what to do

- Do nothing
- Ask me what to do
- Stand by
- Hibernate
- Shut down

[OK] [Cancel] [Apply]

4. **Choose a new function for the power button from the drop-down list.**

   Five options are available, as shown in Figure 22-4. These are described in Table 22-1.

If you really want the power button to turn off the computer, choose the Shut Down option. If you have a laptop and you want it to go into Hibernation mode when you press the button, choose that option.

5. **Click OK after making your choice.**

Table 22-1	Power Button Options
Option	*Pressing the power button does this*
Do nothing	Nothing; the power button is ignored.
Ask me what to do	The standard Turn Off Computer dialog box is displayed, just as though you chose the Turn Off Computer command from the Start button's menu.
Stand by	The computer is put into Standby (Sleep) mode.
Hibernate	The computer is put into Hibernation mode.
Shut down	The computer begins the shutdown process, by closing programs and shutting down Windows. When that's done, the computer turns itself off.

Even though you can change the function of the power button, you still need to shut down Windows properly (or as best you can) whenever you're done working on the computer.

✔ Not all of the five power button options show up on every computer.

✔ If you set the power button to Do Nothing, the only way to turn off the computer is to properly shut down Windows. If that doesn't work, you have to unplug the sucker.

✔ Selecting the Do Nothing option for the power button doesn't affect the 8-second rule; no matter what option you choose for the power button's function, pressing and holding it for 8 seconds turns off the computer.

✔ Laptop computers have many more options available in the Power Options Properties dialog box, including options for a sleep button (if one is available) as well as options for what to do when the user closes the laptop's lid.

Part III
Preventive Maintenance

The 5th Wave   By Rich Tennant

"I know my modem's in the microwave. It seems to increase transmission speed. Can you punch in 'defrost'? I have alot of emails going out."

In this part . . .

I know only a few people who truly practice the art of preventive maintenance. They're the ones who read their cars' manuals and who stick to the oil- and filter-changing schedules. They read the handbooks for their new washer-dryers and actually perform the few recommended maintenance checks. They clean the coils on their refrigerators every three months. They wash out their lawn mowers. Call them diligent. Call them anal-retentive. But you can't call them desperate because when it comes to troubleshooting, they really don't need any.

There is such value to preventive maintenance. It's that confidence you would expect from Dad in a 1950s sitcom: "Oh, darn!," says Dad, driving the family's Buick on a 2-lane highway in the middle of nowhere. "There goes that tire! Fortunately, I just filled the spare with air, not to mention that little Timmy and I spent all last week practicing how to change a flat tire. We'll be on the road again in minutes. And I'll bet no one will say the word *fudge*." You too can experience such self-assurance, as long as you practice a few bits and pieces of preventive PC maintenance.

Chapter 23

Maintaining Your Disk Drives

● ●

In This Chapter

▶ Using various disk tools

▶ Fixing minor disk problems

▶ Defragmenting a drive

▶ Saving disk space

▶ Running the Disk Cleanup program

▶ Scheduling your disk maintenance

▶ Using the task scheduler

● ●

Disk drives hold more importance for your computer because they contain all your stuff — not only the operating system (important) and your applications (more important), but also all the documents and data you create and rely on every day (most important). So, although you can be a whiz-bang at troubleshooting common hard drive burps and glitches, and perhaps you can install a new hard drive in less than 30 seconds, what would work best for you is an ounce of preventive disk drive maintenance. That saves some agony and hair-pulling later.

Disk Maintenance Tools

Windows gives you two tools for maintaining your hard drive and helping its performance: Check Disk, which is also known as ScanDisk, and Defrag.

✔ The Check Disk utility is used to scan a hard drive for errors, potential problems, and damage. It then tries to fix the situation as best it can.

✔ The Defrag utility is used to optimize the hard drive's performance.

A third disk maintenance tool is Backup. It's covered in Chapter 25.

✔ Check Disk and Defrag aren't the best tools available for maintaining your hard drive. You can find better versions of these tools in third-party utilities, such as Norton Utilities Disk Doctor and Disk Optimization tools.

✔ Another good alternative for the Defrag tool is Vopt ("vee-opt"), from Golden Bow Systems:

```
www.goldenbow.com
```

✔ You must have an Administrator-type account to run the disk utilities Defrag and Check Disk. Those utilities don't run otherwise.

✔ Hard disk performance decreases as the amount of stuff on your hard drive increases. You can't do anything about this; it's just a simple truth. It takes longer to access and sift through more information than it does for little information.

Accessing the disk tools

Windows keeps all its handy disk tools near to the bosom of your PC's hard drives. Here's how to get at this common tool chest:

1. **Open the My Computer icon on the desktop.**

2. **Right-click the icon for hard drive C.**

   Or, you can open any hard drive's icon, such as Drive D, if you want to use the tools on that hard drive instead.

   Note that these tools are available for use only on a hard drive.

3. **Choose Properties from the pop-up menu.**

4. **Click the Tools tab.**

   You see a list of the three common disk maintenance tools, as shown in Figure 23-1. The error-checking tool is Check Disk. The defragmenting tool is Defrag. And then, you see a button for backup, if your version of Windows has Backup installed.

The following subsections cover the tools found on the Tools tab in the disk drive's Properties dialog box.

✔ You can also find the Defrag and Backup commands on the Start menu: Choose Programs (or All Programs) and then Accessories⇨System Tools, and then look for the program name, either Backup or Disk Defragmenter.

✔ Some versions of Windows XP Home don't come with a backup program.

✔ Some third-party utilities may install buttons or options on the Tools tab. Figure 23-1 shows the standard Windows configuration, so if you see anything extra, it's specific to your computer and not a part of Windows in general.

Figure 23-1: Where Windows hides the disk tools.

Is not the disk drive riddled with errors?

The Check Disk program is designed to check for and repair common errors on a hard drive. It's not really a performance-enhancing tool.

On most systems, Check Disk is run automatically, thanks to a maintenance robot that Windows runs every few days (via the Task Scheduler). But, you can always run Check Disk manually — and you should, especially if you don't leave your computer on all the time and the maintenance robot doesn't have time to run.

Follow these steps to run Check Disk:

1. **Don't do anything else.**

   This isn't a rule — it's just good advice: Check Disk works best when it has your computer all to itself while it runs. Doing something else, especially something involving disk activity, may cause Check Disk to stubbornly restart, which wastes time.

2. **Start Check Disk from the Tools tab in the disk drive's Properties dialog box; click the Check Now button.**

   Refer to the steps in the preceding section.

   The Check Disk dialog box opens, as shown in Figure 23-2. Feel free to check either option in the dialog box, which merely expands upon the things Check Disk looks for (and adds time to the total operation).

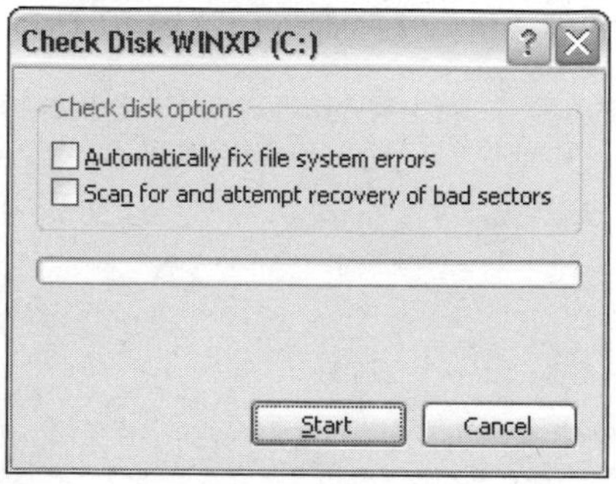

Figure 23-2:
Starting
Check Disk.

   If you don't check the box labeled Automatically Fix File System Errors, Check Disk stops and prompts you to fix the errors, if any are encountered.

   Sometimes, choosing the option Automatically Fix File System Errors requires that Windows be restarted.

3. **Click the Start button to check your disk drive.**

   Check Disk does its thing. Watch the pretty green squares. Try not to read anything into the display.

   After the check is complete, a simple "I'm done" dialog box appears.

4. **Click the OK button to close the dialog box.**

   You can also close any other dialog boxes or open windows.

What does it all mean? Who really knows? When nothing exciting happens, consider your disk checked and everything okay. Feel free to move on.

When errors are found, you're alerted via a warning dialog box. Heed the instructions in the dialog box. Check Disk tries its best to fix things it can fix. But, note that a hard drive with serious problems simply needs to be replaced. Refer to Chapter 15 for more information.

Does Check Disk increase performance? No. It fixes errors. So, if the errors are stopping up performance, Check Disk improves things. For the most part, running Check Disk doesn't make anything run faster.

✔ You have to check each hard drive in your system individually. Keep in mind that just checking Drive C, for example, doesn't ensure that Drive D has also been checked.

✔ Sometimes, ScanDisk runs automatically when the computer first starts up, especially if the computer was suddenly, unexpectedly, or improperly shut down. This is a good thing.

✔ The Norton Disk Doctor utility does some of the same things as Check Disk, but in a more cautious and thorough manner. Disk Doctor is also capable of recovering from some errors that seize Check Disk cold.

✔ Check Disk was the name of the old, original DOS disk-checking utility, though in DOS it was called CHKDSK. (Well, actually, it's still called CHKDSK in Windows XP!)

Fragment me not

Defragmenting a hard drive isn't only a necessary maintenance tool, it's a performance-boosting one. By eliminating most fragmented files and reshuffling popular files to the beginning of the disk (like the head of the line), you see a modest performance improvement.

File fragments aren't bad things. Windows tries to make the best use of the hard drive, so what it does is to split some files into smaller pieces — *fragments* — so that disk space is used more efficiently. But, all those little pieces require overhead to keep track of and to reassemble when the file is accessed. After a while, disk space may still be used efficiently, but disk performance drops like the GPA of two teenagers in love. To fix the problem, you need to run a tool like Defrag every so often.

To run Defrag, abide by these steps:

1. **Open the My Computer icon on the desktop.**

2. **Right-click the icon for hard drive C.**

   It doesn't really matter which hard drive you right-click for Defrag; you choose which drive to defragment in a later step.

3. **Choose Properties from the pop-up menu.**

4. **Click the Tools tab.**

5. **Click the Defragment Now button.**

   The Disk Defragmenter window appears, as shown in Figure 23-3. A list of available hard drives, or disk drives, that can be defragmented (no CDs or DVDs) appears in the top part of the window. The middle of the window contains an entertaining display while Defrag runs.

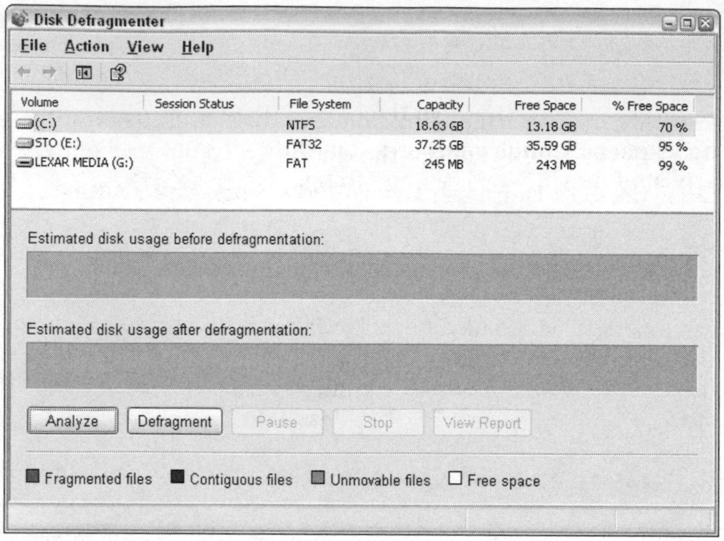

Figure 23-3:
Thrill-a-
minute disk
defragment-
ing goes
on here.

6. **Choose a drive to defragment.**

   You can clean up only one drive at a time. In Figure 23-3, Drive C is chosen.

7. **Click the Analyze button.**

   Defragmenting can be done on any disk drive at any time, but for the best payoff, the percentage of fragmented files needs to be quite large. How large? I don't know. But Windows does, and it tells you in a dialog box displayed on the screen.

8. **Obey the dialog box.**

   For example, if the computer believes that defragmenting is a good thing at this time, click the Defragment button. Otherwise, click the Close button and skip down to Step 11.

   You can optionally choose the View Report button here. In the Analysis Report window, scroll down to the Volume Fragmentation area to review how fragmented the drive is.

9. **Sit back and watch defragmenting in action!**

   It takes a while for the computer to clean up the hard drive. The graphical display keeps you occupied, though I usually get up and do some yard work while the operation takes place.

   Defragmenting can take anywhere from several minutes on up to a few hours to complete. How much time it takes depends on how fragmented the hard drive is, which is related to how long it has been since you last defragmented the drive. That could be ages.

> Feel free to click the Stop button if the insanity of waiting too long over-comes you. Also click Stop if you notice that Defrag keeps trying to start over again. (Read more about that in the following bulleted list.)

10. **Click the Close button when you see the dialog box telling you that defragmentation is complete.**

11. **Close the Disk Defragmenter window when you're done.**

    Or, you can choose another drive to defragment, starting over again with Step 6.

Because Defrag dramatically improves performance, I recommend running it at least once a week, or as often as the program indicates that defragmenting is necessary. The more often you run it, the less time it takes Defrag to do its job.

- ✔ Defrag needs at least 15 percent free disk space to work properly. If you have less than that amount of disk space free, Defrag doesn't run. See the following section for more information.

- ✔ The key to testing a Defrag utility is to run a second one after the first one. For example, running Golden Bow's Vopt after running Windows XP Defrag results in even more optimization. That's because Vopt is a better disk defragmenter than Defrag; it takes less time to do a better job:

  ```
  www.goldenbow.com
  ```

- ✔ Defragmenting takes time! Be sure to set aside several minutes to a few hours for your hard drive to fully defragment.

- ✔ If Defrag poops out on you, just get Norton Utilities and use its Disk Optimizer or get Golden Bow's Vopt and use it instead.

- ✔ Defrag runs best when it's the only program running. Other programs may interfere with Defrag, by slowing it down or sometimes causing it to start over.

- ✔ Refer to the later section "Scheduling Automatic Maintenance" for information on automating the defragment process.

Increasing Disk Storage

Another potential problem with a hard drive is that disk space suddenly runs dry! At first, this situation is suspect with me because today's hard drives hold lots of information and it would take a busy person to fill things up quickly. But, with popular graphics files, videos, and especially online music, you can see the free space on an 80GB hard drive dwindle like you would watch ice melt in the sun.

Checking disk space

To quickly peek at your hard drive's disk usage situation in both numerical and graphical terms, use the disk drive's Properties dialog box, as shown in Figure 23-4.

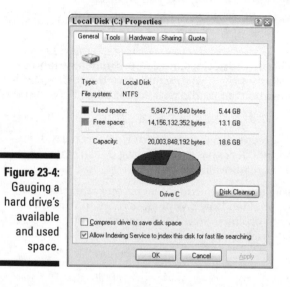

Figure 23-4:
Gauging a hard drive's available and used space.

To see this dialog box, open the My Computer icon on the desktop. In the My Computer window, right-click your hard drive's icon and choose Properties from the pop-up menu.

The remainder of this section references this dialog box, so remember how you opened it.

Some space-saving suggestions

If you're collecting more than one type of a specific file — such as graphics, video, or music files — consider putting all that stuff on CD-R discs. Archiving is the name of the game! Just wait until you have a collection of enough files (more than 500MB, for example), and then burn 'em all on a CD-R.

If you absolutely must have all that stuff on a hard drive, however, consider getting a second hard drive for your computer. It's relatively cheap and easy to install — especially an external model. A second hard drive is a valuable addition, specifically when space is scarce.

Finally, *do not* use disk compression on your hard drive to get more space. In the hard drive's Properties dialog box (refer to Figure 23-4), note the item labeled Compress Drive to Save Disk Space. Avoid it! Do not put a check mark there! Compressed files on hard drives are something I never want to trouble-shoot. Please use one of the preceding suggestions or any of the other disk cleaning advice in this chapter before you even think about disk compression.

✔ After you burn your stuff to a CD-R, you can freely delete it from the hard drive and save yourself oodles of space.

✔ The most common disk compression troubleshooting question I get is "How can I uncompress 65GB of data from my 50GB drive?" My answer is "Only by getting a second, larger hard drive" — which, incidentally, is one of my earlier suggestions. That would have saved some time.

Disk Cleanup

Your greatest weapon in the hard drive space battle is the Disk Cleanup tool. It puts several handy features in one place, which allows you to instantly reclaim lots of hard drive space in one easy step. Here you go:

1. **Click the Start button thing.**

2. **Choose All Programs.**

3. **Choose Accessories⇨System Tools⇨Disk Cleanup.**

   Windows modestly asks which drive you want to clean. This drive should be C, the busy drive. (Clean other drives on your own.)

4. **Click OK to select Drive C.**

   A brief analysis is made. Sit and hum.

   Eventually, results are posted in a dialog box, as shown in Figure 23-5. Note the items you can select *plus* how much disk space is freed by selecting them. In the figure, you see that half a megabyte of crap is sitting in the Recycle Bin. Wow!

5. **Click to check off those items you want to delete, and thereby clean up disk space.**

   Scroll down the list and note the Compress Old Files option — a great way to save space. (File compression isn't the same as disk compression.)

6. **When you're ready to free disk space, click the OK button.**

   Are you serious?

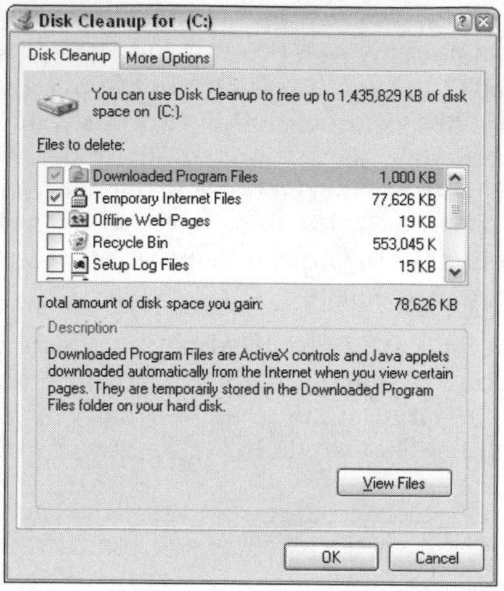

Figure 23-5:
A few of
the many
things
needing
cleaning.

7. **Click Yes when you're asked whether you're sure.**

    You're sure. By clicking the Yes button, you put Disk Cleanup to work for you, to eliminate rogue and unwanted things from your hard drive and generously give that valuable storage space back to you.

8. **Click the Yes button, if prompted, to restart Windows.**

The program ends with no fanfare; it just quits. But, your hard drive is much slimmer! (My Windows 98 system crashed when I last ran Disk Cleanup. Yes, it happens to everyone.)

If you click the More Options tab, just before Step 6, you can see three short-cuts to other places in Windows where you can delete stuff to clean up disk space. Here are the options listed:

> **Windows components:** Clicking the Clean Up button here gives you access to the Windows components part of the Add/Remove Programs dialog box. There, you can pluck through the many applications, or *applets,* that Windows uses, to remove those that you don't want to free up space.

> **Installed Programs:** Clicking the Clean Up button here takes you to the Add/Remove Programs window. There, you can remove programs you no longer use. Note that you can click to select a program listed in the Add/Remove Programs window and Windows tells you how often you use that program. Removing unused or rarely used programs can save on disk space.

> **System Restore:** Clicking the Clean Up button in this case displays a Yes-No dialog box that prompts you to remove older Restore Points.

It's a good idea to uninstall things you don't need, especially if disk space is tight. Otherwise, don't worry about it. Also, I recommend against removing older restore points. Instead, refer to Chapter 21 for information on adjusting the amount of disk space used by System Restore.

- ✔ The Disk Cleanup button in the disk drive's Properties dialog box (refer to Figure 23-4), can be clicked to run the Disk Cleanup program on that particular drive.

- ✔ No, you can't run Disk Cleanup on a CD or DVD disc; the files on those discs are read-only, and you cannot delete them.

- ✔ The Windows components and Installed Programs options (on the More Options tab) can also be accessed from the Add/Remove Programs dialog box. You open that dialog box by using the Control Panel.

- ✔ Note that selecting certain options from the scrolling list causes an additional button to be displayed in the dialog box. For example, clicking the Compress Old Files option brings up an Options button. Clicking that button displays more options or allows you to refine your choices, if you're a refined type of person.

- ✔ Use the View Files button to review what's being deleted before you click the OK button. This button appears only when certain file categories are chosen from the scrolling list.

- ✔ The Downloaded Programs option refers to internal upgrades (add-ons or plug-ins) for Internet Explorer. The option doesn't refer to any shareware or other utility you have downloaded.

Other things to try

Please, O, please, don't sit and stew over your disk space usage. The disk is there for you to use, and Windows works fine with either a full or empty hard drive. In fact, if space gets too low, Windows lets you know. If you're like most people, your computer will most likely die before you get a chance to fill up its hard drive.

Even so, and even with Disk Cleanup and all that, you can try a few more things to keep disk space usage low:

Decrease the size of the Internet cache. Set the Internet cache, or temporary file, allocation to a small size:

1. **Open the Internet Options icon in the Control Panel.**

2. **On the General tab, click the Settings button.**

   The Settings dialog box appears, as shown in Figure 23-6.

Figure 23-6:
Adjust
the Inter-
net cache
size here.

3. **Set the cache size by adjusting the slider labeled Amount of Disk Space to Use.**

4. **Click OK and then close the Internet Properties dialog box.**

Decrease the space used by the Recycle Bin. Here's how you can change the disk space allocation for your deleted files:

1. **Right-click the Recycle Bin icon on the desktop.**

2. **Choose Properties from the shortcut menu.**

   The Recycle Bin Properties dialog box is displayed, as shown in Figure 23-7. The Global tab sets the usage for all drives. Other tabs set drive usage individually, but only if you choose the Configure Drives Independently option.

3. **Adjust the slider to the left.**

   Sliding the gizmo to the left means that less disk space is used by the Recycle Bin. You can then use more disk space for your own junk.

   Or — if you want to risk it — you can click to select the option labeled Do Not Move Files to the Recycle Bin, Remove Files Immediately When Deleted. Choosing that option means that there's no chance of file recovery, but you do get more disk space that way. (No, I don't recommend it.)

4. **Click OK after making your adjustments.**

Remove the Online Services folder. Many new computers come with a folder named Online Services. It may be on the desktop directly, or it may be a folder in the Program Files folder. Wherever — it's something you can freely delete.

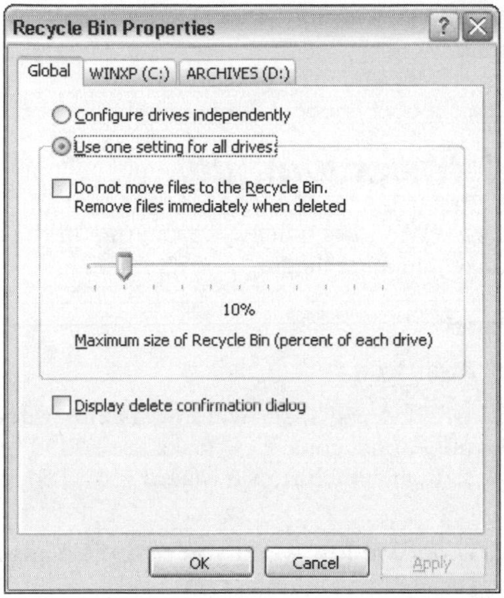

Recycle Bin Properties

Global | WINXP (C:) | ARCHIVES (D:)

○ Configure drives independently

◉ Use one setting for all drives:

☐ Do not move files to the Recycle Bin.
Remove files immediately when deleted

10%

Maximum size of Recycle Bin (percent of each drive)

☐ Display delete confirmation dialog

OK | Cancel | Apply

Figure 23-7:
Setting the
Recycle
Bin's
allocation.

The Online Services folder contains program stubs that let you sign on to various online services, such as AOL, CompuServe, and whatever else is out there. If you don't plan on using those services, zap that folder.

If you get a warning about deleting program files, it's okay. Those programs install only larger programs that you don't plan on using anyway. Yes, you have my permission to delete them — despite my constant admonition never to delete any file you didn't create yourself.

Scheduling Automatic Maintenance

You can use the Task Scheduler in Windows to arrange for ScanDisk and Defrag to be run automatically, according to your own schedule. In fact, you can arrange to have Backup and even other disk utilities running on a regular basis. This section explains everything.

✔ You can use the Windows Task Scheduler to have specific programs run at certain times or on a regular schedule.

✔ Yes, the computer needs to be *on* for the programs to run. You cannot schedule the computer to turn itself on, at least not by using the Task Scheduler.

✔ Using the Task Scheduler is considered an advanced thing.

✔ Go for it!

The Scheduled Tasks window

You cannot schedule tasks for Windows unless you can dig up the Scheduled Tasks window. Grab a mouse and start digging:

1. **Open the Control Panel.**

2. **Open the Scheduled Tasks icon.**

   And there you have the Scheduled Tasks window, as illustrated in Figure 23-8. The tasks appear as icons. New tasks are added by using the Add Scheduled Task icon, which runs a wizard (covered in the next subsection).

3. **Close the Scheduled Tasks window when you're done a-gawkin'.**

Using the Scheduled Tasks window is covered in the following subsections.

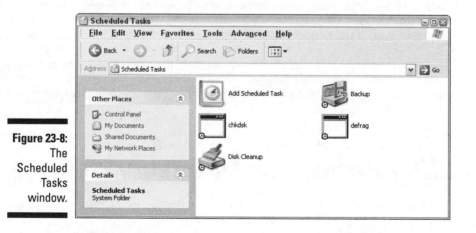

Figure 23-8: The Scheduled Tasks window.

Adding a task

To create a new scheduled task, you need to know the name of the program you want to run and then use the Scheduled Task Wizard to set things up for you. That's easy. But, for computer maintenance, there's no option for specifying the two key disk programs Defrag and Check Disk. That's hard, but I help you out in the following steps.

To add a new task to the Task Scheduler, heed these steps:

1. **Open the Scheduled Tasks window.**

   Refer to the preceding subsection for the details.

2. **Open the Add Scheduled Task icon.**

   This step runs the Scheduled Task Wizard, which helps set up the task.

3. **Click the Next button.**

4. **Locate the program you want to schedule by selecting it from the Application list, and then click the Next button.**

   You find Disk Cleanup in there, as well as Backup and any other software you have installed. You don't find Defrag or Check Disk. To find them, as well as other programs not on the list, complete this sneaky set of substeps:

   a. **Click the Browse button.**

   b. **Use the Select Program to Schedule dialog box to find the program.**

      This dialog box works like any Open or Browse dialog box. Use its controls to locate the program you want. For example:

   c. **Open Drive C (if necessary).**

   d. **Open the Windows folder.**

   e. **Open the System32 folder.**

   f. **Click to select the program named DEFRAG.EXE.**

      Or, to run Check Disk, select the program named CHKDSK.EXE.

   g. **Click the Open button.**

5. **Optionally, rename the task.**

   The wizard names the task after the program, though you're free to change it.

6. **Select how often you want to perform the task.**

   Choose Daily, Weekly, or any of the other options, as shown in Figure 23-9. Don't worry about specific times of day, the day of the week, or so on. That comes next.

7. **Click the Next button.**

8. **Set specific items for the schedule.**

   For example, if you chose to schedule your task daily, you now set the time of day and so on. For scheduling the task weekly, you choose the time of day, days of the week, and so on. The times selected depend on what you selected in Step 6.

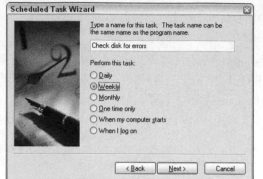

Figure 23-9:
Scheduling
options for
the task.

9. **Click the Next button.**

10. **Enter your user name and password (twice).**

    This step is required because every program must be "owned" by a user on the system. When the program runs, it's as though you were running it yourself. This is a security feature.

11. **Click the Finish button.**

    You're done.

The task now appears as an icon in the Scheduled Tasks window, and it's all set to run on schedule.

Test-running a task

Immediately after creating a new task, you should test the task. That way, you can ensure that everything was created properly and that further fine-tuning isn't necessary.

To test-run a task, right-click the task's icon in the Scheduled Tasks window. Choose Run from the pop-up menu. This command runs the task as though its scheduled time has come around. Sit back and watch and ensure that everything goes as planned. If not, you may need to tune the task.

When things go normally, the task should end and that's that. Otherwise, you may need to adjust things. To do so, right-click the task in question and choose Properties from the pop-up menu. Review the settings in the dialog box and ensure that everything is as you like it.

Checking on your task's progress

Tasks should run as scheduled. But, how would you know? Obviously, you don't want to set your alarm clock for 4:30 a.m. on Saturday and try to ensure that Check Disk is running. That's insane! Especially after that party Friday night. You and that lampshade, I tell ya. . . .

There's a simple way to confirm that tasks are running, as well as to check on how the tasks work. In the Scheduled Tasks window, choose Advanced⇨View Log. This command displays a text file, kept on disk, that lists all Scheduled Task activity.

The newest items are found at the bottom of the list. Scroll down to check on your task's status. Figure 23-10 shows the log, as it appears in the Notepad program. There, you can see that the Check Disk program, CHKDSK.JOB, was started and finished — hopefully, on schedule.

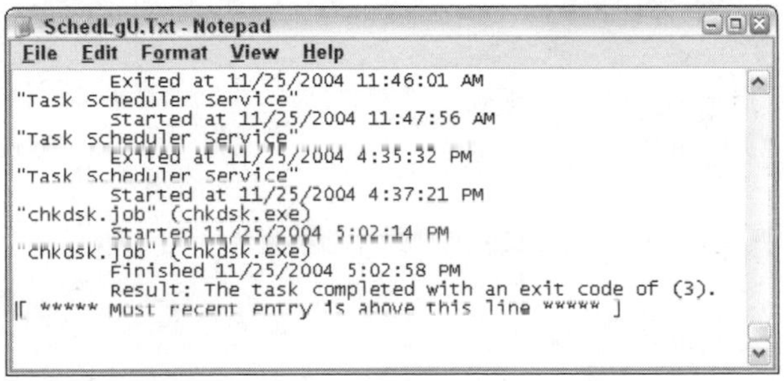

Figure 23-10:
The task
list log.

```
SchedLgU.Txt - Notepad
File  Edit  Format  View  Help
        Exited at 11/25/2004 11:46:01 AM
"Task Scheduler Service"
        Started at 11/25/2004 11:47:56 AM
"Task Scheduler Service"
        Exited at 11/25/2004 4:35:32 PM
"Task Scheduler Service"
        Started at 11/25/2004 4:37:21 PM
"chkdsk.job" (chkdsk.exe)
        Started 11/25/2004 5:02:14 PM
"chkdsk.job" (chkdsk.exe)
        Finished 11/25/2004 5:02:58 PM
        Result: The task completed with an exit code of (3).
[ ***** Most recent entry is above this line ***** ]
```

Any problems appear on the list, so be sure to review it every so often to ensure that things are running just fine.

You can also choose Advanced⇨Notify Me of Missed Tasks to have the Task Manager alert you to any tasks that, for whatever reason, have not run. (Usually, they don't run because the computer was turned off.)

Removing a task

This job is cinchy: To remove a task, and stop it from running ever again, delete its icon from the Scheduled Tasks window. Do this like you would delete anything: Click to select the icon and press the Delete key on your keyboard. Thwoop! It's gone.

Better than deleting a task, just consider disabling the task instead:

1. **Right-click the task's icon in the Scheduled Tasks window.**

2. **Choose Properties from the pop-up menu.**

    The task's dialog box appears.

3. **Click the Task tab, if necessary.**

4. **Remove the check mark by the item labeled Enabled (Scheduled Task Runs at Specific Time).**

5. **Click the OK button.**

When a task has been disabled, the tiny clock image on its icon changes to a white X in a red circle. That shows you that the task exists, but it doesn't ever run.

You can reenable the task by repeating the preceding steps and putting the check mark back in Step 4.

Chapter 24

Useful Tools and Weapons

· ·

· ·

*R*unning a computer is easy. Running a computer successfully requires effort. That has always been true, and the more complex and capable a computer is, the more difficult it is to manage the whole thing. Microsoft has done a good job of making Windows as effortless to use as possible. But, that's no excuse for ignoring things or letting problems persist until even good ol' forgiving Windows tosses in its hand and goes kaput.

Windows comes with a whole clutch of utilities, tools, programs, and techniques you can employ to help keep your computer happy. Many of these are discussed or demonstrated elsewhere in this book. This chapter is merely a locus where the rest of those utilities are explained and detailed.

Also included here are some third-party utilities, ones that I highly recommend to help you fight the endless battle with the bad guys on the Internet.

Weapons within Windows

Windows comes with so many useful and interesting utilities that I could write an entire book on each of them. The following sections detail a few of the more common utilities, with an emphasis on using them for troubleshooting your PC.

The System Configuration Utility (MSCONFIG)

The System Configuration Utility, as shown in Figure 24-1, is your main weapon in fighting the PC's startup battle. This handy dialog box provides a platform from which you can view just about anything that goes on when Windows first starts up.

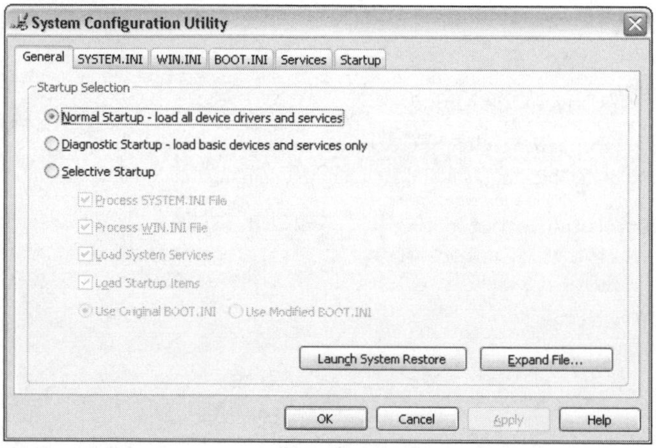

Figure 24-1:
The System Configuration Utility.

To start the utility, type **MSCONFIG** in the Run dialog box. (You can summon the Run dialog box by pressing Win+R or choosing Run from the main Start menu.)

The General tab contains three options for starting Windows:

- ✔ **Normal Startup:** This option runs the normal Windows startup.
- ✔ **Diagnostic Startup:** Run the computer in Safe mode.
- ✔ **Selective Startup:** Choose various options to enable or disable during startup (used mostly by tech support).

The SYSTEM.INI and WIN.INI tabs list settings made by older Windows programs (though most of those programs no longer run in Windows XP). The tabs remain for compatibility reasons.

The BOOT.INI tab contains startup information specific to Windows XP, including some diagnostic options.

The Services tab contains a list of services that Windows normally starts, which you can temporarily disable for diagnostic purposes.

Finally, the Startup tab contains programs that Windows automatically starts — programs you don't find by choosing Programs⇨Startup Menu.

The System Configuration utility provides that central location from which you can disable just about anything that happens when Windows starts. Keep in mind that this utility is for troubleshooting only! By turning certain things off, you can determine that the thing is causing trouble. Then, you have to fix the problem or permanently disable the thing elsewhere.

   ✔ Refer to Chapter 8 to troubleshoot Startup programs.

   ✔ Chapter 21 discusses permanently disabling services. Refer to the section "Processes and Services Here, There, and Everywhere."

The Device Manager

The *Device Manager* is the place where Windows lists all your computer's hardware, gives you access to the software that controls all that hardware, and tells you whether that hardware is functioning. Obviously, this is a handy and useful window to know.

Here's how to display the Device Manager:

1. **Open the Control Panel's System icon.**
2. **Click the Hardware tab.**
3. **Click the Device Manager button.**

The Device Manager lists hardware by category, as shown in Figure 24-2. To see specifics, you must open a category. To see your PC's specific disk drive information, click the plus sign [+] to the left of the Disk Drives item.

To find information on a specific piece of hardware, you must double-click to open that hardware item. Doing so displays the item's Properties dialog box, where you can make adjustments to the hardware or just check to see whether it needs attention.

You can use the Driver tab in the Properties dialog box to install or update a new driver (software) for the device. You do that by clicking the Update Driver button (though it's assumed that you already have the driver downloaded or available on a CD or floppy disk).

You can also disable a device, which prevents Windows from loading software or recognizing the device the next time Windows starts up. That way, you can troubleshoot the device or its driver software; if the computer works better without the device enabled, you have a problem with the device.

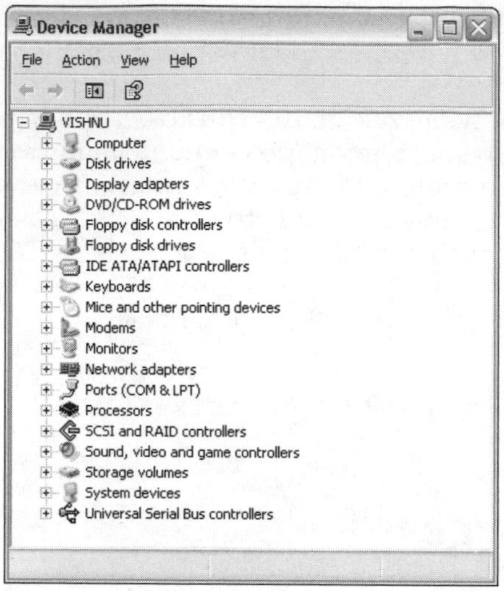

Figure 24-2:
The Device
Manager.

When a device isn't working, it's flagged in the Device Manager. That category with the bad hardware is open and the hardware flagged by a yellow circle icon. In the middle of the yellow circle is an exclamation point. That's your key to instantly find bad hardware. To get further information, double-click to open that item. In its Properties dialog box, you see a detailed description of what's going wrong.

✔ The Device Manager *does not* list printers. For those, you must open the Printers window. That's where new printers are installed, drivers updated, and problems dealt with. Refer to Chapter 14 for the details.

✔ The Device Manager doesn't list all hardware problems. Some hardware trouble cannot be detected by Windows, so just because the hardware isn't flagged as bad, don't assume that it's working properly.

✔ Similar information about devices also appears in the various Control Panel items. For example, the Display Properties dialog box also has a link to information about your PC's video hardware, the same as the information found in the Device Manager.

✔ The supersecret, budding-guru, command-line way to summon the Device Manager is to type DEVMGMT.MSC into the Run command's dialog box.

System Information

The System Information tool is a handy thing to have — plus, it's a great launching spot for running many other tools or utilities in Windows.

Start the System Information program by clicking the Start button and choosing All Programs⇨Accessories⇨System Tools⇨System Information.

The System Information tool's main job is to report about your computer, as shown in Figure 24-3. This dialog box provides a central location for listing all sorts of information about your computer's hardware, software, environment, and the various applications you run.

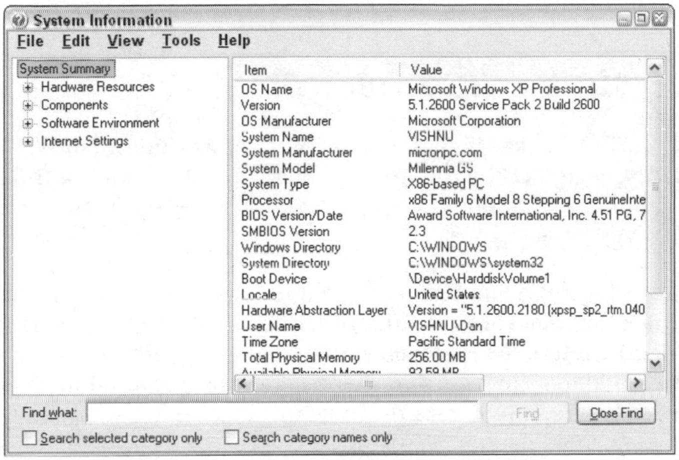

Figure 24-3: The System Information tool.

For example, to see whether your computer has any hardware conflicts, open the Hardware Resources item (click the [+] to its left) and then select Conflicts/Sharing. The System Information tool then lists any shared or conflicting devices in your computer.

Another bonus to this tool is its incredible Tools menu. Plenty of other handy Windows tools are listed on that menu, including some or all of the following:

- **DirectX Diagnostic Tool:** A massive (and relatively unknown) utility for analyzing various gaming components of your PC, as controlled by the DirectX standard.

- **Disk Cleanup:** Discussed in Chapter 23.

- **Dr. Watson:** Covered later in this chapter.

- **File Signature Verification Utility:** Confirms that signed files are valid. A *signed* file contains a digital signature, designed to ensure that the file is sent by a responsible source and performs the advertised duty (that the file isn't a virus or worm or Trojan horse, for example).

- **Hardware Wizard:** Runs the Add New Hardware Wizard.

- **Net Diagnostics:** Runs a troubleshooter or diagnostic tool (as part of the Help system).

- ✔ **Network Connections:** Opens the Network Connections window.
- ✔ **Registry Checker:** Similar to ScanDisk, but used for the Registry.
- ✔ **ScanDisk:** Checks your disk drives for errors (refer to Chapter 23).
- ✔ **System Configuration Utility:** Covered elsewhere in this chapter.
- ✔ **System File Checker:** Covered elsewhere in this chapter.
- ✔ **System Restore:** Discussed in detail in Chapter 4.

The System File Checker

The System File Checker is perhaps the most powerful tool in Windows, one that is, sadly, neglected by too many people. In fact, if more of those tech-support wieners knew about it, they would rarely recommend reinstalling Windows. Ever!

SFC stands for System File Checker. What it does is to verify the condition of the core files that make up the Windows operating system. When any file is missing or corrupted, it's replaced with a fresh new copy. So, in a way, running SFC is like reinstalling Windows, but only when necessary and without having to delete anything.

The SFC utility is a command-line program, though it also uses graphical windows. Even so, to run SFC, you must start up a command-prompt window. Follow these steps:

1. **Get a copy of the original Windows XP CD.**

    You must have a copy of the CD to run SFC. This is the original CD you used to install Windows.

    If you don't have the Windows CD, don't run SFC! The program relies upon the original CD for replacing files. No CD, no SFC.

2. **From the Start menu, choose All Programs⇨Accessories⇨Command Prompt.**

    This step opens a Command Prompt, or DOS, window on the screen.

    Commands must be typed — and spelled properly. If you make a mistake, use the Backspace key to back up and erase.

    You can type in upper- or lowercase. This book uses UPPERCASE for the examples.

    The Enter key is pressed after typing a command to send that command off to Windows.

3. **Type** SFC /SCANNOW **and press the Enter key.**

   That's **SFC**, a space, a slash, and then **SCANNOW** with no space between SCAN and NOW. The line doesn't end in a period. Press the Enter key after confirming that you have typed it all correctly.

   Follow the instructions on the screen.

   This operation can take quite a while!

4. **If any files need replacing, SFC asks for the Windows CD to be inserted. It does this so that it can read a replacement file from that disc.**

   Inserting the CD may start the Upgrade or Install program. Just close that window and continue.

   SFC may pull some false alarms and not recognize the CD after it's inserted. If so, click the Retry button. (This may happen several times.)

5. **When SFC is finished, you see another command prompt that is waiting for you to type another command.**

   SFC is done. You can close the command-prompt window.

6. **Type** EXIT **and press the Enter key.**

   The EXIT command closes the command-prompt window.

I recommend running SFC only when you suspect system trouble that even System Restore seems unable to fix. In that case, SFC may be able to pull needed files from the Windows CD and put the system back into order.

I don't recommend running SFC as regular system maintenance! Consider it a disaster-recovery tool only.

Automatic Updates

Every so often, Microsoft releases *updates* for Windows, also called *patches.* These are introduced to address specific issues, mostly security-related problems or exploited weaknesses in Windows or programs like Internet Explorer. This isn't unusual: Every major operating system developer releases patches and updates — though some not as frequently as Microsoft!

Once upon a time, automatically updating Windows with the various updates or patches was a risky thing. But, it's my opinion that Microsoft has recently gotten better at playing the patching game. Therefore, I think that it's a good idea to turn the Automatic Updates feature on. Here's how to check on that:

1. Open the Control Panel's System icon.

You can also display this icon by right-clicking the My Computer icon on the desktop and then choosing the Properties command from the short-cut menu.

2. Click the Automatic Updates tab.

The dialog box looks like the one shown in Figure 24-4. This is where you can tell Windows how often or whether to automatically update your computer.

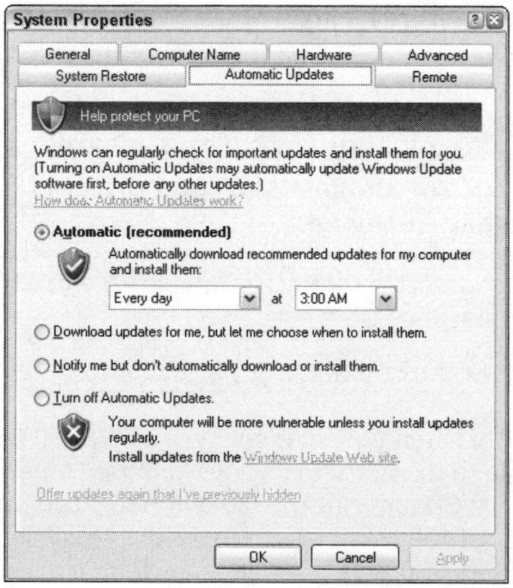

Figure 24-4: Automatically update Windows.

3. Set Automatic Updates for your needs.

If you have updated or have Windows XP SP2, I highly recommend that you set Automatic Updates to Automatic, as shown in Figure 24-4. Otherwise, choose whichever options best suit you.

4. Click OK when you're done.

Obviously, Automatic Updates requires an Internet connection. If you have broadband, the update checking goes on automatically. Otherwise, it works in the background, by sneakily downloading information whenever you're connected to the Internet.

✔ You can also display the Automatic Updates dialog box by opening the Automatic Updates icon in the Control Panel.

✔ If you're using an older version of Windows, I advise you *not* to update. If the system is running smoothly — plus, if you have a firewall and antivirus software installed, you're probably okay and don't need any updates that may imbalance your computer system.

✔ If your computer is running in a mission-critical situation, don't update it — especially if it's not connected to the Internet.

✔ In fact, most security warnings are related to the Internet. If your computer isn't on the information superhighway, most of the security releases don't apply to you. Choose the option labeled Turn Off Automatic Updates.

Dr. Watson

I am not a Dr. Watson fan — ever since he first showed up in Windows Version 3 for DOS, back in 1993. At first, he sounded like some miraculous Peter Norton-like tool for finding out what's wrong with Windows. (Yes, it had trouble even back then.) But, no, Dr. Watson is merely a disaster-reporting tool — a CNN for your computer that neither makes the news nor resolves any issues.

To start Dr. Watson, type **DRWTSN32** into the Run dialog box. This action displays the complex-looking Dr. Watson interface, as shown in Figure 24-5. Looks powerful, right? But keep in mind that Dr. Watson only reports on the situation; he doesn't fix anything.

Overall, I assume that the Dr. Watson tool has some value, though I personally don't find it good for much.

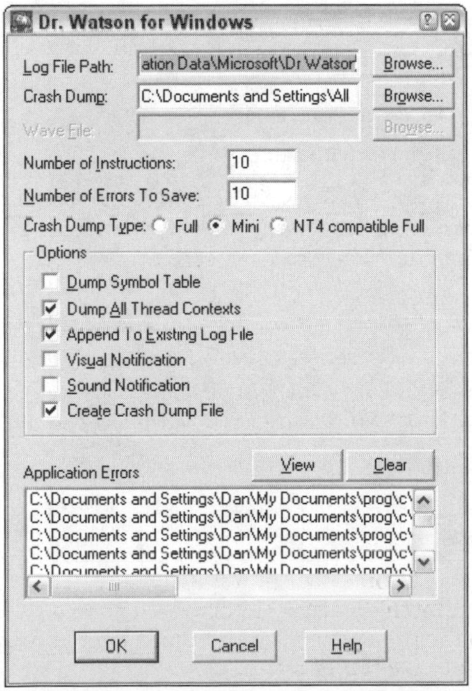

Figure 24-5:
The impressive-looking Dr. Watson interface.

Welcome to Safe Mode

The only question I have is "Why does Windows need a 'safe' mode?" Shouldn't it be safe to use Windows all the time? And, if it's called Safe mode, does that make the normal mode of operation *Dangerous mode?"*

Once again showing a knack for improperly naming things, Microsoft gives Windows users *Safe mode*. (It's an industry-wide, not just Microsoft, problem with naming things.) Safe mode really should be called Diagnostic mode or even Slim mode because in Safe mode you can run Windows with no extra drivers or options, which are often the cause of any trouble you may be experiencing.

Starting in Safe mode

You have many ways to get into Safe mode in Windows.

The first way happens under Windows own decree: The computer just starts up in Safe mode. You can tell by the low resolution plus the words *Safe mode* in all four corners of the screen, as shown in Figure 24-6. When that happens, Windows is telling you that something is wrong. Indeed, it may even announce why it's going into Safe mode before you even see Safe mode.

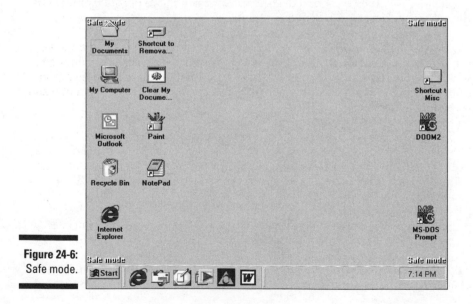

Figure 24-6: Safe mode.

The second way you can enter Safe mode is manually, when the computer starts. Immediately after the "Starting Windows" text message appears, you can press the F8 key to see a startup menu. (I cover this subject in Chapter 8.) You can select one of the Safe mode options from that menu to start your computer in Safe mode.

Finally, you can direct the computer to start in Safe mode from the System Configuration Utility. On the General tab, if you select the Diagnostic startup, Windows starts in Safe mode the next time around. (Conversely, if you would rather have Windows not start in Safe mode, select Normal from the list in the System Configuration Utility.)

✔ Accept and realize that you use Safe mode to *fix things*. That's it. You don't work on projects there. You don't gather and reply to e-mail. You fix something and then start the computer in Normal mode.

✔ Starting Safe mode may be one of the few times you see the Administrator's account appear as a login option for Windows. Log in as the Administrator only if you're directed to do so in order to fix some problem.

Fixing things in Safe mode

The idea behind Safe mode is that, with various options and features disabled, it's easier for you to work at fixing them. You can change certain settings that the computer doesn't allow you to change when you're in Normal mode.

For example, I recommend using Safe mode if someone has changed the settings on the Appearance tab in the Display Properties dialog box. Suppose that someone has changed the text to be very small or changed the graphics to be very big or use black-on-black text. You can fix all this in Safe mode and restore your settings.

If the computer just spontaneously goes into Safe mode, check the Device Manager. If your computer has a problem, the device appears flagged with a yellow circle and an exclamation point. Open that device by double-clicking it and then read what the problem is. Follow those instructions to fix the problem.

Generally speaking, disabling a device in the Device Manager or reinstalling an older device driver is the solution that puts the computer back to normal.

Note that you change just about any Windows settings in Safe mode. Those changes may not appear immediately, as they would when Windows is run normally. The changes are made nonetheless; you see their effects when you restart the computer and return to Normal mode.

- ✔ Yes, many things don't work in Safe mode. Those things, such as networking, are disabled to provide a better environment for troubleshooting.

- ✔ Refer to Chapter 4 for more information on running System Restore to fix problems in Windows XP.

- ✔ The changes you make may not have any visual effect in Safe mode, but they have an effect when you return to Normal mode.

You're done with Safe mode

When you have finished making Safe mode corrections, simply restart your PC. Do this part properly! Even Safe mode must be restarted the way Windows normally is.

When your computer comes back to life, the problem should be fixed. Then, you can get on with your duties.

If the computer continues to boot into Safe mode, check the Device Manager. Read any startup messages that appear. Open the System Configuration

---

The Windows XP Recovery Console

There's a special tool you can use specifically for troubleshooting massive Windows problems. This tool belongs only to the Windows XP operating system, so it's called the Windows XP Recovery Console. It's nothing fancier than a beefy version of the command prompt (like DOS), but with a whole boatload of utilities for fixing problems in Windows.

To install the Recovery Console, you need the original Windows CD. (It cannot be installed without the CD.) Insert the CD into your CD-ROM drive. Open the Run dialog box and type the following command, where *D* is the drive letter of the CD-ROM drive containing the Windows CD:

```
D:/I386/WINNT32.EXE /CMDCONS
```

Follow the instructions on the screen to complete installation.

After installing, the Recovery Console appears as an option when you start your computer. One option is to run Windows XP; the other, to run the Recovery Console. (You may see other operating systems as well, depending on how your computer is configured to start.)

When you run your computer with the Recovery Console, you can use its command-line tools to fix certain problems in Windows or to diagnose certain situations that would be difficult to observe when Windows runs normally. The list of available commands is extensive; use only those that you're recommended to use by your dealer, tech support, or computer guru.

To close the Recovery Console and restart your computer, type the **EXIT** command at the prompt and press the Enter key.

Utility (MSCONF, which is covered elsewhere in this chapter) and switch back to the Normal Startup option to see whether that helps.

As a next-to-last resort, connect to the Internet and visit the Microsoft Knowledge Base (refer to Chapter 5) to see whether you can find a solution to your predicament there.

Internet Tools

Hooking your computer up to the Internet opens the entire online universe for your perusal, information, and play. That's good. What's bad is that being on the Internet opens up your personal computer for lots of nasty things to creep in and "play." Yes, that's something you want to avoid.

Windows has a handful of tools and techniques to help keep you safe from the nasty things on the Internet. But, most of the tools you really need must come from somewhere else.

I have split up the necessary tools you need into five categories:

- ✔ Antivirus
- ✔ Anti-spam
- ✔ Anti-spyware
- ✔ Anti-hijacking
- ✔ Firewall protection

Each of these categories is covered in the five following subsections, along with my recommendations on how best to protect your PC.

Antivirus

Viruses are nasty programs that come into your computer to do evil things. They may, for example, program your computer to relay spam or unwanted e-mail. The virus may program your computer to attack other computers. Or, it may simply propagate itself, by sending more viruses out to everyone in your e-mail address book. Viruses are nasty!

To protect yourself against viruses, you need antivirus software. This software isn't a part of Windows, though many computer dealers often bundle either the Norton AntiVirus program or the McAfee Virus Protection program. Many other sources of antivirus programs are on the Internet. Table 24-1 lists some popular ones.

Table 24-1	Antivirus Programs and Sources
Program	Web Site
Avast	www.avast.com
AVG	www.grisoft.com
Kaspersky	www.kaspersky.com
McAfee Virus Protection	www.mcafee.com
Norton AntiVirus	www.symantec.com/avcenter/

Use antivirus software to scan your system, but not all the time. Some antivirus programs allow you to manually scan the system every so often. That's good. But, antivirus programs that constantly scan the system waste resources. Unless your computer is in a high-risk situation, such as in a very public place, don't bother with a constant scan.

Configure your antivirus software to scan all incoming files, such as e-mail attachments and programs downloaded from the Internet. Those two door-ways are the most common paths for viruses and other nasty programs to mince into your PC.

With antivirus software installed and running on your PC, you have one less thing to worry about and one less major problem to troubleshoot.

- ✔ Cleaning up after a computer virus requires great effort and lots of time. It's not something you want to do. In fact, many folks pay huge sums of money to others to clean up a virus mess.

- ✔ Virus programs generally require you to subscribe to a service to keep your computer up-to-date when fighting the latest viruses. Do not neglect to pay for these services! They're worth every penny!

- ✔ You can have two antivirus programs installed on your PC, though you don't run both at the same time. For example, use Norton to do a full system scan, and then use Kaspersky to do the same thing. Often times, one antivirus program catches something the other one misses.

- ✔ Avoid Web-based antivirus scans. Sure, some of them may be good and legitimately do their job. I just don't feel right recommending such a thing to you.

- ✔ Refer to Chapter 21 for information on disabling antivirus software so that you can install new programs on your computer.

Anti-spam

I suppose that spam is a common enough term these days that I don't need to explain it, but I will anyway: *Spam* is unwanted e-mail. Or, call it junk e-mail. It floods nearly 50 percent of the average computer user's e-mail inbox every day. In fact, they say that more than 90 percent of all e-mail that's sent will be spam, or unwanted and unrequested advertising.

The best way to deal with spam is to create *e-mail filters,* which Outlook Express called *Mail Rules,* to help weed out which messages are advertising and which are legitimately intended for your own eyeballs. This task can be tough because spam-senders are often very clever at disguising their messages.

✔ Refer to my book *PCs For Dummies* (Wiley Publishing, Inc.) for more information on creating mail rules to block spam and other suspect e-mail messages.

✔ I suggest avoiding such major spam-fighting tools as Earthlink Spaminator. Those packages tend to be overly aggressive at blocking legitimate e-mail as well as spam.

✔ I also recommend avoiding those e-mail verification services that require legitimate e-mail users to do a puzzle or reply to a secret message before they can send you e-mail. Although such services are popular and they do work, many people (such as myself) who are very busy don't have time to deal with such things.

✔ Legitimate e-mail that is misinterpreted as spam is referred to as *ham* by the computer geeks.

✔ A good program that helps eliminate spam before it even gets on your computer is Mailwasher. Unlike having to writing e-mail filters, you can train Mailwasher to sort out the good from the bad e-mail. This program is free to download and use for 30 days. I recommend it!

```
www.mailwasher.net
```

Anti-spyware

Spyware is a rather new category for computer software. Basically, it's unwanted programs that are installed on your computer to monitor your Internet habits. Based on that information, specific advertising is then targeted to you. Although this doesn't sound malevolent, many spyware programs are devious and impossible to uninstall. Plus, often people don't really want such software on their computer without their knowledge.

The best way to get rid of spyware is with anti-spyware software. Table 24-2 lists some packages I recommend. Be careful out there! Some programs that advertise themselves as anti-spyware programs are, in fact, spyware of the worst type!

Table 24-2	Recommended Anti-Spyware Software
Program	*Web Site*
Ad-aware	`www.lavasoft.de`
Spybot	`www.safer-networking.org/en/index.html`
Spyware Blaster	`www.javacoolsoftware.com/spywareblaster.html`

✔ Computer feeling slow? Chances are that *massive quantities* of spyware software are running on your computer — sometimes, multiple copies of the same program running at once!

✔ It seems like fighting spyware would also be a function of antivirus software, but it's just not the case. Spyware, though it's just as evil, isn't the same thing as a virus. Even so, recently I have noticed that many antivirus programs now offer anti-spyware protection as well.

How you can tell whether your computer has spyware

The frustrating thing about spyware is that you cannot really tell what's spyware and what isn't. Consider this: Most spyware isn't advertised as such. It's given away freely on the Web, often as some friendly tool or shopping helper. Though some spyware sneaks into your computer, most of it is downloaded by choice: shopping assistants, calendar minders, free utilities, free wallpaper or desktop backgrounds, free screen savers, or any of a number of seemingly innocent programs.

The problem occurs, and you probably first notice that you have a problem, when you try to uninstall the software you downloaded. That's when you discover that the program keeps coming back — like an unwanted cat! Nothing you try removes the program! You complain to the developer, and it claims that you agreed to keep the program on your computer when you downloaded it — which you did, but who reads all those software licensing agreements?

The next step you need to take is to get the anti-spyware software that this book recommends. Run that software. Then, remove the unwanted program. Then, use the SpywareGuide link (shown in the nearby "Anti-spyware" section) to confirm any and all programs you want to download from the Internet, to ensure that you're not downloading more spyware into your computer.

✔ To confirm whether a given program is spyware, you can use the spyware database at SpywareGuide:

```
www.spywareguide.com/
```

✔ Some spyware advertises itself as helpful programs you download. I could name a few of these programs, but the likelihood is that my publisher or I would be sued for calling those well-known spyware programs "spyware" in a book. This gives you just a small taste of how nasty these programs — and their developers — can be.

✔ The best way to remove some unwanted program, which is usually spyware, is with anti-spyware software.

Anti-hijacking

I almost included this category with spyware because it's that similar. On the Internet, a *hijacking* program is one that takes the home page you have selected and changes it to some other page on the Internet — generally, some advertising portal or, often, pornography.

The annoying thing: You didn't make the change. You don't even remember making the change.

Even more annoying: You cannot change the home page back. Or, if you do, the next time you run Internet Explorer, the annoying home page is back from the dead! Creepy!

What's happening is that your Web browser's home page has been hijacked. This can be done legitimately; most Web browsers, including Internet Explorer, *temporarily* reassign the home page if an update or newer version is available. But, that happens only once. Otherwise, hijacking occurs all the time and often to Web pages that have nothing to do with legitimate computer products.

There are two ways to fix a hijacked home page. The first is to run anti-spyware software. Most of those products have anti-hijacking features installed because hijacking the home page is a common spyware technique. The second way is to get anti-hijacking software. The one I recommend is Hijack This, though it's very technical. You can find it at

```
www.spywareinfo.com/~merijn/downloads.html
```

Finally, there's a technical thing you can try. Most hijacking is done by modifying a file named HOSTS.TXT in Windows. The file is used to associate certain IP addresses with host names, which can be handy for some networking operations, but is mostly used to hijack Web pages.

To open HOSTS, browse to this folder:

```
windows\system32\drivers\etc
```

The HOSTS file is plain text, so you can use Notepad to open it. When you do, peruse the bottom of the file for any new entries. What you may see in the case of a hijacked Web page is something like this:

```
365.10.23.145          google.com
```

What this entry does is to redirect any traffic intended for the Google domain to the server at the IP address 365.10.23.145 — which is probably some bad guy's address.

When your home page has been hijacked, look for an entry matching the home page Web site. If you find it there, just delete that line in Notepad. Then, save the HOSTS file back to disk.

Note that this may be only a temporary solution: The program that rewrote the HOSTS file may do it again when the computer restarts. That's why I recommend using anti-spyware or anti-hijacking software first.

- ✔ Refer to Chapter 18 for information on changing the home page — legitimately — in Internet Explorer.

- ✔ Yeah, if you know what you're doing, the HOSTS file can be a fun place to play. But, don't mess with it! Most anti-spyware programs assume that any modification to the HOSTS file is *bad*.

TIP

A quick way to tell whether a tool is crap

It's a scary world out there on the Internet. Tons of tools and helpers are available, many of which seem like they do good. Or, do they? It's often hard to tell whether a promising tool does what it advertises or whether it may cause more trouble than it's worth.

Whenever I encounter a computer utility that I want, I do a brief test. First, I go to Google and do a quick search for the tool's name. For example, if the tool is named AntiBlorf, I type "AntiBlorf" into the Search text box on the Google main page (www.google.com) and click the Search button. I then peruse the results to see whether anything might be wrong.

Generally speaking, if a program is junk, the search results shown by Google indicate so. In the listing, you find references to the program name you entered, along with various bad words and accusations. Typically, the opinionated links go to various online forums, where disappointed users discuss the software. Or, if the software is good, users praise the program. Either way, you get some good feedback right away.

Firewall protection

The Internet was designed by people who were very trusting of each other. Picture the Internet as a big neighborhood where all the neighbors originally liked each other so well that they not only left their doors and windows unlocked, they also left them all open all the time. In a trusting environment — and especially one in a nice warm climate — that's a perfectly acceptable thing to do. But, not these days.

The Internet is still designed with all open doors and windows. To close those doors and windows, you need extra software on your computer, in the form of a firewall. The firewall guards those open doors and windows — officially called *ports* — to limit access both in and out to only those programs you allow.

Windows XP comes with a firewall, though its abilities are rather limited. The SP2 update comes with a better firewall, though it monitors only incoming traffic. Therefore, to truly protect your computer, you need a third-party firewall. Norton makes one. McAfee makes one. And, you can get a decent free one, from Zone Labs, named Zone Alarm.

    www.zonelabs.com

The idea behind using a firewall is to train it to recognize which programs are okay to use the Internet and which are not. This is done as you use the firewall software. As you do, you see a pop-up window asking whether such-and-such a program can access such-and-such a service on the Internet, similar to what's shown in Figure 24-7. You then click a button to allow or deny access or, if access has already been denied, you click OK, as shown in Figure 24-7. That's how the firewall is trained, and how it works.

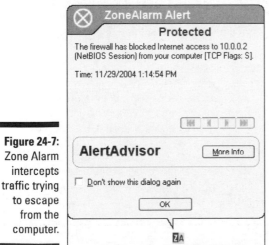

Figure 24-7: Zone Alarm intercepts traffic trying to escape from the computer.

When you get a request for Internet access — in or out — from an unknown or unlikely program, you click the Deny button. Deny! Deny! Deny! That's how you keep the bad guys out of your computer.

Chapter 25

The Benefits of Backup

*B*ackup is drudgery only if you have never, ever, had a disk problem at any time in your entire life, and maybe even before then. Otherwise, those who use Backup and have benefited from its goodness sing the Daily Praises of Backup song every doo-dah day:

> O Sing we now of old Backup
>
> That good utility;
>
> Our data's safe, no disk blow-up
>
> Will cause anxiety

So, I won't sit here and debate myself while you read. Instead, if you're wise, you'll heed my backup advice. If you're foolish, you'll rip these pages from this book's binding and make yourself a most excellent paper hat.

What to Back Up, What Not to Back Up

A *backup* is nothing more than a safety copy — a duplicate — of your files, data, and important stuff. It exists "just in case." So, if anything happens to the original, you can always rely on the good old trusty backup. Sounds kind of wholesome, doesn't it?

The main problem with backing up is that performing the operation is time-consuming. (In the old days, backing up to floppy disk was labor-consuming as well because you had to continually exchange floppy disks.) Backing up is time-consuming because it must create a fresh copy of all the information on your hard drive. But, does it need to be *all* the information?

Back up everything! Purists argue that a full hard drive backup is the only way to fully restore your computer. After all, if a virus infects a slew of files, the easiest way to restore those files is from a full backup.

Back up just your stuff! On the other hand, why back up files that you can easily copy from an installation CD? If the worst happens, you can reinstall Windows and reinstall drivers and applications. Then, use the backup disks to reinstall all your own stuff. That too works, and it saves backup media and time as well.

Which option do you choose? How about a compromise? When you first do a backup, back up *everything* — the entire hard drive. From then on, just back up your own stuff. If you ever revamp the system or install upgrades, do another full disk backup.

Then again, the choices and options available for backing up are limitless, so it depends on your patience, experience, and willingness to do the backup in the first place.

- There's no need to back up the applications installed on your computer; it's easier just to reinstall them. No, the most important thing on your computer is your data — the stuff you created and stored.

- You can restore Windows and your software only if you have a copy of the original installation CD or a reinstall disk that came with the computer. Don't throw that stuff out!

Various backup terms

Backup programs may use some interesting terminology. Sometimes, the backup manual explains the terms; sometimes, it doesn't. If not, here are my own handy definitions of various backup terms.

Full backup: This term refers to a complete backup of the entire hard drive. All the files backed up are marked "backed up" by the computer. That way, you can easily spot new files created after the backup.

Specific backup: Only those files that are selected are backed up.

Incremental backup: This term refers to a backup of only those files created or modified since the last full backup.

Differential backup: This type is the same as an Incremental backup in that only files modified since the last backup are archived. However, unlike an incremental backup, the files backed up are *not* marked as having been backed up (a rare option to select).

Copy: Files are backed up, but they're not marked as having been backed up, as they would be for a full backup.

✔ Keep copies of all the software you install on your computer. I keep the
     original CDs in the boxes the software came in.

How to Back Up

A *backup* is nothing more than a file copy. Here's how to back up any file:

   1. **Open the My Documents folder.**

   2. **Click to select any document.**

      It doesn't matter which one.

   3. **Press Ctrl+C to copy the file.**

   4. **Press Ctrl+V to paste the file.**

      The file is copied into the same folder, but given a new name with the
      prefix Copy of.

What you have done is to duplicate a file. It isn't a shortcut because the
duplicate is identical to the original: same size, type, dates, and contents,
but different names because two files in the same folder cannot share the
same name.

The problem with this type of backup is that there's no safety. Sure, you can
use the backup if something happens to the original file. But, if the folder is
deleted or the entire hard drive is damaged, the backup or file copy is useless.

No, the key to backing up is to store the backup on another media: a CD-R,
DVD-R, a Zip disc, a flash drive, a disk drive on the network, or a second
physical drive inside of or attached to the computer.

You may freely delete the duplicate file you just created.

   ✔ *Media* is a general term describing a place where information can be
     written, such as a hard drive, floppy disk, CD-R, or Zip disc.

   ✔ Also included in backup media is the tape drive, though tape drives aren't
     as common (or as cheap) as they were just a few short years ago.

   ✔ The best backups are those you can make to a separate media, such as
     any removable disk or an external disk drive. That way, you can remove
     and lock up the disk, just to be safe.

   ✔ Simply copying a file counts toward creating a backup. In fact, when I "back
     up" this book's files at the end of the day, I simply copy the files' folder
     to a flash memory drive. I just copy and paste using Windows Explorer.

✔ If you have a second physical hard drive, you can back up your files to it rather than to a removable disk. This method isn't as safe as using a removable disk (which can be locked in a fire safe), but it's better than merely copying the files to the same disk. Refer to Chapter 15 to find out how to tell a physical disk from a logical disk.

✔ Expensive software and hardware backup solutions are available, though they're mostly used by large institutions or corporations. These solutions include DAT drives, RAID drives, and other high-end methods of data protection that you needn't worry about.

Backing up without backup software

To merely *copy* a group of files (to back up without using backup software), you just need to drag and drop the clutch of icons from one disk to another — from the hard drive to the CD-R disc or from the hard drive to a Zip disc. It's a simple file-copy operation, and it works.

This process has two limitations. The first is that it's up to you to determine whether all the files will fit on the destination disk. For example, you cannot copy 1,300MB of your stuff to a 720MB CD-R disc. It just doesn't work. Ditto for copying 400MB of files to a 250MB Zip disc. No amount of suitcase-sitting gets those extra bytes on the disc. No way!

The second limitation is simply automation: "Real" backup software automates the process. Plus, it may even let the backup span across multiple disks, which certainly saves some time.

In any event, suppose that you want to back up using the old file-copy method:

First, decide what you want to back up. Because space is limited, perhaps you should back up only the contents of the My Documents folder. Or, if you suppose that's too big, back up perhaps only a handful of folders in which you have current projects.

Second, determine the size of those folders. You can do this task by examining the folder's Properties dialog box. The following steps assume that you're trying to gauge the size of the My Documents folder:

1. **Open the My Documents icon on the desktop.**

   To calculate the folder's size, you must visit the *parent* folder, the folder that contains the folder you're working in. You do that by clicking the Up Folder button.

2. **Click the Up Folder button.**

3. **Right-click the My Documents folder.**

4. **Choose Properties from the pop-up menu.**

   If you see the Target tab in the folder's Properties dialog box, you have stumbled across one of the many Windows shortcut icons. Heed these steps:

   a. Click the Find Target button.

   b. Repeat Steps 3 and 4.

   You should see the General tab of the folder's Properties dialog box, as shown in Figure 25-1. Note the size! In Figure 25-1, it's 124MB, which is enough to fit on a 250MB Zip disc or a CD-R disc.

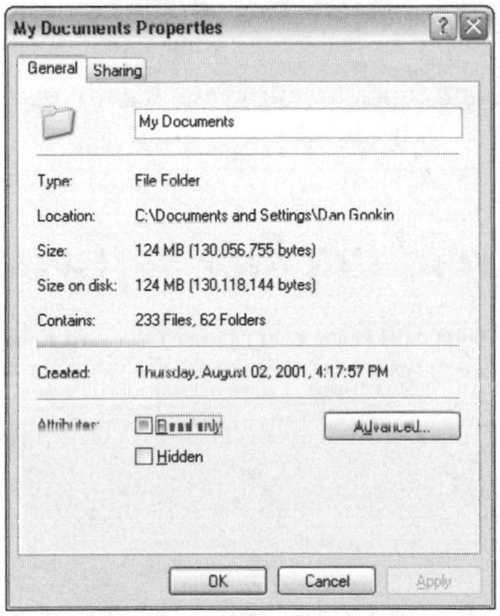

Figure 25-1:
A folder's
Properties
dialog box.

5. **Close the Properties dialog box.**

6. **Close any other open windows, except for the original window you opened.**

Third, prepare the backup disk. Insert a CD-R disc into the drive and prepare it for receiving information (*format* the disk). Or, insert a Zip disc or scout out a location for the files on a second hard drive.

Fourth, copy the files. Use any one of the numerous Windows file-copying commands to duplicate the files on the backup disk.

Fifth, put the disk in a safe place. Remove the disk from the drive. (*Burn* the CD-R/RW disc.) Properly label it. Date it. And then, store it in a safe place.

Sixth, repeat these steps every so often. The more often you back up, the better the chances of recovery if anything nasty happens.

If these steps are all you follow to back up your stuff, that's great. The drawbacks are obvious, however. First, you can effectively back up only stuff that fits on a single disk. Second, you really can't tell the difference between what's backed up and what's new, so performing an incremental backup between major backups is fairly impossible. Third, if you're that religious about things, you may as well get real backup software anyway.

- ✔ Honestly, for backing up a single folder, project folder, or today's work, the file-copy is perhaps the best way to go.

- ✔ Not every My Documents folder handily fits on a removable disk. In fact, the computer I'm writing this book on has 1,200MB of files in the My Documents folder and its subfolders — far too many to stick on an individual disk. In those cases, you must use real backup software, which can archive files across multiple disks — and keep track of everything.

- ✔ I keep all my backup disks and tapes in a fire safe. It's not expensive or anything fancy. Most office supply stores carry them.

Backing up with real backup software

The difference between merely copying files and using real backup software is immense. Real backup software tries as best it can to automate the process, and it can access a variety of backup devices, from special tape drives to CD-R, Zip discs, and other removable disks. Plus, you have filters and other ways to select which files get backed up and how often. Backup software can organize backups by "set." You can do scheduling. It's pretty amazing stuff, and most of the programs are easy to use.

The following steps outline how you would perform a backup of your stuff using the less-than-impressive Backup program that comes with Windows XP.

1. **Start the backup program; from the Start button's menu, choose All Programs➪Accessories➪System Tools➪Backup.**

   This step normally runs the Backup or Restore Wizard. Otherwise, the Backup Utility window is seen. (To return to the wizard, which I recommend, choose Tools➪Switch to Wizard Mode from the Backup Utility window's menu.)

2. **Click the Next button.**

3. **Choose the option labeled Backup Files and Settings.**

   The next screen narrows down your choices for what to back up, as shown in Figure 25-2. The first three options are very clever, as described on the screen and in the figure.

   Choose the last option to back up specific folders or projects. When you make this selection, in this or any Backup program, your next step is to select the files you want to back up. When you choose one of the first three options, the computer already knows what to back up.

4. **Click the Next button.**

5. **Select the backup media.**

   Backup media is fancy talk for the location where the backup file will be stored. You see, all the files and stuff you back up are balled into one huge thing — like a giant rubber band ball. The backup program can put that all on one large storage place or split it into pieces for storing across several CD-R discs, for example.

   Please do not choose the floppy disk option for backup! Even on a new Windows computer, it would take more floppies to store your backup files than any Office Max has at any given time. Nope: Choose a removable drive for the backup file.

   (As this book goes to press, Windows Backup does not recognize or back up to CD-R discs. This may change in the future.)

   You can use the Browse button to choose a location on a specific drive. Browse to the My Computer window, and then open the drive's icon to use that drive.

6. **Type a name for the backup set.**

   Here's where I take advantage of the long file-naming rules in Windows. I like to name a backup set by the date and contents. For example:

   ```
   2005-10-01_My Documents
   ```

   This filename tells me that the backup set was from October 1, 2005, and that it contains the My Documents folder and its subfolders. I suggest that you be equally as clever when assigning a name to your backup.

7. Click the Next button.

Review the summary screen. Use the Back button to go back and make changes, if necessary.

8. Click the Finish button.

You're not really done.

9. Watch the screen.

Or, you can go off and do something. Depending on what you're backing up, the operation could take a while. Figure 25-3 shows a sample Backup Progress window. Pay attention to the Estimated Remaining Time, as shown in the window. That tells you whether you have time to take a hot bath or whether you need to stick close to the PC.

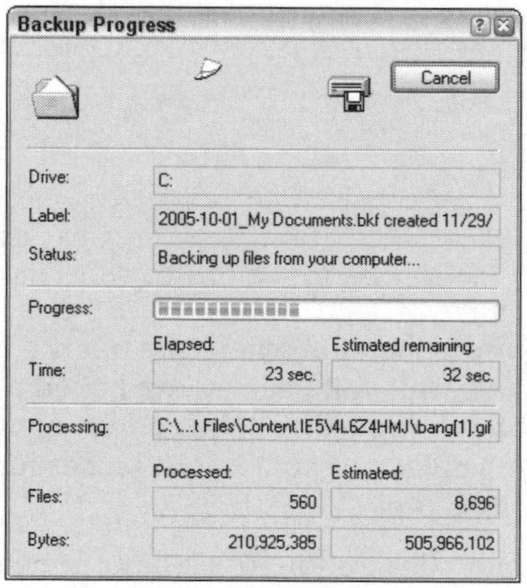

Figure 25-3:
The backup progresses and gives you something entertaining to watch.

Backup Progress				? □ ✕
				Cancel

Drive:	C:
Label:	2005-10-01_My Documents.bkf created 11/29/
Status:	Backing up files from your computer...

Progress: ▮▮▮▮▮▮▮▮▮▮▮▮▮

	Elapsed:	Estimated remaining:
Time:	23 sec.	32 sec.

Processing: C:\...t Files\Content.IE5\4L6Z4HMJ\bang[1].gif

	Processed:	Estimated:
Files:	560	8,696
Bytes:	210,925,385	505,966,102

10. Swap backup disks, if prompted.

Remove the old disk, insert a new disk, and continue.

11. Avoid reading the detailed summary screen.

12. Click the Close button.

The backup is done. But you aren't!

13. Remove the last backup disk, if necessary.

14. Store the backup disks in a safe place.

Now you're done.

Now you can sleep easier, knowing that your stuff is backed up. That safety copy means that any accident, hardware failure, virus, or runaway 13-year-old "computer genius" can damage your hard drive all it wants. You can restore your stuff quickly and easily.

- Some versions of Windows XP Home don't have a Backup program. If so, you may want to check the Windows CD to see whether the program is there. If so, you can install it per the instructions on the CD.

- Backup's sister, Restore, is covered in Chapter 4.

- One third-party backup program I can recommend is Dantz Retrospect Professional. You can download a free 30-day trial version from

  ```
  www.dantz.com/
  ```

- Try to keep within earshot of the PC when you're backing up. There are audible warnings in case something goes wrong and audible prompts for inserting new disks, if necessary.

- *Audible* means that the computer makes noise.

- It's best to back up to removable media, such as CD-R or CD-RW discs.

- I recommend using CD-R discs rather than CD-RW. The former are cheaper than the latter. So, rather than keep and reuse CD-RW discs, it makes more sense to just throw away an old CD-R when you're done with it. (Or, dispose of it properly per your location's recycling laws.)

- Get a fire safe for holding your backup disks. You can find inexpensive fire safes at most office supply stores. Note that it helps to put the back-ups *in* the safe and close the safe's door for things to work best.

When to Back Up

If you can get yourself into a regular backup schedule, great! It doesn't have to be rigorously followed. After all, if you use your computer only every so often, there's no point in backing up new stuff that doesn't exist.

For everyone, at least once, do a full backup of everything on your computer. That only needs to be redone after you install new software or update something.

Here's the schedule I recommend for diehard office environments:

- On Friday, a backup of everyone's documents and settings (see the second option in Figure 25-2). Use three sets of backup media: A, B, and C. Rotate the sets so that you do a full backup with a different set every week.

- Every day, do an incremental backup and back up only those files that were changed, modified, or added during the day. You set an incremental backup by clicking the Advanced button (after Step 7 from the preceding section). Then, choose Incremental from the drop-down list.

These two steps are the most thorough way to cover all bases. Any disk mishap means that you're out of only a day's worth of work.

For the casual user, the same type of schedule can be employed, but do the full backup once a month and the incremental backup once a week. Because you're probably not creating as much stuff as you would in an office environment, you don't need to be as rigorous about backing up. However, if you want to be really safe — and for those folks who fall between each system — also perform this operation:

> At the end of the day, do a full backup of your main project folder.

For example, at the late evening hour when I finish today's work, I shall close down Word and back up this book's folder by copying it to a flash memory disk. I could also schedule a sophisticated backup program to do that for me automatically, but it's not really a bother to perform the operation myself.

- ✔ I suppose that any schedule works as long as you stick to it.

- ✔ Also check out your backup program's automation features to see whether you can schedule backups for times when you're away from the computer.

Part IV
The Part of Tens

The 5th Wave   By Rich Tennant

"Well, that's the third one in as many clicks. I'm sure it's just a coincidence, still, don't use the 'Launcher' again until I've had a look at it."

In this part . . .

1 don't feel that a list has any legitimacy unless it has at least ten items in it. Top three lists? A joke. Anyone can come up with three things. It's silly. Top five? Nope. Odds are that if five things are on the list, there are most likely five more and the person concocting the list has done only half the research. Ten things? Whether they're the top ten or just ten things, you *know* that they're all good things — or at least that the list will have enough good things to make up for the mediocre things. The odds are in your favor!

In this, the traditional final part of a *Dummies* book, I present you with various chapters that contain lists of 10 things dealing with troubleshooting your PC. Actually, I started out with 20 things in each chapter and then pared it down to only the best 10. That way, I'm certain that you won't feel ripped off.

Chapter 26

The Ten Rules of Tech Support

In This Chapter

▶ Don't abuse technical support

▶ Keep paper and pencil handy

▶ Behave

▶ Try to get a name and number

▶ Prepare

▶ Know your computer

▶ Be brief

▶ Be patient

▶ Try to get a case number

▶ Say "Thank you"

I believe you'll find that the task of phoning tech support is made all the easier if you keep the following rules in mind.

Don't Use Technical Support As an Excuse for Not Reading the Manual or Using the Help System

Always look up your problem first in the manual or the online help. Second, visit the company's Web site and look for a Technical Support link, FAQ list, or troubleshooter. If you can find the answer there, great! Even if you don't, the tech-support people will appreciate that you have made the effort.

Have Something to Write On

This advice not only gives you a pad to doodle on while you wait on hold, but also means that you can take down notes and instructions as you're given them. You may also need to write down a case number, in case your issue is unresolved and you need to call back. That saves a great deal of repetition later and helps serve as a record of your tech-support call.

Be Nice

Each new call is a mystery to the tech-support person. The person doesn't know you, doesn't know your problem, and doesn't know how long you have been waiting on hold. None of those things is that person's fault, and he doesn't need to hear you scream about any of it.

The tech-support person is there to help you. That person didn't cause the problem and isn't out to get you. The friendlier and more informative you can be, the better for the other person.

Be Sure to Get the Person's Name and a Number Where You Can Call Back

Before diving into the problem, get some basic information about your tech-support person. Generally speaking, the person says his name when he answers the phone: "This is Satrajit in technical support. How can I help you?" Write down "Satrajit" on your notepad.

If possible, ask for a direct line on which to call back in case the call breaks off. Sometimes they have it, and sometimes they don't. Accept whatever answer the person gives you.

- ✔ If a tech-support person says that she doesn't have a direct line or that she cannot be contacted directly, it's most likely a lie. Don't get mad! The company typically has a policy not to give out direct lines, so she's being forced to lie on purpose. This is policy, not an excuse to ignore you.

- ✔ You can also try to get an employee number up front.

Prepare: Do the Research before You Call

Exhaust every possibility and potential solution on your own before you phone tech support. Ensure that you're referring to things by their proper terms. If not, carefully describe what things look like.

Have These Items Handy: Serial Number, Order Number, Customer Number

Often, tech support needs confirmation of who you are and that you have a legitimate product before you can continue. You should get items like serial numbers beforehand — especially if the serial number is on the computer's butt and the computer's butt is up against the wall under your table.

It also helps to know which version of Windows you're using. Do this:

1. **Click the Start button.**
2. **Choose the Run command.**

   Or, press the Win+R key combination, which summons the Run dialog box.
3. **Type** WINVER **into the text box.**
4. **Click OK.**

   The WinVer program displays a dialog box that details which version of Windows you're using.

You may also see which is your CD-ROM drive, whether it's D or E or whatever.

Don't Spill Your Guts

The tech-support person needs to know about the problem, not about what doom and peril await you if you can't get your computer working in time. Remember that most tech-support people are under the clock; they may have only 12 minutes to deal with you, so be as direct as possible.

Be Patient

Tech support always assumes that you don't know anything about your computer. Don't bother saying, "But I really know computers. My wife calls me a 'computer genius.'" That doesn't speed things up!

Often, tech-support people must follow a script and check things off despite your insistence that you have already done such a thing or another. Just follow along and eventually they catch up with you.

Get a Case Number

Before the call is over, try to get a case number, especially if the result is inconclusive or doesn't meet with your liking. The case number ensures that the next time you call, the support person can read over the incident and you have less repeating and reexplaining to do.

- You don't need a case number if the problem is solved.
- Some tech-support people give case numbers whether the problem is solved or not. Write it down and keep track of it for later.

Thank the Person

Whether your tech-support person solves the problem or not, thank the person for her time and efforts at assisting you. I'm not sure why, but it's just one of those things that was beaten into me as a child. (Heck, I even thanked the bullies who stole my lunch money.)

Chapter 27

Ten Dumb Error Messages

. . . .

. . . .

*H*oo, boy, this could be one long chapter! If only computers had just ten dumb error messages. But they don't. They have thousands. Back when I wrote the original *DOS For Dummies* (in 1991), I asked for and received from Microsoft a list of all possible error messages in DOS Version 5 — all 20,000 of them. And, that was only DOS! Over the evolution of Windows, I can imagine that several *hundred thousand* error messages are possible — so many that I doubt Microsoft has them all listed.

This chapter lists what I consider to be the most popular, annoying, or just frustrating dumb error messages. Obviously, it's not the entire list. That would take too much room to print — and too much booze for me to write them all down.

The Program Has Performed an Illegal Operation and Will Be Shut Down; If the Problem Persists, Contact the Program Vendor

In our modern "What is legal?" society, this error message often induces uncalled-for terror in the bosom of its victims. What is *legal*, anyway?

Relax! In the computer world, the word *illegal* is used to describe a programming operation that isn't allowed. The computer programmers could have used the words *prohibited* or *corrupt* instead, but they didn't.

Another popular word to use is *invalid*, as demonstrated by the next several error messages. The word is pronounced "in-VALid," as in "not valid." It's not "IN-valid," as in "incapacitated by illness."

Anyway! The program has done something beyond your control. Too bad. Shut down the computer. Restart Windows. Start over.

Don't bother contacting the "program vendor." Odds are that the vendor doesn't want to hear from you, knows about the bug, and won't fix it. You can try if you want, but my experience has shown that they really, really don't care. And, that's too bad.

Invalid Page Fault

This message has to do primarily with *virtual memory,* or disk storage that's used to bolster physical RAM. When a program attempts to access a chunk of virtual memory that doesn't exist, has been damaged, or is used by another program, you see the "Invalid Page Fault" gem of a message. There's nothing you can do about it.

Page is a term closely associated with virtual memory in Windows. Though virtual memory is one big, contiguous chunk of disk space, it's accessed through smaller chunks, called *pages.*

General Protection Fault

Who knows? Apparently, something is wrong, but Windows is unsure about the specifics; hence, the word *general.* From the word *protection,* you can assume that one program tried to stomp on some other program's turf. Windows responds by immediately killing the offending program and issuing this error message.

This is one instance where the Dr. Watson tool can be effective. Watson must be running in order to catch this one, and even if it is, good luck trying to find someone who can interpret Dr. Watson's results. (I'm not a big Watson fan; refer to Chapter 24.)

San Andreas Fault

I'm just checking to see whether you're paying attention.

Optional and fatal exceptional information

The *0D* in Fatal Exception 0D is a *number,* not a code. In this case, it's a hexadecimal number, which we humans would read as 13 — unlucky 13. Likewise, the 0E in Fatal Exception 0E is another number, 14. Here are the official Fatal Exception Family Error Numbers, their official names, and their brief meanings:

00 Divide Fault: Some idiot program tried to divide a number by zero.

02 NMI Interrupt: This hardware problem is too complex to explain in the space provided.

04 Overflow Trap: The washing machine is dumping water faster than the pipes can handle it.

05 Bounds Check Fault: Something is out of whack, so far that the whack woke up the microprocessor, which generated this error.

06 Invalid Opcode Fault: The microprocessor has encountered an instruction of a type it hasn't seen before. Yet, unlike the intrepid voyagers in a *Star Trek* episode, the microprocessor decides that it's time to cash in the chips and call it a day.

07 Coprocessor Not Available Fault: Because all Pentium computers come with a coprocessor installed, either the program is being run on a very old computer or the program is just being stupid.

08 Double Fault: The service changes sides in a tennis match.

09 Coprocessor Segment Overrun: The floating-point number is so large that it floats up and lodges in the cooling fan. The system has to stop while it unheats.

0A Invalid Task State Segment Fault: This message is rare ever since they banned alcohol from the fraternities over at Task State.

0B Not Present Fault: This message is commonly found in areas unaccustomed to earthquakes.

0C Stack Fault: See "Leaning Tower of Pisa Error."

10 Coprocessor Error Fault: The microprocessor misses the plane because the coprocessor is still in the bathroom *and* she has the tickets in her purse.

11 Alignment Check Fault: The computer sends a donation to the wrong political party.

Fatal Exception 0D

The first of the Fatal Exception brothers (and I suppose that Fatal Exceptions 0A, 0B, and 0C exist, but they have apparently passed on to a higher realm — possibly Unix), Fatal Exception 0D occurs when a program does something unusual or unexpected. In this case, the problem can be local to the display, to multimedia, or to other device drivers being corrupt or evil.

Fatal Exception 0E

A variation on the Invalid Page Fault error, this one crops up (again) when the program does something unusual or unexpected or somehow touches invalid or forbidden data. This error and the Invalid Page Fault error have subtle differences between them — subtle enough not to care about.

Perhaps the biggest difference between this error and the Invalid Page Fault error is that your Fatal Exception 0E requires that the computer be restarted in order to recover. Nasty.

Windows Protection Error

Whereas the other faults and errors described in this chapter seem to be rather vague (or involve virtual memory), this error is straightforward: You have a problem with a VxD, or virtual device driver. The solution is to boot into Safe mode and reinstall the virtual device driver in question (refer to Chapter 24).

Numerous other problems can also induce a Windows protection error. The error message text states the specific source, such as memory, or a specific file or the Registry, for example.

Errors Involving KERNEL32.DLL

The kernel file gets blamed for lots of problems, but it causes relatively few of them. In fact, it's because the kernel file is so robust that many mishaps are caught and error messages displayed. In other words, KERNEL32.DLL is the messenger, and we don't kill the messenger, boys and girls.

Errors tossed back at the KERNEL32.DLL file include problems with the swap file, damaged files, injured-password lists, smashed Registry entries, microprocessor troubles, bad software programs, corrupted drivers, viruses, and low disk space. The KERNEL32.DLL file catches lots of flack.

- ✔ As usual, restarting Windows fixes this problem.

- ✔ If you *clock* your CPU (run the microprocessor at a higher speed [MHz] than it's rated), you can get frequent KERNEL32.DLL errors.

- ✔ Hardware trouble — such as a hot PC, a broken power supply, static, or radio frequency noise — can also produce KERNEL32.DLL errors.

Blue-Screen-of-Death Errors

When it's a big and important error, Windows doesn't mess around with a dialog box or cute graphics and icons. No, it goes straight back to its soul: DOS! And the error message is displayed on a text screen; white text on a blue background. It's called the *Blue Screen of Death*. Generally, these errors are either fatal or important enough that they require immediate attention.

- ✔ If the error message says something along the lines of "Wait for window or press any key (or Ctrl+Alt+Delete) to reboot," then reboot. You can try waiting — especially if you feel that you can fix the problem or the problem will fix itself — but it's normally Ctrl+Alt+Delete+Pray.

- ✔ Sometimes, the error message is simply urgent and not life threatening. For example, you may be asked to reinsert a disk that the computer was using. If so, obey the instructions, and the computer continues working.

Stack Overflow

Technically a programmer's error, a stack overflow happens when a program runs low on a specific type of memory. The memory is called the *stack,* and it's used to store information for the program — like a scratch pad.

The problem is that the stack has only so much room and a sloppy or damaged program can use up that room quickly. When that happens, the microprocessor must take over and rescue the program, lest it bring down the entire computer system. The microprocessor steps in by halting the program and issuing a "stack overflow" error message.

There's nothing you can do about it other than complain to the program developer.

Divide By Zero

Another error caught by the microprocessor is the *divide by zero* error. When you try to divide something by zero on your pocket calculator, you get an *E* to indicate an error. The computer equivalent of the E is that the microprocessor steps in, stops the program, and issues a divide-by-zero error message.

No, there's nothing you can do about this error message either. You can try complaining to the software developer, but it usually blames you for it.

Bad or Missing Command Interpreter

This error is more of a DOS issue, but because the command prompt is still a part of Windows, you may see it from time to time.

The command prompt itself is a program named COMMAND.COM or CMD.COM (same thing). It's the program that displays the command prompt and runs other DOS programs and commands. Nerds would call it "the shell" program, for some obscure beach reference. Anyway.

When a DOS program closes, it's supposed to return control to COMMAND.COM. If memory space is tight or the program that was just run is corrupted, COMMAND.COM often can't be found. In that case, the DOS session hangs up and issues a "Bad or missing command interpreter" message.

Fortunately, this message doesn't mean disaster or instill the terror that it once did with DOS users. When you see the message, simply close the DOS window and get on with your life.

Chapter 28

Ten Things You Should Never or Always Do

*Y*ou should always brush your teeth before you go to bed. No! You should always brush your teeth when you get up in the morning. No, better still, just walk around all day with a toothbrush in your mouth. Constantly brush your teeth! And floss!

Oh, boy! I hate lectures. But, I thought that I would end this book with one just because I have been really good this time and haven't done much finger wagging. You see, it really isn't your fault! If you still have shame, consider reading through these ten things you should or shouldn't do. That should sate your guilt gland.

Never Run Your Computer in Safe Mode All the Time

Safe mode is for troubleshooting and fixing things. It's not the computer's standard operating mode. And though you can get work done in that mode, that's not what that mode is there for.

- ✔ I know that this advice makes sense, yet I get e-mail from people who do run their computers all the time in Safe mode.
- ✔ Perhaps it's the name. Maybe it should be called Fixing mode or Troubleshooting mode.
- ✔ Refer to Chapter 24 for more Safe mode stuff.

Never Reinstall Windows

Reinstalling Windows is a bad idea, especially considering that most problems can be fixed without having to reinstall. Only if your computer is ravaged by a virus or some other catastrophe is reinstalling the operating system ever necessary.

- ✔ Lazy tech-support people suggest reinstalling Windows just to get you off the line. Don't give up that easily!
- ✔ Also refer to Chapter 20.

Never Reformat the Hard Drive

You have no reason to do this. It's not a routine chore. It's not required. It's not a part of owning a PC.

As with reinstalling Windows, reformatting a hard drive is necessary only if the system is utterly destroyed by some catastrophe. Otherwise, this is a rare and unnecessary thing to do.

Never Randomly Delete Files You Didn't Create

I think that the emphasis in this heading is more on "randomly" than on "files you didn't create." In many instances in this book, you have permission to delete certain files that you didn't create or cause to come into being. My point is merely to be careful with what you delete. Don't be hasty. Don't assume just because you don't know what something does that it's okay to delete it. That gets people into trouble.

Never Let Other People Use Your Computer

Windows XP is designed for multiple people to use the system — as long as each person has their own account. So, give them their own account! Don't let them use your account. There's no point in that!

Treat the computer like you would your wallet: Never loan it out to anyone unless you expect to have it returned in a different condition. Your computer is a private thing. Keep it private.

✔ Especially avoid letting visitors — relatives, specifically — use your computer. All it takes is one grandnephew to infect your computer with all sorts of viruses.

✔ If visitors really want to use a computer, they can bring their own or go to the library.

✔ Be firm. Say "No."

Never Use Pirated Software

Pirated or stolen software — or any software you didn't pay for — is often the source of computer viruses. Sure, it may be "free." But, who knows what idiot put what virus on that CD-R?

Pirated games are perhaps the single greatest source of viruses in the PC world. You just run a terrible risk — not to mention that it's legally and morally wrong to steal.

Always Shut Down Windows Properly

Use the Shut Down Windows dialog box to make the operating system die a peaceful death. The idea is to try to avoid the situation where you just turn off the computer. That leads to major problems down the road.

Of course, if the system doesn't let you shut down properly, you have to just flip the power switch. Refer to Chapter 22 for some help.

Always Back Up

Whether it's just copying today's files to a removable disk or using real backup software, you would be wise to have a spare copy of your data handy (refer to Chapter 25).

Always Set Restore Points before Installing New Software or Hardware

The System Restore utility is a must-use tool for whenever you upgrade your system. Remember that change introduces problems in many computers. Having the ability to "go back in time" with System Restore is a blessing. Set those Restore Points!

Refer to Chapter 4.

Always Scan for Viruses

I highly recommend using antivirus software. It's a must. In fact, it's shocking that such a utility isn't a part of Windows. (Oh, but I could go on. . . .) Instead, I recommend investing in a good antivirus program, such as Norton AntiVirus or any program that offers updates via the Internet.

Computing in this decade is a dangerous thing. Make it safer. Use antivirus software. Refer to Chapter 24.

Keep your antivirus subscription up-to-date! New viruses are introduced all the time. Be safe! Protect yourself.

Appendix

Windows Startup Program Reference

● ●

*I*t would take a mighty thick appendix to list the thousands and thousands of Windows startup programs that are available. Even then, the list is continually growing, with new applications and programs (not to mention new viruses and worms) being developed all the time.

Rather than list everything here, I present you with a selection of Web pages you can visit. These pages list startup programs, describe what the programs do, and specify whether the program is legitimate or spyware or a virus. Also, these pages are updated often, so you know that the information you're getting is fresh.

- ✔ http://www.sysinfo.org/startuplist.php
- ✔ http://www.lafn.org/webconnect/mentor/startup/
- ✔ http://www.windowsstartup.com/wso/search.php

This list was current at the time this book went to press. Note that the list is by no means complete; other Web pages documenting the startup programs undoubtedly exist.

Index

• F •